LABYRINTH

LABYRINTH

Selected Poetry and Prose of
Lorenzo García Vega

Edited and Translated by

CHRISTOPHER WINKS

Station Hill Press

BARRYTOWN, NY

Published by Station Hill Press, the publishing project of the Institute for Publishing Arts, Inc., 120 Station Hill Road, Barrytown, NY 12507, a not-for-profit, Federally tax-exempt organization [501(c)(3)].

Online catalogue: www.stationhill.org
E-mail: publishers@stationhill.org

Design: Susan Quasha

ISBN: 9781581772395
Library of Congress Control Number available upon request.

Special thanks to the late poet/publisher Mark Weiss (Junction Press) for developing and keeping faith in this project until his untimely death.

Earlier versions of some of these translations appeared in the online journal *Truck* (halvard-johnson.blogspot.com) and in *The Whole Island: Six Decades of Cuban Poetry,* ed. Mark Weiss (Berkeley: University of California Press, 2009).

This book is for Milena Deleva:

"*Y tú, yo, inventándonos, amándonos, bajo el liso desquiciamiento de la nada.*"

Contents

Acknowledgments

My special thanks go to Lorenzo García Vega, who encouraged this project and sent me several of his virtually unobtainable books to assist me in making my selection. During one of his rare visits to New York for a reading at New York University's King Juan Carlos Center, I was able to meet and talk with him and his wife Marta Lindner, and it was an encounter that will always remain in memory. I regret that he did not live to see this anthology, but at least I know that the project enjoyed his support. (In a characteristically strange touch, some of my e-mails to him and an excerpt from an earlier draft of the introduction to this anthology ended up in Jorge Luis Arcos's comprehensive study of his work, *Kaleidoscopio: La poética de Lorenzo García Vega* (Madrid: Colibrí, 2012).

José Kozer has generously allowed his poem "Homenaje a Lorenzo García Vega," along with my translation, to serve as a poetic prelude to this anthology; I have always been thankful for his friendship and inspiration. Gratitude also goes to Ladislao Aguado, director of Hypermedia Ediciones, for granting permission to reproduce García Vega's writings. I extend a warm salute to Roman Antopolsky for his scrupulous work in typing and correcting the typographical errors in the published Spanish originals into a computer file.

My colleagues in the Department of Comparative Literature at Queens College/CUNY have, as always, been exemplary and supportive friends and interlocutors

The late poet Mark Weiss encouraged me to undertake a comprehensive translation of García Vega's writing. Throughout the protracted process of what turned out to be a more formidable task than either of us could have contemplated, Mark was always patient and encouraging, even as he never hesitated, skilled editor and accomplished translator that he was, to point out errors and weaknesses in my versions. Whatever misprisions may remain are exclusively my responsibility.

Note on the Selection and Translation

This anthology seeks to cover every stage of Lorenzo García Vega's vast creative oeuvre (some of which has only recently been published in Spanish), from the early vanguardist poems written following his entry into the Orígenes milieu to selections from the final collection published in his lifetime, *Erogando trizas donde gotas de lo vario pinto* (*Distributing Scraps When Drops of the Varicolored*), along with representative if necessarily (though no less regrettably) brief selections from his prose anti-memoirs *Los Años de Orígenes* (*The Orígenes Years*) and *El Oficio de perder* (*The Vocation of Losing*). Since *The Orígenes Years* remains his single most-often-cited work, the one that earned him both admiring and depreciative notoriety from Cuban writers, I have chosen to break chronological order and begin the anthology with representative extracts from that memoir, which depict, often painfully, the stiflingly philistine cultural ambience against which *Orígenes* (nobly but ultimately unsuccessfully, in García Vega's view) rebelled, the intolerance and dogmatism of the post-Revolutionary period, and the poet's psychic anguish, mingled with desperately neurotic humor, in attempting to come to terms with his shipwrecked exilic condition in New York and Albino Beach alike. It can be said that *The Orígenes Years* marks a settling of accounts with his previous poetic work and clears the way for the generically unclassifiable texts of his subsequent "notarial," "non-writer" years. As such, it sheds light on his entire writerly trajectory.

I have compiled a set of reference notes at the end of this volume which readers may find particularly useful in the frequent instances when García Vega mentions figures from the Cuban artistic and literary scene who may not be widely known to anglophone readers.

Translating a writer as idiosyncratic and difficult as Lorenzo García Vega involves numerous challenges, not the least of which is a temptation to smooth over many of his rough edges, awkwardness, compulsive repetitions, formulations that sound odd even in Spanish, and convoluted syntax. I have almost completely resisted such temptation, not being at all enamored of the unfortunately still-common tendency of some translators to attempt to "improve" the source text. At the same time, I am concerned with ensuring that García Vega "speak" convincingly in English (a language he himself almost defiantly, after decades in the United States, never chose to learn) and with doing justice to his verbal music, dissonant as it tends to be. It is, after all, the irritated oyster that engenders the pearl.

Introduction

A Labyrinth Before Dying: Lorenzo Garcia Vega's Neo-Baroque Poetics

In 1949, the prominent Cuban intellectual Jorge Mañach, author of *The Crisis of High Culture in Cuba*, published an open letter to the poet José Lezama Lima in the magazine *Bohemia*, in which, after much preamble, he confessed with respect to the poetry of Lezama and his cohorts (among them Gastón Baquero, Eliseo Diego, Fina García Marruz, Virgilio Piñera, Ángel Gaztelu, Octavio Smith, and Cintio Vitier) associated with the literary journal *Orígenes*: "I admire it in parts, but I don't understand it," and concluded, after reiterated statements of utter bafflement at the poetry's "sibylline" qualities, with the rather back-handed valediction, "I admire you very sincerely, more for what I can guess at than from what can be understood." Mañach speaks here as a self-appointed gatekeeper of a purportedly authentic Cuban national culture, reproaching his rebellious juniors for what he considers a kind of unregenerate aestheticism, fit only to be read by other poets and not by the larger "national" public.

All of this would amount to a tropical variant of the age-old clash of generations were it not for the specific historical context in which the alleged hermeticism of the *Orígenes* project originated: the prevalent violence and corruption of 1940s Cuba, where a nominally democratic order marked by progressive social legislation was undermined by gangsterism, aggravated disparities of wealth, economic dependence on the United States, and a generalized frustration at the persistently unfulfilled promises of an independence so often invoked but never really lived. With its firm dedication to maintaining the integrity of culture in general and poetry in particular, *Orígenes* emerged as an ethical as well as cultural challenge to the dominant philistine intellectual ambience of Cuba. Advocating a poetics that has since become known as "neo-baroque," and has exercised immeasurable influence on generations of experimental poets in the Spanish-speaking world, Lezama and his associates found precursors in the syntactical and imagistic convolutions and sinuosities of the Spanish Golden Age poet Luis de Góngora and the 19th-century French poet Stéphane Mallarmé. If Lezama was to declare that "only the difficult stimulates," it was not out of abstract aestheticism. Rather, his perspective stemmed from a desire to change the terms of cultural discourse, to posit values that went beyond the dominant careerism and opportunism, and to mobilize what the Martiniquan writer Édouard Glissant would later call opacity in the interests of a greater diversity, grounded in Cuban history and culture but also open to poetries in other languages. It was, in short, an intellectual adventure embarked upon—as such adventures tend to be in the Caribbean—within and against adverse conditions. The obstacles the journal encountered can be summed up in its low circulation—only 250-300 copies of each issue were printed, and most of these were hand-delivered to its readers, since bookstore sales in Havana amounted to a mere dozen or so copies per issue.

When in 1946 the 20-year old Lorenzo García Vega encountered José Lezama Lima in a Havana bookstore—whose name "La Victoria" carries an ironic resonance in view of García Vega's lifelong dedication to the "vocation of losing" (the title of his memoirs)—he was recovering from eight psychologically damaging years in a Jesuit school, with ambitions of being a writer but hesitant to enter into an inimical literary milieu. Thus uncertain of his goals and direction, he heard a voice behind him enjoining, "Young man, read Proust!" Thus began a master-disciple relationship in which García Vega would faithfully and obsessively read all the books that Lezama would loan him weekly as part of the Master's "Delphic Course of Study," whose curriculum was adjusted to suit what Lezama saw as the intellectual needs of each student. (García Vega's started, not with Proust, but with Lautréamont's *Les Chants de Maldoror*, where, as Lezama with delphic prescience told his protégé, "everything begins.")

The youngest of the Origenistas, García Vega was evidently among the most tempestuous and confrontational (well summed up in his iconoclastic "Into the water with Apollinaire," which appeared in his first collection of poems): the benign Lezama dubbed him the "Protestant Jesuit" in a group made up of practicing Catholics, and in his *roman à clef De peña pobre*, the poet and later ultra-orthodox guardian of the flickering Origenista flame Cintio Vitier called him "Rancor." But, as García Vega was to admit in later years, the group—Lezama in particular, who became for him a surrogate father as well as a teacher and mentor—saved his life. *Orígenes* published his first collection of poetry *Suite para la espera* (*Suite for Waiting*) in 1948—when he was 22—as well as his first novel (of linked short stories) *Espirales del cuje* (*Spirals of the Withe*), which won him the Cuban National Prize for Literature in 1952. But none of this was a guarantee of a successful career, particularly in the perilous years of the Batista dictatorship; *Orígenes* depended on the munificence of its patron, José Rodríguez Feo, who cut off the publication in the late 1950s and switched his sponsoring allegiance to Lezama's poetic and philosophical adversary, Virgilio Piñera, and the publication *Ciclón*. Yet when the Cuban Revolution triumphed in 1959, most of the Orígenes group did not greet it with enthusiasm, and their generational contemporaries were more drawn to the unadorned anti-bourgeois style of Piñera, considering the Baroque affinities of Lezama *et al.* obscurantist and pompously verbose. For his part, García Vega welcomed the Revolution, and was eventually given a post with UNESCO.

In a reversal of fortune typical of the first decade of the Revolution, García Vega would later fall out of favor with the post-revolutionary cultural bureaucracy, while the initially skeptical Vitier, García Marruz, and Diego would end up as supporters of the regime, and do so precisely in the name of Orígenes. Beginning in 1968, García Vega would embark on an exilic odyssey that would take him from Cuba to Spain to New York City to Venezuela to his final home in Miami, a less-than-scintillating territory which he renamed "Albino Beach." In the process, he clarified and refined his vocation of losing, accepting jobs on the order of a doorman at Gucci's, a messenger at the art publisher Abrams, and most enduringly in terms of its echoes in his literary work, a 10-year stint as a "bag boy" at a Publix supermarket in Miami, bagging groceries and loading up and conveying shopping carts to the customers' cars: all this with doctorates in Law and in Philosophy and Literature from the University of Havana.

These "faces of the reverse," as he entitled his 1975 collection of diaries (*Rostros del Reverso*), had definite psychic and physical consequences: mental breakdowns, chronic alcoholism, two major heart attacks. As he dryly declares in his memoirs: "Life, like the mambo, has its peculiarities." Through and indeed because of it all, he took a long look at the formative experience of his youth in the Orígenes group and, in his controversial 1978 memoir *Los años de Orígenes* (*The Orígenes Years*), submitted the practices and theories of that group—even those of his beloved Lezama Lima—to a stringent and uncompromising critique. Refusing all nostalgia, García Vega considers that, for all its aspirations to transcend its impoverished cultural milieu, *Orígenes* in the end reproduced a version of Cuban nationalism that aggravated the pernicious cultural kitsch it sought to transcend, adding to the Cuban canon a new set of "marble derby hats"—in the colloquial Cuban speech of the 1902-1959 Republican era, a metonym for a self-important opportunist and political climber—that would weigh heavily on a new gallery of heroes, literary or otherwise, in order to usher them fully into the soap-opera of Cuban history. (It should be noted that Cuba did in fact give the Spanish-speaking world the first radio soap-opera.) Among other things, García Vega attacked the restrictive, silencing effect of the group's Catholic pieties—comparing it to an "iron lung"—as well as Lezama's tendency to evade frank discussion and to play the role of patriarchal teacher without questioning what García Vega calls the "frame" the group placed around itself. But García Vega's aim is not simply parricidal; his critique of Lezama is intended less to debunk and gossip than to humanize, to indicate the intrinsic flaws and failings that made the Orígenes group into much less than what it had promised to be: a renovating force in Cuban intellectual life.

If I have lingered on the details of García Vega's biography, it is because, of all major Caribbean and Latin American writers, the autobiographical mode is central to his poetic work. Along with *Los años de Orígenes,* he published diaries and the immense anti-memoir *El oficio de perder* (*The Vocation of Losing*), and his work, from his earliest poems to the his later unclassifiable texts or "boxes," bears all the marks of the "autistic" creator he humorously called himself: obsessively focused on dreams, minuscule details of his immediate environment, recurrent memories of childhood, and, in his later years, the tacky sterility of Albino Beach (an endless source of sardonic wonder). Deliberately refusing whatever might link him too closely with the hackneyed repertoire of Cuban images, be they baroque, conversationalist, committed, or boringly patriotic, whether emanating from the exhausted, ideologically bankrupt island itself under the sway of what García Vega variously calls "the Castrato" and the "Castroist shitpile," or in the pre-Batista simulacrum that is the land of exile, García Vega declared himself a "non-writer writer," preferring the title "notary," one who inscribes his work with the "doy fe" or "witnesseth" of the passive observer who registers without interpreting.

An example of García Vega's demystification of Cuban iconography is the poem "Martían Text," in which he takes on nothing less than that most fetishized and most marmoreal derby-hat of all, José Martí, whom he manages to rescue from the tattered flags and neon detritus—those "electronic shells"—of the pseudo-patriotic kitsch in banquet halls and ballrooms of a pathetically imitative exile. Interrupting the project that has imprisoned him—"Founding the Nation"—the Martí of the poem compassionately lays to rest a (homeless?) corpse on a park bench at night. The dead bury the dead; as with many of Martí's own poems, the poem is haunted. The poet's spectral double appears in a hallway chair, in tune with the dissolution into nothingness of the poem itself.

Rejecting the Origenista aim of composing a Cuban literary canon, García Vega claims as ancestors and inspirations the literary Cubism of Max Jacob, Surrealism, Pop Art, the playfully reiterative language-games of Gertrude Stein, Marcel Duchamp's profoundly anti-philosophical anti-art, the conceptual/performance art of Joseph Beuys, the musical experimentalism of John Cage, Conlon Nancarrow, Karlheinz Stockhausen, and Giacinto Scelsi, and kitsch objects from the plastic world of Albino Beach. He avails himself of the insights of psychoanalysis in its zen variant (marking a further distance from Orígenes, which dismissed Freud as "boring," as Fina García Marruz put it). In proudly affirming his "chronic immaturity" and consequent refusal to submit to the tyrannical hierarchy of Form, he situates himself in the topography of literary negation mapped by Witold Gombrowicz and Virgilio Piñera. The deadpan, mechanistic, yet exuberantly expansive writing procedures of Raymond Roussel, whom García Vega admired (because, as he told me in conversation, "what he writes looks dumb, but it actually isn't") appear in the guise of García Vega's verbal obsessiveness. Realizing that not everything can be said with absolute precision, he seeks to compensate for the lack with the obsessive repetition, reconfiguration, and reworking of certain phrases for long stretches. Like Gertrude Stein, he bangs repeatedly at the door of language to see what might lie behind it. Like Fernando Pessoa, he deploys heteronyms, notably "Doctor Phantom," the anti-protagonist of the sequence "Phantom Plays the Game," who incarnates García Vega's own sense of himself after definitively moving to Albino Beach; "Vilis," an oneiric emanation of Miami; and the "Builder of Boxes" (who is also Tokol, a demented Hungarian mulatto from García Vega's natal Jagüey Grande).

Michel Leiris, García Vega's most notable predecessor in the domain of meticulous and extended memoir-writing, prefaced the republication of his *L'age d'homme* with an essay that compared the author's effort at complete self-revelation without concealment or evasion to the bullfighter who confronts the bull in the ring. Though the writer does not obviously face mortal danger, the challenge he sets himself—to expose himself to himself and his readers via the cultivation of a rigorous and uncompromising style—is for Leiris entirely analogous to the risk assumed by the matador when he faces the horns of the bull.

For his part, García Vega fights that bull in the manner of the Mexican clown Cantinflas (see his routine on YouTube): the effect may be comic, but the bull is no less present. In stylistic terms, there is indeed an element of the *cantiflesco*—convoluted and hilarious circumlocution—in the way García Vega self-consciously entangles himself in his observations, suddenly becoming aware, while writing, of the limitations of his language, the absurd artifice of his phrases, the figurative dimension lacking any referent in lived reality. But such entanglement is in keeping with the way he describes his memoirs, which could easily designate his *oeuvre* as a whole: "...perhaps I have been writing something that's attempting to be *the vocation of losing*, that is, attempting to be something like an autobiography of my vocation of non-writer writer, and at the same time I want to write a *Don't Die without a Labyrinth*, that is, the narrative of my kaleidoscope, my circularities, my corridors that end in the same corridor, etc. [...] I need to know that I want to write my autobiography... but that this narrative is at the same time about a Labyrinth that is attempting to raise itself before the very eyes of the Reader." He goes on to ask himself: "Can I go back to the beginning, without eliminating everything I've written? That is the question, and that is the question that's depressing me."

That beginning, for him, is Jagüey Grande, and his childhood discovery that the vocation of poet was consonant with the vocation of losing; his fateful train journey from Jagüey Grande to Havana at the age of 10, in what he calls "the cabalistic year 1936," through the "leaden, stale" landscape of the Cuban countryside where he spent his early years. In fact, whatever childhood memories he has managed to hold onto are leitmotivs of his entire work ("Young man, read Proust!"), along with a persistent note of tumbledown decrepitude—sugarcane fields in the dead season, pianolas, flickering silent movies, a portrait of Lautréamont's Maldoror, grown old and toothless. "When one decides to write, delirium is always lying in wait...The present, space of my past." And further: "I've said again that the Labyrinth of what I was is what has to be within my present, in this Albino Beach."

Although García Vega, in keeping with his disdain for labels and literary schools, explicitly rejected any attempt to link him to the neo-baroque movement in Latin American poetry, his choice of that quintessentially baroque construction, the labyrinth, as a metaphor and locus of his life's work invites such comparisons. In his open letter to Lezama Lima, Jorge Mañach complained of not even being able to understand the grammar of his poems, and García Vega, while not following Lezama's poetic sinuosities, operates on a similar level of grammatical idiosyncrasy, albeit by means of a logic of compression and collage, eliding verbs and connectives, juxtaposing images as if they were concrete physical elements, objects in verbal form. His labyrinth, then, is a box that contains in palimpsest all his poem-text-story boxes—he seeks to achieve on the verbal plane what Joseph Cornell's collage-boxes achieve on the visual. One might also invoke in this context *El laberinto de mi mismo* (*The Labyrinth of Oneself*), a pioneering "magical-realist" (or more properly, "gasiform") novel by the virtually-forgotten 20th-century Cuban writer Enrique Labrador Ruiz, a series of internal monologues of an obsessive isolate who dwells in a private fantasy.

In short, if the labyrinth is site and substance of his creation, García Vega himself is the bull or Minotaur with which he does battle, risking his mental health as the *torero* does his life, transforming his doubts, anxieties, neuroses, fears, *idées fixes*, and bouts of anguish and depression into so many winding passageways, armed only with the fragile thread of a language he questions, doubts, and even mocks. He invokes, with his customary uncertainty, the concept of Myth intrinsic to any labyrinth: "In that the Myth was what I lived, what I lost is also the Myth for me, which I can't manage to grasp." But even that loss enters into the labyrinth, in the form of the broken thread that prevents him from going back to the beginning as he would wish. The Labyrinth, after all, is constructed on the long threshold of death; it is a monument that annihilates itself in the moment of its fulfillment.

As Michel Foucault remarks in an essay on Raymond Roussel that could equally apply to García Vega: "At the most enigmatic moment, when all paths stop and one is at the point of being lost, or at the absolute beginning, when one is on the threshold of something else, the labyrinth suddenly offers the *same*: its last puzzle, the trap hidden in the center—it is a mirror behind which the identical is located. This mirror teaches that life before coming alive was already the same, as it will be the same in the immobility of death. The mirror which reflects the birth that's explained by the labyrinth is the one where death looks upon itself, in turn reflected by it." If García Vega's labyrinth is constructed against death, it is only complete—and complete in its disintegration—at the moment of death foretold by the moment of birth, and fulfilled in the labyrinthine convolutions of life, where the poet is "entangled, dramatically entangled." The thread of language not only breaks, it fetters, and García Vega's work is the tragicomic chronicle of his attempts to break away, which only bind him further. As he would put it, "Why do I keep on with all this botheration which consists of always asking myself about the same thing?"

"The Toad's Leap," from his 2004 sequence *Textilandia Albina*, is a good example of his "late style," where he wrestles with the intractability of conveying the movement of thought in a language seemingly imprisoned in commonplaces, and where the immediacy of the poem as process is conveyed through sudden leaps, doubling-backs, parataxes, repetitions, juxtapositions, only to annihilate itself at the end by surrendering to whatever its listeners (not readers) make of it, if indeed that matters.

But far from greeting such poetry with a variation on Mañach's "I don't understand," the generation of Cuban poets that emerged in the 1990s welcomed Lorenzo García Vega as a distinguished elder capable of showing them an alternative direction not dependent on the aesthetic prescriptions of recycled Origenismo or any kind of discipleship. Notably, one of García Vega's champions on the island, Antonio José Ponte, followed the poet's irreverent lead by writing an essay on José Martí's overcoat, which proposed a demystification and hence humanization of Martí that met with the uncomprehending outrage of none other than Cintio Vitier, who generations earlier had enthusiastically participated in the debate with Mañach. The semi-underground Diaspora(s) group of avant-garde poets—whose aim was to "forget Orígenes," that is, to supersede it instead of mythologizing and thus freezing it—published an anthology of their work in Mexico (*Memorias de la clase muerta*), which García Vega prefaced. Nearly all these poets have gone into exile, but amazingly for a living exiled poet (a distinction he shared with his friend José Kozer), an anthology of García Vega's poems (*Lo que voy siendo*) was published in Cuba under the auspices of the poet Reina María Rodríguez and edited and prefaced by his close friend, the late literary critic Enrique Sainz. On the other hand, Rodríguez's efforts to publish *Los años de Orígenes* in Cuba have so far come to naught—García Vega's mordant, often scathing criticism of Cuban culture, literary icons, and official policies (cultural and otherwise) is evidently still too much for the bureaucracy to digest, even forty years after its first publication. Notwithstanding, a July 2019 presentation in Havana, held in an independent cultural space, of a new edition of *Los años...* published by Cubans living in Mexico, concluded with the publishers' giving away several copies of the book to those in attendance.

Beyond Cuba, García Vega's work has found enthusiastic readers in Spain and Latin America: *Los años de Orígenes* has been reprinted twice (in Argentina, and more recently in Mexico) since its initial 1979 publication in Venezuela, and much of his late work has been published by small enterprises in countries from Guatemala to the Netherlands. The exiled Cuban poet and former member of the *Diaspora(s)* project Carlos A. Aguilera has done excellent work in publicizing García Vega's writings and editing his posthumous diaries. In short, after years of remaining unread and unpublished, Lorenzo García Vega, in the final stages of constructing his labyrinth before his death in 2012, could be said to have found a certain victory in his lifelong experience of defeat. But really, does it matter what I or any critic says of him? Referring to what academics like myself like to consider "our profession," but which may simply be a disguised vocation of losing that dares not confess itself as such, García Vega declared (in a 2001 interview with Carlos A. Aguilera): "I don't want explanations from those people. Let them go on with their conferences and their learned presentations. I don't want them to shit on my testimony with any kind of dissertation-type explanations." The rest is reading. Witnesseth.

A Note on the Text

The original Spanish versions of García Vega's poetic and prose-poetic texts have been reprinted *en face*; the extracts from his memoiristic writings appear in English-only versions.

Labyrinth

Homenaje a Lorenzo García Vega

José Kozer

Ábrete verbena, cae a tierra,
crezca roya, luto
universal.

Luz del mundo cae a tierra, luz
eléctrica del sol.
no hay existencia a corto
plazo para nadie, un solo
campanero en el Orbe,
zancadilla universal

Lorenzo el Descontento por
antonomasia le
dijo a Marta quiero vivir,
al morir: no pudo ser,
dejemos los libros
quietos, leer es de
ciegos, en los nichos
el invidente tantea
nada a rastras,
desconoce (en ese
sentido nada ha
cambiado) ceniza
desovar universal.

Homenaje a Lorenzo García Vega
sentado
al borde de un catre de

Homage to Lorenzo Garcia Vega

José Kozer

Open up, verbena, fall to earth,
spread, rust, universal
mourning.

Light of the world, fall to earth,
electric light of the sun,
there's no short-term
existence for anyone, a lone
bell-ringer in the Orb,
universal trip-up.

Lorenzo the Malcontent par
excellence
told Marta I want to live,
while dying: it was not to
be,
let's leave the books
be, reading's for the
blind, in the recesses
the sightless one stumbles
toward nothing reluctantly,
unaware (in this sense
nothing's changed)
of ash, universal spawn.

Homage to Lorenzo García Vega
seated
on the edge of a folding

tijera, un cono de luz
en la mirada (luz
natural) sus pupilas
la corroboran en toda
la Peninsula de La
Florida adonde fue
a parar: *in extremis*
todo lugar es el
mismo, no hay
triciclos, casas de
jagüey, ya vio y no
cree, pasa a ras de
su mirada una Garza
y no distingue pájaro
de copa (a posarse
Muerte posarse) de
jagüey: delante de
casa, donde la madre
sale en refajo a llamarlo
a merendar, termina
Marta quiero vivir la
historia universal.

Años, ido, al borde de un catre,
oía ruidos
vecinos, hubiera querido
creer en San Policarpo,
santo patrono de los
ruidos: como tantas
cosas en su caso no
pudo ser. Lo desnudaron
para lavarlo con agua
inminente de ceniza, lo
acicalaron camisa blanca

cot, a cone of light
in his gaze (natural
light) his eyes
bear this out in the entire
Florida Peninsula
where he ended up:
in extremis every place
is the same, there are no
tricycles, houses of
jagüey, he saw and
doesn't believe, a heron
passes at eye level
and he cannot tell bird
from the jagüey crown
(alight Death alight):
In front of the house,
where his mother
comes out in a
slip to call him inside
for lunch, here it ends
Marta I want to live
universal history

Years, disoriented, on the edge
of a cot, he heard noises
nearby, he'd have wanted
to believe in St. Polycarp,
patron saint of
noises: like so many
things in his case it was
not to be. They stripped
him
to wash him with imminent
ash water, they

de manga larga, yugos
dorados, pantalón beige:
lo prefería. Medias
blancas, perdió el
rumbo, también lo
perdió la candela, y
si resucitó, lo duda, al
borda de una renovada
desolación: desdibujo
un laberinto, hizo
aparecer un Minotauro,
una ternera de madera,
y donde iba a narrar la
historia de Pasifae, el
toro blanco, Poseidón
y Minos ay Lorenzo
García Vega una vez
más se encoge detrás
del tronco de un jagüey,
narra, no se le oye, da
la cara, no se mueve.

dressed him up in a
long-sleeved white shirt,
golden yokes, beige pants:
he preferred that. White
socks, he lost the trail,
and also the flame,
and if he revived, he doubts it,
at the edge of a renewed
desolation: he blurred
a labyrinth, he made
a Minotaur appear,
a wooden calf,
and where would he tell
the tale of Pasiphae, the
white bull, Poseidon
and Minos ah Lorenzo
García Vega once again
shrinks behind a
jagüey trunk,
tell, he can't be heard,
he shows his face,
he doesn't move.

from

Los años de Orígenes / The Orígenes Years

(1979)

The Gucci Doorman

Working in the Fifth Avenue store for millionaires. It's the Gucci doorman, but things are going badly, because Dr. Gucci's been observing his behavior, and it appears, as he operates the revolving door, that he's not behaving like a real doorman.

The Argentine manager came by in the afternoon. He told him they were making him a new doorman's uniform, but they were still watching his behavior—yesterday morning, he put his hands in his pockets! The manager advised him to put on a show for the customers, emphasizing that working for Gucci was like working for the opera. He commented that others had commented that the doorman looked like a mummy. He advised the doorman to identify with his job, since being a doorman involves a certain art. He ordered the doorman when it rained to make a beeline for the customers' umbrellas and then place them in an umbrella stand shaped like an enormous boot.

All through the day, next to the revolving door, he says *good morning* when the customer enters and *good bye* when he leaves. He calls the men Sir and the women Madam. He's writing his memoirs on the *Orígenes* years, but he's aware of two things. The first thing he's aware of is the Argentine manager's warning about putting his hands in his pockets. The second thing he's aware of—as the doorman of a store for millionaires—is Juan Goytisolo's warning: "My idea in this regard is of a complete commitment that begins with language, with absolute honesty about who one is, and on that basis I move towards a social commitment, towards the struggle for a much more humane, more just society than the one we know."

The revolving door is a good Origenista image. It's useful for hypostasis, for confusion in its purest state.

The Gucci doorman remembers his Orígenes *years*, a title for a best-seller.

In the store, the Gucci flag must be hoisted. The doorman hoists the Gucci flag.

What does *Orígenes* have to do with this? In Gucci, there's an Italian assistant, about eighty years old, who amuses himself by touching the butt of a young American girl who sells men's belts. The old guy looks like someone out of a Fellini movie, but he also looks like someone out of the movie of the Cuba of before, the movie of the *Orígenes* years.

(You had to leave Cuba, you had to leave what could have been a revolution, to return to the machinery of the millionaires.)

The Gucci doorman thinks that *elegance* is the reverse of the latrine.

Orígenes. Gucci. What the former was. What the latter is. It's always the reverse. It seems too unreal. How much nightmare do you have? The unreal, the image. The image in New York. The image in *Orígenes*. Which is the reverse of what? *The Gucci doorman remembers his* Orígenes *years.*

Through the Gucci revolving door, Lezama, Fina, Cintio, Father Gaztelu could enter. Because everything resembles a Felliniesque carnival, a carnival bringing together the dead and the living. It's because the moment of unreality has arrived, as if something were becoming Zen-Nirvana, Sankara, John Cage: a confusion that Octavio Paz stirs up in a poem. But what remains then? Does the void remain?

Tillich at the moment of his death: *I have rejected with horror the idea of casting a flower into the void of the current of time. The latter must remain a void.*

But this unreality can be offered up as a memory, as an emotion. Because the Gucci doorman sees, through the glass of the revolving door, the St. Patrick's Day parade. Some girls are marching. But then, there's the memory of Judit. But then, since everything can interchange as if in a masked ball, it's as if the *Orígenes* years were arriving through the *void of the hollow current of time.*

Because *nothing is*—the Gucci doorman says to himself—but everything can begin, or end, with the *Orígenes* years. Because the stupid, cruel idiocy of working in a store for millionaires leads to the other stupid, cruel idiocy of having been a *voluntary worker* in Castro's

Cuba, and that's something like a consequence of the *Orígenes* years.

Because before he hoisted the Gucci flag, the Gucci doorman was told by the Cuban head of a Gucci department:

– In the end, they're asking you to bow down to the bosses. In the end, and in a word, you're a servant.

And one morning, performing *voluntary labor* in the cane fields, the poet X—who had to stay in Cuba, and that's why his name is X—told the Gucci doorman:

– You have to swallow all this. You've got to submit. You can't protest. We writers are shit.

That's why the Gucci doorman has a third warning to deal with. A warning that isn't the Argentine manager's about putting one's hands in one's pockets, a warning that isn't Juan Goytisolo's about total commitment, but the Origenista Cintio Vitier's warning:

Don't ask me for false
collaborations, games
of misunderstanding and confusion:
ask me to bring
my being towards its bleeding sun.

Don't ask me for signatures,
photos, credits for an abominable
development of duplicity: ask that
we be like brothers
opening our hearts to each other until death.

Don't flatter my vanity, seek my strength,
which is yours. Don't love me, with your delicacy
that betrays me. Don't pretend
you're going to believe in my pretense.
Let's not make another world of lies.

Let's make a world in truth, with truth
divided like terrible bread for all.

That is what I feel that each day, implacably,
the Revolution demands of me.

And here's a verse of Octavio Paz about Nirvana and Samsara—A verse that can't be quoted because *the comrades* take away the books of everyone who leaves Cuba—the Gucci doorman, on break—How elegant and high-toned Fifth Avenue is during the break!—tries breaking that *terrible bread for all* that Cintio offers him, just as he returns again and again to the memory of the *Orígenes* years.

The Coffer

Bravo! A chapter about a coffer. With nothing missing. Now this is the most difficult chapter of the *Orígenes* years. It's about appearing in the midst of an idiotic destiny. Telling... Because we've already said it, we're stuffed full of lies.

A fine paradox, that: narrating the destiny of a few Cuban writers. If I tell you that it's in order to call on, to assemble all of them. My dear professors, my dear men of letters, my same old Cubans: here we are with a coffer. Yet another show. Keep on selling your theses. I offer them up to the late, great Lezama. Spit into the air, fill up your resumes with an essay on poverty in the *Orígenes* years. We present ourselves as clowns for those who might have a devout interest in the labor of our journal.

You may also come to Miami to accumulate more data. Oh, the Miami heat! Or go to Cuba, gratis, merely by painting yourselves in a leftist hue, with a bit of Sartrian doubt and some slight interest in the poor. Go pay the great whore of the Casa de las Américas. Tourism for assholes. Since the Orígenes years are all-purpose.

Because I fell in a park. I don't know how to say it. A superficial matter, almost ridiculous. Some show we've put on! Cintio, Eliseo, Lezama, transformed into non-conformists for the opportunistic refinement of the phony Latin American left. A show for castrated intellectuals with their homosexual dreams of powerful men.

Because we're going to talk about almost everything. Not everything, almost everything. Because you can't play the fool in these times when the *boom* and other things like the *boom* are walking around God's barnyard. Because Fausto Masó, in a letter from Venezuela, told me: "Paz liked your article. Why don't you send him some columns from the subway? Call it *from the underground*, propose it for his new publication. That style would be excellent for him, but when you get started, be careful about coming off Cuban—political, anti-Castroist, enemy of Communists; later, you'll know what to do, but for Latin American publications that's not the first concern, or at least, it shouldn't appear to be." No, nor is the first concern anything that's not cute and well-scrubbed. Because, come on, if you're going to be anti-Communist, you have to be an operator who says lovely things about North American institutions. Because in the subway, you can't talk about spilling your guts, since the *Orígenes* years have only served to make us act like clowns.

Get it together. Okay, let's go back to this chapter. Cintio Vitier said: *Don't pretend you're going to believe in my pretense. Let's not make another world of lies.* So I've fallen off a bicycle. I'm almost knocked out. I'm seeing stars, like in the comics.

I want a chapter in which I talk about an Airport. I've already talked about Aristides Fernández. Cartula's appeared as well, with his piano in a silent movie theater.

A chapter that talks about an Airport. I've fallen off a bicycle, in a park. I'm talking about everything. I'm talking about Fausto's letter. I'm quoting the words of an Origenista homage: "If we got along for ten years with your indifference, do not bestow on us, we entreat you, the fetid fruit of your admiration. We thank you, but we decidedly prefer your indifference. Indifference was useful to us; but we don't know what to do with admiration. It would confound all of us, as there is nothing more harmful than an admiration corrupted at its root. You are vitally incapable of admiring. You represent the *nihil admirari*, the shield of the oldest decadences. You have built your house with defective material, lined with lead for the simian and the chafing-dish stone."

But now they've bestowed more fetid fruit upon us. They're trying to turn Lezama into a mummy of the *boom*. Cintio's talking about the sun of a moral world. Everyone wants to see how Eliseo's father said: *The Republic*. More theses, more books will come out.

I'd never ridden a bicycle before. I got on a bicycle at the top of a little hill, in a New York park. I went down the hill, on the bike. I fell. I'm almost knocked out. In the Airport I was put inside a cage. The cage had a glass door. Judit, my daughter, was five years old. She was playing, and she was looking through the glass door. I had to say goodbye to Judit. When people went into the cage I had to say goodbye to Judit. Judit was five years old, she was playing, but when I left the cage and boarded the airplane, Judit was there crying.

I'm almost knocked out.

Let me write, in the subway, cute things about North American matters. Or let me not be an anti-Communist. Or I should recite Paul Valéry. Because my friend Fausto Masó has given me good advice as an exiled Cuban. Because Víctor Batista tells me I shouldn't overdo it when talking about the *Orígenes* years. Because Mario Parajón believes I'm going to make enemies if I talk about the *Orígenes* years. Because Carlos M. says he's also worried about my *Orígenes* years. Because Julián Orbón says I'll regret telling the story of the *Orígenes* years. Because I fell off a bicycle. I want to talk about an Airport. But what does a coffer have to do with an Airport? I'll explain my stars. I'll explain the comic book. I'll explain the Airport where the mummy couldn't leave, the mummy fabricated by the *boom*. *Lezama transformed into Ramses II*, as Octavio Armand would say.

But I'm raving again. I have to get a hold of myself. A little more order! Well, it's about... Now I'm getting started! It's about an airport, the same airport in which I had to see Judit from a cage. Cintio was with the kitsch mystic. Goddamned stars! Comic books. Falling off a bicycle. Order: it wasn't that, exactly like that. Cintio would be at the Airport. Cintio had gone to wait for the mystic at the Airport. The mystic said that the cages belonged to the Most Holy Trinity. Cintio said that now we really were with the Revolution.

But I have to be careful. I'm on the grass, almost knocked out. Knocked out in a New York park. Too old to learn how to ride a bicycle. Better for me to have learned to ride a bicycle during the Orígenes years. But that was serious. Those were serious years. Let's see if I get started! A little effort, less stars, and you'll see how I end up writing a perfect essay on the coffer of the *Orígenes* years. Wait, professors, wait a little longer!

So—Lezama had a coffer. I remember the afternoon when he showed me the little box. Mario Parajón, in an article, also talked about the little box. The cage in the Airport wasn't there, it was during the Orígenes years, but there were other cages. The little box was a golden coffer, with a hunting scene embossed on it. Lezama had spent the little left over from his salary to buy the coffer. Rialta, the mother of Orígenes, thought it was crazy to spend what was left over from a wretched salary to buy a coffer. Lezama felt shitty because of what Rialta told him. A mummy, then, could leave via the Airport. Not even I, at that time, was surrounded by stars, like in the funny papers. But we were fucked, because somebody bought a coffer, but somebody was left without the remainder of a wretched salary.

The kitsch mystic landed in an old Russian airplane. It was raining. Cintio told him that *they had just received a hard blow. The ten million didn't happen.* The great harvest of 1970 didn't work out. *Fidel was almost in tears when he said it. He (Cintio) wept when he heard it.* Judit couldn't walk through the glass door, and she cried too when I left. Lezama felt shitty. He always had to be stuck in that little room in his house on Calle Trocadero. He had a wretched salary. And Cintio wept when he learned that Fidel wept, but some Origenistas, comfortable petits-bourgeois, didn't know the story of the golden coffer.

Sugar went up, and went up again. In Europe, during World War II, millions of people died. Millions of people were crushed. In Europe, children underwent bombardment, but in Cuba, sugar went up. And it was okay that millions of people died so that sugar would go up, and Cubans became chauffeurs, and Cubans had houses. But Lezama had a coffer. And in Cuba, poverty never ended.

So there they were, those sunny Sunday mornings. Sunday winter mornings, sunny Sundays. Sundays with the winter that was invented in Cuba. *We're up here, the ones with the lust for Art,* a black man said, up there, in the upper balcony of the Auditorium. Lezama said that black man was smiling, and that his teeth shone like piano keys. It was the black man who sat up high, in the upper balcony, to hear the Sunday concerts in the Auditorium. Lezama had dreamed about that black man, since in Cuba there never was anything, nor was there such a black man. Only the sunny morning, the Sunday morning, with an invented winter, in that Auditorium, filled with satisfied bourgeois, belching bourgeois listening to Beethoven. A Sunday concert for chauffeurs who liked Beethoven. But that morning there was a premiere of something by Julián Orbón, and Julián Orbón was Orígenes's musician. I was with Lezama, Lezama was the black man, and we were in the upper balcony. It was a dreadful Cuba. A dreadful Cuba with *El Carmelo*, for the bourgeois who went to the Auditorium. Lezama was still laughing, he laughed back then, but Lezama was the black man. Lezama had a coffer, and *El Carmelo* was the big café where the cabbies and busdrivers went. Lezama also quoted Langston Hughes: "They send me to eat in the kitchen / When company comes, / But I laugh, / And eat well, / And grow strong. // ... Tomorrow... // They'll see how beautiful I am / And be ashamed—// I, too, am America."

The comic book! the stars continue. Wait a bit! You'll see how I work it all out. I can't manage to put things in order. That worries me. People might whisper... I have some experience and I know how they can squeal on you. They could put me into a frame. Baroque phantoms can have disembodied voices, and they can also fit themselves into a frame. It wouldn't be the first time they've done that. They start out, let's say, by catching us unawares. They'll say: he fell off a bicycle. He compared the *Orígenes* years to the stars of the funny papers. What do I know? They'll even feel sorry for me. I'll be the Origenista with a disembodied voice surrounded by stars. I'll be the neurotic who was in the cage of an Airport. They'll mix up everything. So I'll be the voice of the phantom Lorenzo, the phantom that still isn't sorry for speaking badly of the *Orígenes* years.

In this Airport that's the same Airport, I'm not waiting with Cintio for the Nicaraguan mystic. I'm in a cage attempting a discourse on a beginning, an end, an end that could be a beginning. There's an old Cuban protesting. The bastard's going to screw us all! The old Cuban is speaking, protesting, and the *comrades* are looking grim. Because of the goddamned old man, the *comrades* could prevent us all from leaving. Lezama, in the upper balcony, didn't talk about Charles V, nor was Lezama, in the upper balcony, the Baroque ghost with a disembodied voice. On the contrary, he quoted Langston Hughes, and talked about a black man who said: *We're up here, the ones with the lust for Art.*

But the *comrades*, the grim types at the Airport, aren't going to let the old man go if the old man keeps on protesting. Judit is behind the glass door. Cintio wept when he heard that the leader wept. That phantom Aristides Fernández, who wasn't the Baroque phantom with a disembodied voice, was the phantom face of Cuban poverty. And sugar kept on going up, but Lezama, who had spent the rest of his salary on a coffer, was invited, with Gastón Baquero, Editor-in-Chief of the *Diario de la Marina*, to the house of a member of the *Orígenes* group. In Cuba everything was, and wasn't. Some Origenistas were, and weren't. Because of this, the member of the *Orígenes* group was very interested in receiving Gastón Baquero, Editor-in-Chief of the *Diario de la Marina*. Gastón Baquero had been a member of the *Espuela de Plata* group, and the member of the *Orígenes* group had also been a member of *Espuela de Plata*, but the member of the *Orígenes* group wasn't interested in Gastón Baquero, the member of *Espuela de Plata*, but in Gastón Baquero, Editor-in-Chief of the *Diario de la Marina*. So the member of the *Orígenes* group had ordered *torrejas*.

Now, in a New York park, I've turned into a comic-book gossip. I'm seeing stars, I'm half knocked-out, and I'm becoming a gossip. Wasn't I in an Airport? Judit was behind the glass door. The poor old man was protesting. The sadistic *comrades* wanted to keep him from leaving. It was raining that afternoon. And what about those *torrejas*? I already said it, they're going to label me a comic Origenista, with gossip, stars, everything.

But this was what I was thinking in the Airport, when I was about to leave my country. That in Cuba, everything was, and wasn't. So Lezama wanted another helping of the *torrejas*, but Gastón Baquero hadn't yet tried the *torrejas*. So the member of the *Orígenes* group was nervous because Lezama was going to eat the *torrejas*, and the

Editor-in-Chief of the *Diario de la Marina* wasn't going to eat the *torrejas*. It was then that Gastón, smiling, turned to Lezama and said: "Lezama, don't ask for more *torrejas*: the *torrejas* are for the important people."

I'm half knocked-out, and this comic-book gossip. But the *boom* turned Lezama into a Baroque mummy, and a Baroque mummy can't leave via the Airport. So that, according to sound logic, the stars of the comic book are getting to be like the Baroque mummy. But Lezama wasn't just that, and as a result, in this Airport, with Judit behind the door, the *comrades'* grimness, and the old man protesting, I remembered the *torrejas* platter of the *Orígenes* years, the coffer of the *Orígenes* years, the humiliations Lezama had undergone, and the humiliation that being a writer in Cuba implied. And Cintio and the mystic would later be in the Airport and they'd talk about the harvest of the seventy millions, and they wouldn't talk about Lezama's coffer, but everything would keep on being the same, everything would keep on being lamentable.

I'm almost knocked-out, my dear professors, so have a little patience with this thesis on *Orígenes*. You'll see, maybe I can recover from the comic book. We Origenistas didn't always act like clowns. But the thing is that not only did Cubanness in poetry exist, but also Cubanness in the reverse, and Cubanness in the grotesque. That's why, just as the Baroque phantom could speak in a disembodied voice, the *boom* turned Lezama into a mummy. That's why Cintio wept along with the Nicaraguan mystic. But also, my dear professors, our story, the story of the *Orígenes* years, was pretty sad. Because, look, a black man wanted to laugh, out of lust for Art, in the upper balcony of a theater for constipated bourgeois. Because a poet bought a coffer with leftovers from a miserable salary. Because the success of a journal, in a hostile and petty milieu, culminated in an Airport, an Airport where Judit was behind a glass door, and where a Nicaraguan mystic got off an old Russian plane.

I'm surrounded by stars, but I can't stop remembering what I remembered at the Airport. There were other mornings in the Calle

Obispo. The set-up was so stupid, like the stupid set-up of the Teatro Auditorium. Every day, the painter Mariano sat in a café. Mariano had his studio in an old room in an old building, in Old Havana. Mariano earned nothing, or almost nothing. The set-up was stupid. That Cuba of ashes would never end. But Mariano kept on painting, kept on going to his studio, kept on going to his café. And he was like the poor shadow of poor Aristides Fernández. And that was a vocation in the face of sordidness, in the face of absurdity. And it was, and wasn't. But it was, and so we were able to keep ourselves together, in the face of Cuban stupidity, during those *Orígenes* years. But it wasn't, and so we ended up asking questions in the rainy afternoon at the Airport.

And the tale of all this is the tale that's behind the baroque disguise that is *Paradiso*. And Lezama had told it, a tale that wasn't a disguise, a non-*boom* tale, a *tale* tale without Charles V, without Racine, without the dandy Casal, without lost grandeur. And it was this tale that almost can't be talked about, because it wasn't. That it wasn't, but where there was the tender occurrence, our own, of our poverty that was. It wasn't, and we knew that couldn't be said. But it was, and although it couldn't be said, it was what we were always saying behind our images, behind our searches. It wasn't, and because of that Loveira, Carrión, our novelists, had not written their novel. But it was what it was, and because of that Loveira, Carrión, our novelists, had left the almost tangible trace of that novel. Because it wasn't only Cubanness in poetry, it was Cubanness in poverty, and Cubanness in the reverse.

(Parenthesis for a chapter about a coffer.

A narrator would have to make reference to the poverty of circumstance. Putting things together, in his home-made archive, the narrator could locate a few pieces.

What was and wasn't. Referring, within a context that cannot be grasped, to what was poor and chaotic about a specific moment. Because the *Orígenes* years don't present themselves within the cultural quality of a landscape, but in the amorphousness of a faceless circumstance. That's why the narrator has to fashion his vision out of unrelated elements which he has to continually question.

The reverse in the impoverished Cuban narrative tradition. A piece of the phantom with the voice of our poverty. So if we survey the writings of Cuban novelists—e.g., Loveira and Carrión—prior to the *Orígenes* years, we'll encounter two points: number one, anachronism, superficiality, and carelessness; but number two, the contrasting possibility of a hidden Cuban story. So that here we have the perplexity of a decision: a decision to seek—seek while inventing?—this...how to put it? unexpressed voice which, however, peeps out.

The junkyard. Objects, images, memories. Outside a cultural tradition, but demanding its landscape. And here's the *poor anecdote*: that occurrence which one doesn't know how to relate, since it's out in the open, but which, with its *gusts*, asks for a manner of speaking, a voice.—Martí achieved this in a Cuban way: "Lola, *jolongo*, weeping on the balcony."

The other history, the other story. That which is ours belongs to the reverse, or in that *invisible landscape* that Mallea talks about. Because that which is ours is besmirched with lies. Because of this, when a narrator looks at the *Orígenes* years, and wants to write about a coffer, the narrator catches *the other history* by surprise. So in France, where a cultural tradition exists, a writer like Céline can say: "...my 'memorial' will appear in high schools...you had an unexpected stroke of luck seeing as how you're so greedy for entertainment I'll make you live through moments that you'll only learn about before a hundred years are out...I'm sure you'll appreciate it, with you being born and me in complete 'relativity'!" But where there's a landscape, this *relativity* is there, it's palpable. But we who lack *relativity*, we have to arrive at a game of phantoms, or invent a soap-opera. Because when we say history, we have to invent a story, but also, when we invent a story, we have to struggle with a history that we don't know how to talk about.)

And, since I have the above parenthesis, perhaps I can get away from those comic-book stars. But it remains difficult. So I'm going to repeat the beginning of the story of the coffer.

It's a golden coffer with a hunting scene on it. Rialta, the mother of *Orígenes*, was displeased because Lezama spent the rest of his miserable salary on the coffer with the hunting scene. Mario Parajón told the story. Mario Parajón also said: "Lezama did nothing but read his books, smoke his cigars, eat his *fresh crab* in *La Zaragozana*, the cheap Spanish restaurant decorated in green, right near his favorite street, Obispo." Mario Parajón also said that back then *times changed*, because "in 1957 and 1958, the then-director of Culture, Guillermo de Zéndegui, published *La Expresión Americana*, which he first presented in better-paid lectures." What happens is that in Cuba everything gets besmirched. Everything becomes another history, another story. Now there's a story that *he did nothing but read*... but there's another story which isn't the one about how *he did nothing but read*... Now there's a story that says that back then *times changed*, and that *the then-director of Culture*, but there's another story that says that back then *times* didn't *change*, and that it's best not to touch that. I never knew that Lezama was Azorín, nor that times back then had changed, nor did I know that Lezama lived at the rhythm of a petit-bourgeois from Madrid. And Mario Parajón never knew that Lezama was Azorín, nor that times back then had changed, nor did he know that Lezama lived at the rhythm of a petit-bourgeois from Madrid. And Mario Parajón is my friend, and Mario Parajón was with me when I wrote *the Cuban operetta in Julián del Casal.* Mario Parajón, my friend, is an absurd man, he's solitary, he'd prefer to live with a few dogs, and he knew about Julián del Casal's Cuban operetta, and the Cuban operetta of the *Orígenes* years. But in Cuba everything got besmirched, and Mario Parajón is an actor and my friend Mario Parajón is an absurd actor, but Mario Parajón also, though he's my absurd friend, wants to be an Orteguian Catholic actor, and doesn't want to stop being part of the Cuban operetta of the *Orígenes* years.

That's why Mario also is and isn't. And since Mario is and isn't, Mario Parajón wants a compromise that's like a dream, but what he managed was a compromise that's like a symptom.

Let's continue, then, with the tale of the coffer. Lezama had a coffer and worked in the prison, but working in the prison was horrible. So a friend got Lezama a little job in cultural administration, and when Lezama took a trip, the friend gave Lezama a coat. But the friend didn't get on the telephone when they fired Lezama from that wretched little position in cultural administration, and the friend asked Lezama to lend him the coat he'd given Lezama. And there was a *grand style*, but the *torrejas* were for the important people. And the friend didn't get on the telephone, and several days went by, and Lezama stayed fired, and then the friend got on the telephone and they gave Lezama back his wretched little position in cultural administration. And the thing is that Mario Parajón knows as well as I do, or should know as well as I do, that when Lezama read his *Expresión Americana*, we, his friends, were the ones who paid for his lectures and no director of culture paid for his lectures.

Because most of the directors of culture behaved abominably. And González Palacio, the director of culture, published a poetry anthology of Cintio's, but at the price of Cintio's including González Palacio in the poetry anthology. And Lorenzo García Vega won the National Literature Prize, but since the director of culture González Palacio didn't want Lorenzo García Vega to win the National Literature Prize, González Palacio demanded that Lorenzo García Vega turn over half the prize to a charitable fund. And there was a *grand style*, but people stuck their heads in the sand, and it was only Lezama, with his wretched little position in cultural administration, who told Lorenzo García Vega that if he wished to protest, he himself was prepared to resign his wretched little position in cultural administration.

And afterwards it was said that times had changed, and Castroism came, and the young people came. And the young people had published only one story, but they appeared in the anthologies. And the young people had written only one essay, but they became ambassadors. And the young people entered cultural administration wanting to know if the wretched little position Lezama held wasn't the wretched little position Lezama held. And the young people were rebels, but they only wanted to know Seix Barral. And the young people, contributors to the supplement *Lunes*, wanted to create a body of work by means of political power. And there arrived what appeared to be a Revolution, but Lezama, and the work of *Orígenes*, was always looked down upon. But Mario Parajón had a mother-in-law who was the director of culture, so Mario Parajón had a position in cultural administration. So Lezama, since he had a friend with a mother-in-law, could get a better job in cultural administration. And so Lorenzo García Vega, since he had a friend with a mother-in-law, could get a job in cultural administration. And so a few Origenistas, since Mario had a mother-in-law, could stop going to *voluntary labor* in the countryside, and maintain a position as *absolute Christians*. But because, with Castroism, the Origenistas had only improved their position through a mother-in-law, and not for the work they had achieved, the cultural functionary Vicentina Antuña could ask that, when the edition of Góngora's poetry was being prepared, Lezama not be allowed to intervene in the edition of Góngora's poetry.

But back to the comic books. When will the nightmare of this tale of a coffer end? What to do with so many stars? I feel uncomfortable like this, half knocked-out. There's the Airport, I'm getting all mixed up. What order am I going to establish? Alemany told me, in Madrid, when this festival of exile began, that this was the unfolding of the Absolute Spirit. Hegel entered our history on horseback. Let's see, I'm trying, I'm moving, I'm pulling myself together on this park grass! Soon I'll get out of this knocked-out condition. And all those too-dark years. Press, publicity, University. It was like a solid meringue that squashed us all. We could never get out of it. Now we've pulled ourselves together, on this grass, soon I'll be on my feet. Less stars, but you can't do anything with this world. And Rector Cadenas, who didn't want Juan Ramón to speak at the University, because this is what Rector Cadenas asked: "Come on now, boys, is this

Señor Jiménez really important enough to speak here?" But there was another University, the Villanueva of the priests: all nice and clean, orderly, utterly mediocre. Being with those nice and clean Catholic professors was also like being half knocked-out. So Max Henríquez Ureña told Lezama that he was doing what he could to get him off the grass, but he couldn't, because Lezama's resume lacked certain necessary prerequisites for being a professor at Villanueva.

Because what was ugly was ugly. Ugliness got mixed up with ugliness. Because in Cuba there never was anything, nor is there anything, nor will there be anything. The *Orígenes* years had passed, but that was too ugly. This unnameable feast, in the grass, knocked out. After years with the journal, the rich guy was going to take the journal away from us. The rich guy told Lezama: from now on the rich guy is *Orígenes*. That one with a press and publicity, and a few resentful professors. Keep on with the stars, but don't keep on with *Orígenes*. And *Orígenes* was full of caution and etiquette and stereotypes. And *torrejas* for dessert. And one was and wasn't. The meetings at Bauta were meetings with a chill. And in these conditions you couldn't be a friend, nor even almost human. It's shameful to play the clown. Knocked out in an Airport. But it has to be said, even with the comic-book stars. Now there was so much caution, so many fears, that Lezama distrusted some members of *Orígenes*. And it wasn't true, and the members of *Orígenes* remained faithful to the *Orígenes* years. But *torrejas* for dessert, and those disguises. Because a painter of the *Orígenes* years had gone off with the rich guy. A painter from *Espuela de Plata* agreed with the rich guy. And Lezama called the Origenistas to Julián Orbón's house. Lezama said that he had to get hold of the Origenistas on the spur of the moment, because if not, some Origenistas could go off with the rich guy. And the old man was protesting at the Airport, and the *comrades* wanted to keep him from leaving. Too somber, too lamentable. A whole circle of friendship, a whole style, all those *Orígenes* years, but you had to go running over to Julián Orbón's house so that a few Origenistas wouldn't go off with the rich guy. And maybe Lezama was paranoid, and maybe no Origenista would go off with the rich guy. But that was too somber, but the Origenistas always lived inside an iron lung. And there was the press, the publicity, the professors, all of which despised the work of the *Orígenes* years. And a plate of *torrejas* as well. And because of that Lezama was afraid that a few Origenistas would go off with the rich guy.

I don't know how to say this. Because I'm in a New York park, dreaming about an Airport, after falling off a bicycle. Too implacable, in Cuba. It was, and wasn't. Because the rich guy never paid his contributors, nor did he pay for any book by the *Orígenes* writers, but the rich guy was ready to pay contributors in order to finish off the *Orígenes* years. And there was a plate of *torrejas*. And there are the stars. And sometimes it seems as if the intellectual world is a mafia. And that's why I'm fighting with this grass, the bicycle, and this comic-book of stars. Because Alemany said it was the culmination of the Absolute Spirit. But the *Orígenes* years were going to be left all alone. And because of the damned old man, in the Airport, we could all have been prevented from leaving. So Juan Ramón, the personification of poetry and the will to poetry, a universal Andalusian, etc., wrote a diatribe against professor-poets. So Lezama, against the rich guy's wishes, imposed the contribution-diatribe of the poet Juan Ramón. So the rich guy broke with *Orígenes* because of the contribution of the poet Juan Ramón, but the poet Juan Ramón, also quite cautious, pretended not to notice, or played dumb, and he didn't send over a plate of *torrejas*, but he did send ten dollars to *Orígenes* so it could fight the rich guy, but it seemed Juan Ramón understood nothing of the fight against the rich guy or didn't want to know anything about the fight against the rich guy. And Wallace Stevens said that the rich guy was a poet, and many *famous* foreign intellectuals who had contributed to *Orígenes*, played dumb in the fight against the rich guy. And Lezama was paranoid, he raced over to Julián Orbón's house, and he was afraid that a few Origenistas would go off with the rich guy. And I don't believe a few Origenistas would have gone off with the rich guy. What's happening is that I'm surrounded by stars. And Lezama was right to feel paranoid. So the last thing that could happen is to find oneself in an Airport while knowing all this. But I've fallen off a bicycle, as if I were a gossip, and the Origenistas didn't go off with the rich guy, nor do I think they would have gone off with the rich guy. But the Origenistas lived inside an iron lung, and with Lezama, there was a sado-masochistic game, and because of that the Origenistas, despite all the fine words, and despite the lone voice of the Baroque, didn't support the journal financially, and they allowed the *Orígenes* years to die. So the Origenistas were with Lezama. The stars. But the Origenistas were not with Lezama. Because one was, and wasn't. And sometimes Lezama wanted to be the father, but there was a sado-masochistic game with the father.

So Lezama and the *Orígenes* years are also Lezama's nightmare, and the nightmare of the *Orígenes* years. A nightmare with the cage of an Airport. So Lezama had spoken of the Atreides and the fate of the Atreides. And maybe there might be too much pomp and solemnity in these words. But there was a destiny of ashes. And Lezama, despite his *triumph*, lived, during the last years of his life, the final nightmares of his hell. Because in Cuba everything was implacable, and it will go on being implacable. Because the *torrejas* keep coming back. Because the destiny of the Atreides could be a rhetorical phrase, and a phrase of grandeur in decline. But the destiny of the Atreides, as said by the man Lezama, isn't the lone voice of the Baroque, but the voice of the *Orígenes* years.

These are the *Orígenes* years. This is the tale of a coffer. In the Airport, there was an end that could be a beginning. In New York there's a beginning that's an end. The *Orígenes* years have returned, so let's continue with the idiocy of the *Orígenes* years. And there's an albino beach, and everything that's lamentable about an albino beach. Because of this, over the phone, I'm asking Eugenio Florit to recommend me for some kind of job, since I don't have any kind of job, and I'd like to write about the *Orígenes* years. And *Dean* Florit asks me to hang on, and he tells me he's going to get a notebook. And *Dean* Florit brings the notebook over to the phone, and he wants to read me the addresses of some bookstores, so that I could go to some bookstores and ask for a job in some bookstores. Then again, I'm not surrounded by stars, but I remember the tale of a coffer. And in Cuba everything was, and wasn't. That's why I have to tell Florit, over the phone, to forget about the notebook. And I have to tell Florit, over the phone: "Florit, you're going to die in the cold. The worst thing that can happen to a poet is to die in the cold." Because this is a Cuban poet reaching out to another Cuban poet. Because there was a coffer. Because the *Orígenes* years have to mean something. And Julián Orbón says that not only will I regret speaking harshly about the *Orígenes* years, but that I'll also regret answering *Dean* Florit harshly. And I'm in the comic book of a few stars, and I'm rather old to be a romantic, but I'd like the *Orígenes* years to mean something, just as I'd like Florit, as a Cuban poet, not to have the lonely voice of an old man who's going to die in the cold.

Beginning, end, beginning as end, end as beginning, everything weighs on the *Orígenes* years. This chapter is about a coffer. And a coffer is a park, and a bicycle, and an Airport. And I've looked for my identity in the albino beach, and I believe my identity to be the identity of the *Orígenes* years. So Judit stayed behind a glass door, and Lezama was Judit's godfather, and the Origenistas wanted to celebrate saint's days and they wanted to celebrate baptisms. That's why I also picked up the phone, but to call Cintio. I called Cintio from New York. Now there was the tale of a coffer, and I'm an Origenista, and I was with the *Orígenes* years. That's why I told Cintio, on the phone, that Judit stayed behind a glass door, and Judit was my daughter. That's why I told Cintio that I wanted the Origenistas to go see somebody, because an Origenista's daughter stayed behind a glass door. But Cintio talked about working shifts with me. Cintio told me he was only a citizen. But Cintio didn't talk to me about the Origenistas. And there was the tale of a coffer. And everything was much too deplorable. I'm keeping on with my stars. This chapter is a disaster. I didn't know how to put this chapter together.

Meeting in La Victoria

Young man, read Proust.

Dim light bulb. Light bulb, dim light. Layer of insects stuck to the glass of the light bulb. Small stain. Dim light.

The corners are barely lit.

The light, dim, is too intimate. Too domestic. It doesn't light up the corners.

It's like the light of a storeroom. Or like the light of the room where old castoffs are kept.

Layer. Stain. Black stain. Rubbed insects. What's he doing here? Because this isn't the neglected room of an old mansion, but the back room of a bookstore, *Librería Victoria*, or *La Victoria*, as we all called it.

Light bulb, dim. There he was, in front of the bookshelves on the right. He was thumbing through the pages of Jaeger's *Paideia*. He was an adolescent. He was wearing a black suit—maybe he wanted to look like Unamuno—and a tie—he never stopped wearing ties. He also had trembling hands.

Trembling hands. Because of that, even there, under the dim light of that bulb smeared with a layer of squashed insects, dim light that barely lit up the corners, a spectator, positioned next to the small door of the back room—not exactly a door, but the opening of a crude cardboard folding screen—couldn't help perceiving—if back then Alain Robbe-Grillet had been translated into Spanish, we'd know the distance, measured precisely in meters and centimeters, separating the spectator from the adolescent character—the excessive trembling of those hands holding Jaeger's book.

But the spectator was there, at the small door of the back room—not exactly a door, but the opening of a crude cardboard folding screen. And the spectator said:

– Young man, read Proust!

It was José Lezama Lima.

What was he doing there? The adolescent didn't know. It was midday. Lezama left immediately.

There was a desk in the back area of the bookstore. The desk was near—if Alain Robbe-Grillet had been translated into Spanish, we'd know the distance, measured precisely in meters and centimeters, separating the spectator from the adolescent character—the cardboard folding screen that divided the back area. In front of the desk were two chairs. Lezama was sitting in one of these chairs.

Lezama went to *La Victoria* every afternoon, but the adolescent didn't know why the spectator always went, in the afternoon, to *La Victoria.*

But this spectator was—and this is certain—a complete *presence.* A complete presence, and very much a Cuban one. The adolescent remembered him with a cigar, a white suit, and an incredible laugh.

(Because Lezama's presence was unforgettable for all of us who had the immense privilege of seeing him, of hearing him, in the *Orígenes* years, since the few of us in his circle felt the pride, and the responsibility, not only of being close to our country's highest spiritual consciousness, but also, almost paradoxically, its highest ethical consciousness.)

Because the adolescent didn't know who Cintio Vitier was either, nor anyone who was a priest, nor did the adolescent even know about the journal *Orígenes*. Cintio Vitier was a book, *Extrañeza de estar* (*Strangeness of Being*), that the adolescent saw in *La Victoria.* The adolescent asked about Cintio, and about the book, and a Cuban, a professor of literature, answered that Cintio, and the book, had something to do with philosophy, with existentialism, and with the avant-garde, but it was all incomprehensible. The adolescent asked about a priest, a priest in *La Victoria*, next to Lezama, and surrounded by a group of young people.—The thing is, the young people appeared to have great respect for the priest, and Lezama had shown the priest a book –. But the owner of *La Victoria* and the historian of Martí, Don Isidro Méndez, answered with one voice: "He's a priest,

Father Gaztelu, who's part of a group of faggots. He founded with Lezama a journal that was called *Nadie parecía, pero todos lo eran*—Nobody Appeared to Be, But All of Them Were."

What happened was that Lezama was once in *La Victoria*, and Professor Jorge Mañach came in. Mañach said to Lezama: "They say that now you're being called *Maestro*." Lezama answered: "I'd rather be called *Maestro* in jest than *Professor* in earnest."

In *La Victoria*, as in the newspapers, as in the professorial coteries, as in all the little worlds of official Cuban culture, artists and writers were held in disdain. And because of that, for some time in *La Victoria*, they got rid of the sofa and chairs, because every day the old Cuban writer Luis Felipe Rodríguez went to the bookstore, and he sat down, the old Cuban writer, on a sofa or a chair. So for a while they got rid of the sofa and the chairs, because for the Spanish owner of *La Victoria*, and for many Spaniards who went to the bookstore, the old Cuban writer was just *an old pain in the neck*. And only Lezama, who also went to *La Victoria*, respected Luis Felipe's calling, and only Lezama got angry at this indecency.

That's why, in the back area of the bookstore, the adolescent had seen the copies of a journal with a white cover. He had seen the square shape of the copies of a journal. He had seen a journal called *Orígenes*. But the adolescent only read books of philosophy. But the adolescent had never thumbed through the square-shaped journal. How could anything interesting be published in Cuba? So the adolescent didn't know that the man who had said to him, *Young man, read Proust*, was the man who edited the journal.

Because there was a cavalcade of confusion. Because everything in the Cuba of those times was a cavalcade of confusion.

from

Suite para la espera / Suite for Waiting

(1948)

Variaciones

De la tarde a la noche no hubo tránsito. Estaba ahí. La lluvia la presiente, la envuelve. Va como encapsulada en cada gota. Promesa de un otoño eterno. Con acre sabor en los oídos.

El chubasco al lado de la noche persistía. Lamiendo en ondas el agua emponzoñada. Ligeras corrían en breves presagios. Juego minúsculo: pequeñas amazonas que agitadas atravesaban la calle.

Breve mueca que hace la lluvia al tocar la acera. Desgestos y vieja mueca. Mueca de parroquia al insinuar sus campanas.

El estremecimiento de lo viejo, de un algo impensado retenía. Tú, Tú. Parecían venidas de muy lejos las puertas y ventanas. El sueño desenvolviéndose por las casas (confianza de extraños recovecos y dulce melodía).

¡Noches de lluvia que al pellejo se adhieren como gatos! Noches, resbalar. ¡Noches de inhumado eco, con sus pestañas tentando el vértigo de luz! Caminan las calles, son descubiertas en relampagueante zigzag de casa con relicario antiguo. Y encogidos gatos de esparcidos ojos. ¿Luminosos?

¿Tentación? ¿Cruce de calles? ¿Caminar? Oh, sí, tarde como un manto, vívido paisaje. Reminiscencia de cansados niños en el portal tendidos.

Despaciosos pinos se mueven. Carretera de cristal por la luna empapada. Cañaverales meciendo sus ensueños: Torpes. Quedo guiños de estrellas.

La locomotora cargada de tesoros sucios.

Me hieren los minutos. Siento el estremecimiento delirante. Desgárrenseme las carnes: percibo el devenir plástico del día.

Mi mirada inmadura quiere besar las cosas. Tengo el miedo terrible de perder el devenir, perseguido en la colina y en el río.

Variations

Between afternoon and nighttime, no transition. Night was there. Rain anticipates it, envelops it. It walks along as if contained in every drop. Promise of eternal autumn. With a bitter taste in its ears.

The downpour continued at the edge of night. Lapping in waves the envenomed water. Swiftly they flowed in brief premonitions. A tiny game; wee Amazons that crossed the street nervously.

Brief grimace of rain touching the pavement. Expressionless old grimace. The church's grimace when its bells insinuate.

The shudder of the aged retained something unthought-of. You. You. The doors and windows seemed to have come from afar. Sleep spreading through the houses (confidence of strange nooks and sweet melody).

Rainy nights that stick to the skin like cats! Nights, slipping. Nights of buried echoes, their eyelashes tempting light's vertigo! They walk the streets, they are revealed in the zigzag of lightning of a house with an ancient reliquary. And shrunken cats with scattered—luminous?—eyes.

Temptation? Crossroads? Walking? Oh yes, afternoon like a cloak, vivid landscape. A memory of weary children stretched out in the doorway.

Slow pines are moving. Crystal highway drenched by the moon. Cane fields rocking their reveries. Sluggish. Quietly, wink of stars.

The locomotive laden with dirty treasures.

The minutes wound me. I feel the frenzied shudder. Tear my flesh apart: I see day's expressive transformation.

My immature gaze wants to kiss things. I have the terrible fear of losing the transformation, pursued on hill and river.

Las cosas se me presentan, ay, en majestuosidad imponente. Quiero elevarlas al sol y esconderlas en estuche.

Quiero seguir en círculos creciendo.

Es la hora matutina del buitre, ya sus alas azotan los balaústres.

Más, no ha de mirarlo. Callo. Es un triste resabio de ancestral desilusión.

Se insinúa el buitre por las rejas. Con mirada de águila, y latir afiebrado, insinúa torrentes de palabras calladas y parece que esconde mil mares de antaño.

Solitario buitre. De mirada madura, témole a tu pico y a tu canto, desesperadamente. He de seguir tocando el fantasma dormido.

Things present themselves, alas, in imposing majesty. I want to raise them to the sun and hide them in my drawer.

I want to keep growing in circles.

It is the vulture's nocturnal hour, already its wings are lashing the balusters.

But I don't have to look at it. I keep quiet. It's a sad vestige of ancestral disillusion.

The vulture makes its way through the bars. With an eagle's gaze, and feverish wingbeats, it hints at torrents of silent words and seems to be hiding a thousand seas of yore.

Solitary vulture. With a ripe old gaze, I am in desperate dread of your beak and your song. I must keep touching the sleeping phantom.

He de vivir por siempre. Me bañaré en los ríos y habrá lumbre encendida.
Sí, allá en la ciudad de la jerga dulce, el cantar afiebrado ilumina las murallas.
Después, me puedes destrozar buitre. Es mi precio a mi ansia de vida.
(El buitre se extraña inútilmente, con menso de cola escucha a las estrellas.)

Meridiano. Y las porfías de niños se retuercen entre las flores. Y los organillos cercanos a la mar anuncian la llegada del velero.

Reloj. Exactitud y los blancos cristales de las copas. Y los altisonantes gritos del vendedor: últimos gritos y la parranda de las frondas. Y se abren las compuertas de la calle. Mientras las quejas se disipan en la nimiedad de la blancura.

Girar instantáneo. Vuela de nubes. Las casas flotan en su diluvio estremecido. Nimiedad, luz clara. Mediodía.

I must live forever. I will bathe in the rivers and a fire will be lit.
Yes, over there in the city of sweet jargon, feverish singing lights up the walls.
Afterwards, you can rip me apart, vulture. It's the price I pay for my yearning for life.
(The vulture is pointlessly surprised, with a flick of his tail he listens to the stars.)

High noon. And the children's tiffs are entangled in flowers. And the hurdy-gurdies by the sea announce the sailboat's arrival.

Clock. Precision and the goblets' white glass. And the resonant cries of the vendor: last shouts and the procession of branches. And the street's floodgates open. As the complaints dissipate into the excessive whiteness.

Instantaneous whirl. Flight of clouds. The houses float in their shuddering flood. Excess, bright light. Midday.

La noche de los pasmosos

La noche de los pasmosos arlequines.
Los reyes, los astros de euforia rubrican.
¡Qué brincan las viejas campanas!
Madre, ah, sí, en tanto oscuro, vuelven.

Miro. La madre en los lentos portales, las nucas de lloro,
las viejas campanas, taladrados sopores.
Risa, minúsculos dioses, mirad las encíclicas pardas
fuera del naufragio de mi habitación.
Con los papeles a cuestas, atrás ¡como yo mismo!

Lloro las euforias.
¡Ya es tan tarde!
Afuera, el ruido de un tableteo.

Night of the Wondrous

   Night of the wondrous harlequins.
Kings, stars, euphorically certify.
   Let the old church bells leap!
Mother, ah yes, as it's dark, they're returning.

I look. Mother in the slow passageway, napes of weeping,
the old church bells, piercing torpors,
Laughter, minuscule gods, behold the grayish-brown encyclicals
outside the shipwreck of my room.
Burdened with papers, behind, like me myself!

I weep for the euphorias.
   It's so late already!
Outside, the noise of a rattle.

Arrellanado

Arrellenado… uf… Que el lastimero esfuerzo
compense mi prisión.
La tarde recoge los balaústres
(¡Qué no vayan a perderse!)
Comprendo… Todo en calma
en el trillo quedando.
Hasta la herradura ¡qué no robemos su oxidación! nos deja su mueca.
¡Es tarde!
Podemos volver… volvemos.
Choque de carretas.
Yo tanteaba sus nudos, sin bueyes, en abril, siempre.
No sé
Sus ruedas seguían maniatando mi frente hasta la noche.
Pienso ¡soledad!
En los piñales: rojo, rojo —tierra— tiñe, tiñe su cuarto
—cielo—. Rosa hiriente
Resonaremos.
¡Que puedo decir a… hasta el infinito!
Doy con mi pie al polvo.
Mi cuello entre palmas.
Busco, búsqueda, revuelvo mi alma entre caminos.
Bujías, bohíos:
rojos sus patios planchados.
Del mediodía: revoloteo tardo en mí.
Coro… (En la casa una mujer junto a la bomba de agua)
Aguas, salpicoteando en el charquero ¡que los niños no
se acerquen!
Que tanto mediodía así! La tienda ausente ¡yo sé!
Se han ido.
Reconocí ese golpe. Muero en luto, como en trinos.
¡yo sé!

Stuffed Up

Stuffed up…phew… May this plaintive effort
   compensate for my imprisonment.
Afternoon gathers up the balusters
(Don't let them get lost!)
I understand… Everything calmly
staying in the thresher
Even the horseshoe—let's not steal its rust!—leaves us its grimace.
         It's late!
We can go back… let's go back.
         Oxcarts collide.
I was examining its knots, without oxen, always, in April.
         I don't know
Its wheels kept binding my brow until nightfall.
         I think: solitude!
In the pine groves: red, red—earth—dyes, dyes its room
– sky. Wounding rose
         We shall resound.
What can I tell…until the infinite!
         I kick the dust.
         My neck among palms.
I seek, search, I stir my soul among pathways.
         Sparkplugs, huts:
         red their ironed courtyards.
Of midday: a slow fluttering within me.
Chorus… (In the house a woman at the water pump)
Waters, dripping into the mud puddle: don't let the kids
get close!
So much midday here! The missing general store: I know!
         They've gone.
I recognized that blow. I die in mourning, as in trills.
         I know!

Estos pueblos en sus cifras. Mi habitación.
Mi tía puede encontrar mis juguetes.
Río con su hablar ¡qué tanto destino!
Mientras ese curso de hormigas…
Como con ella, su trenza, mi retenido tiempo.
Ahora el hotel luce tan chico.
Ayer vi su jardincillo entre pólvora de la fiesta.
Aún en su ruina, el polvo no destapa.
Miro mis sentidos. Como en el estanque,
hay deshojazón sobre sus ondas.
            Sin saber. Bracear
como estrenar. La noche se ha abierto sobre sí misma.
Todos pueden llorar, sin devenir, sin recoger la llanada.
Se trenzan los contactos como lúpulos de cerveza.
            También río, como en el circo.

These villages in their ciphers. My room.
My aunt can find my toys.
River with its speech: so much for destiny!
While this march of ants…
As with her, her braid, my time held back.
Now the hotel looks so small.
Yesterday I saw its little garden amid the dust of the fiesta.
Even in its ruins, the dust does not disclose.
I look at my senses. As in the pond,
leaves are scattered on its waves.
        Without knowing. Exertion
like beginning. Night has opened onto itself.
Everyone can weep, without becoming, without gathering the plain.
Contacts are braided like beer hops.
        River too, as in the circus.

Ah, que haya visto

I

Ah, que haya visto aquella noche
con los inviernos de cañaverales, lanzando
sus prodigios a plumazos: estragos de la estrella.
Si yo volviera a paso de esperar el carricoche
con la vela de los hombres sabios. Las velas rudas
sosteniendo como bastiones las encíclicas gozosas.
Si volviera el retozo de su humo. De su humo danzando
camafeos en los mármoles.

Y dejaba a ojos los murciélagos
para que tropezasen con los trenes,
con los anaqueles del gris de mis manos.

¡Respondo preguntas, a lo lejos!

II

Atrás… zigzaguea para más: tropos de ferrocarril
Veo:
Las bujías embadurnadas.
Los locos silencios de fiebre, en matojos!
que engendran la ira de exhaustos quehaceres.
El viejo desliza sus palabras coralinas.
Pero… ya estoy en la estación!

Ah, to Have Seen

I

Ah, to have seen that night
with the canefield winters, hurling
their wonders with strokes of the pen: star's drought.
If I could return to waiting for the wagon
with the wise men's candle. The crude candles
supporting the joyous encyclicals like bastions.
If the frolicking of its smoke could return. From its dancing smoke
cameos on the marbles.

And I more or less left the bats
to collide with the trains,
with the shelves of the gray of my hands

I answer questions, at a distance!

II

Behind ...it zigzags still more: railway tropes
I see:
Smeared sparkplugs.
In the bushes, fever's crazy silences!
engendering the anger of exhausted tasks.
The old man lets slip his coraline words.
But...I'm already at the station!

III

Y… vino el después: los trastos sonados, sonando
en refriegas se suman cadáveres de cascos glaciales
¡yo con mi cerebro rasurado!
¡Pronto que este invierno se me viene encima!
Los "puertos seguros". Indios vestidos al desgaire rozan
las cigarras. Mueven en "figurines de clown" carruseles
de euforia tardía.

Pero ¡Dios! ¡Todavía aquí!
Vamos al centro húmedo de los globos ¡sí!
Más ¿qué más? Digan las cabezas partidas:
        —"¿Qué hay, qué tal?"
Y yo corro a lomo de euforia los parques.
Progresión… la niña repercute su pelota sobre
el banco, sobre el banco, sobre mí! Hasta ser "yo",
        "¿Cómo te llamas?"
        "Lucía"
        A secas…
Vástagos de conjuros quedan en el buzón.
Yo irguiendo los lloros
hasta hacer la danza rítmica.
Ayer había visto mi fuerza, caminaba entre tablones.
¡Pero que chicas las flores!

Iluminaciones: id a la Iglesia.
Trompos para aquellos,
"son como niños".

Electrocutada la bujía.
Abollando con mis amigos los parques ya abandonados
                – "y el jodío de una sola cara"…

III

And…the afterwards came: the dreamed-of rubbish, dreaming
cadavers from glacial outbuildings join in brawls
I with my shaved brain!
How quickly this winter descends upon me!
"Secure the gates." Shabbily-dressed Indians brush against
cicadas. In "clown costumes" they set in motion
carousels of belated euphoria.

But, God! Still here!
Off we go to the moist center of balloons, yes indeed!
But, what else? The divided heads say:
"What's up, how are you doing?"
And I run through the parks astride euphoria.
Progression…the girl bounces her ball on
the bench, on the bench, on me! Until I'm "I",
"What's your name?"
"Lucia"
Bluntly…
Shouted exorcisms remain in the mailbox.
Me brandishing my wailing
until the dance be rhythmic.
Yesterday I'd seen my strength, walked between planks.
How small the flowers are!

Illuminations: go to church.
Whirligigs for those,
"they're like children."

The sparkplug electrocuted.
Denting with my friends the now-abandoned parks
– "and the jerk-off with one single face"…

Lima

Conquistadores a zancadas en los almohadones
En Lima
los galápagos jardineros Verlaine las trompetas
lagrimosas
los suburbios de naranja las pirámides de sal
para trinchar la luna
las polvorientas mesoneras a trompicones en el caracol
desnudan sus cabezas piden lila hasta el columpio
   de Júpiter
las liebres en incienso de gaseosa fecha de libro roto
en remiendo de algodonoso indio
los aviones de cartón César Vallejo
los cuentos "Simón Bolívar" en caja de sorpresa
del pez en el estambre de la abuela
los abruptos camafeos en la montaña
los roncos gañanes musitando las endechas del periodista
en las banderas acuáticas
los guerreros del rey Don Juan acampados
en la lluvia como una niña sibilina como un agorero cowboy
         En Lima

Lima

Conquistadors striding forth on large cushions
In Lima
tortoises gardeners Verlaine lachrymose
trumpets
orange suburbs salt pyramids
to carve up the moon
dusty innkeepers in fits and starts on the seashell
bare their heads beg for lily all the way to Jupiter's rocking chair
the hares in sparkling-water incense with a date of a worn-out book
mending a cottony Indian
cardboard airplanes César Vallejo
"Simón Bolívar" stories in a surprise box
of fish in grandma's worsted
abrupt cameos in the mountain
hoarse farmhands humming the journalist's dirges
on the aquatic flags
the warriors of King Don Juan bivouacked
in the rain like a sibylline girl like a cowboy soothsayer
In Lima

En playa recortada

El dios indio porta el tirabuzón en las fiestas del arroz
Arrojan las salinas portuarias al octaedro
para doscientos guerreros en llamas columpios zigzagueantes
Así a barlovento los barcos de papel en el busto de Bach
Como un cancerbero misántropo asoma en la palabra ciclón
          Apollinaire al agua

On an Irregular Beach

The Indian god carries his corkscrew in the festivals of rice
They throw the salty harbors into the octahedron
for two hundred warriors in zigzagging rocking chair flames
Thus to windward the paper boats on the bust of Bach
Just as a misanthropic goalkeeper leans over the word cyclone
          Into the water with Apollinaire

Marfiles ahogados

Chaplin abúlico
su saco de coral fangoso
atrás cleptómanos enlutados de alhelí
Portones carreteando la estrella como una concha
a vista de paraguas encendidos
para que los encendedores de lluvia no asusten
a los huelguistas
La partida toma los discursos del insecto
Así en la pluma al aire los moluscos ensortijados
de tic tac
y los tísicos ovillados en el fuego del coral
En las azoteas cuelgan los payasos
para la cripta de cristales para orinar las bibliotecas
Así las plañideras toserán la mañana
como un trompón
como yo
Adiós

Drowned Ivories

Apathetic Chaplin
his muddy coral suit
to the rear mourning kleptomaniacs of wallflower
Gates hauling the star like a shell
seen by flaming umbrellas
lest the incendiaries of rain frighten
the strikers
The new mother takes the insects' speeches
And thus in the feather in the air the curled-up mollusks
of tick-tock
and rolled-up consumptives in the coral fire
On the rooftops clowns hang
for the crypt of glasses for the libraries to piss
And thus the mourners will cough in the morning
like a bump
like me
Bye

En las lágrimas de las focas

Frío en los guardines terrosos
Parada la luna a estribor en la quinta hora de la tarde
Ahora todos nos iremos como un corcel
torcidamente muertos para llorar la injuria de las cortinas
y los llantos triples de las paredes dormidos truenos
Vaivén de desplegados cabezas hipnóticas calabazas calvas
Crines del estudiante musitan en las cuevas del Rey
lloran las pamelas
Coral absorto en pastillas de luna
Absalón húmedo remiendo lavanderas en los tropos de la sal
   Panderetas para la huida
para los morteros doctores a cruce de jabalinas
así tramposos humeantes piedras jacarandá en la casa vacía

frío en acordeón de la luna focas lloren sus precipicios
así en las fábricas los cadáveres elefantes
cuando los cuaternarios avancen cenicientos
lupa para Dios en los mosquiteros sonrosados
   encantos en los cuartos de baño
gritan las bombas para los inquilinos pacíficos
listones acuáticos en la tierra embadurnada tantanlin

In the Seals' Tears

Cold on the muddy tiller ropes
The moon halted at starboard around five in the afternoon
Now we'll all be off like a steed
twisted and dead to mourn the curtains' insult
and the triple laments of the walls sleeping thunderclaps
Swaying of hypnotic heads bald gourds on display
The student's horsehairs are mumbling in the King's caverns
the sombreros weep
Coral absorbed in lunar tablets
Damp Absalom patching up washerwomen in the tropes of salt
   Tambourines for flight
for the mortar doctors crossing javelins
such swindlers smoking stones jacaranda in the empty house

cold the moon's accordion seals weep their cliffs
thus in the factories elephant corpses
when the ashen quaternaries advance
magnifier for God in the rosy mosquito nets
   enchantment in the bathrooms
bombs scream for the perfect tenants
acoustic strips on the daubed earth teedadum

from

Orígenes / From the Journal *Orígenes*

(1951)

Túnel

Túnel de mi espera, ¿Por qué tu noche labrada
de equívocas cenizas? ¿Por qué tu noche sostenida
por el tributo oscuro, extinguido? (Mi vida
perdiéndose por tus rotas imágenes) Oh morada,

¡oh silencio! ¿acaso anhelada? ¿acaso en el recodo, mía?
Si estabas, todo temblor, como un engaño,
a romper las esquinas de mi sueño. Si estabas por el regaño
de tus paredes rotas, espectrales. Sí, y retenía

tu fulgor la extraña tarde, como una bella
sensación de hastío (un soplo cansado colora
este último tributo de mi frente a tu enjuto

sueño ironizado). Oh leve, oh grande, oh aurora
de lo extraño, oh túnel: rompiendo en el instante, con la estrella
tenaz de tus insomnios, el hosco fulgor de mi tributo.

Tunnel

Tunnel of my waiting. Why is your night carved
from equivocal ashes? Why is your night sustained
by the dark, extinguished tribute? (My life
losing itself in your broken images) Oh dwelling,

oh silence perhaps longed-for? perhaps, in the recesses, my own?
You were there, all a-tremble, like a trick,
breaking into the corners of my dream. You were there in the reproach
of your broken, spectral walls. Yes, and the strange

afternoon retained your splendor, like a beautiful
feeling of boredom (a tired breath colors
this final tribute of my brow to your thin

ironic dream), Oh light, oh great, oh dawn
of strangeness, oh tunnel; that moment breaking, with the tenacious
star of your sleeplessness, my tribute's gloomy splendor.

from

Ritmos Acribillados / Riddled Rhythms

(1972)

El santo del Padre Rector

Llega ese día., el día de fiesta en el colegio: lo siente como un frío. Sin embargo, él va también hasta allí, hasta el borde de ellos. Cerca de ellos, pero no más que para pensar en sus cosas, en sus casi cosas, en su historia. Pero eso, no puede saber cómo son los gritos, las risas, los juegos. Y cuando el jesuita —gordo, sofocado— tira caramelos por una ventana, él se levanta con los demás, se agacha como los demás, llega a recoger bombones en un rincón; pero luego se ve, entrando en la alegría de ellos como el que desenfadadamente penetra en una casa ajena, y se avergüenza.

Ahora unos montan a caballo; otros, cerca del campo de pelota, se acercan al camión que tiene los refrescos: se sofocan, pelean, ríen: él nunca conocerá su secreto. Pero aun insiste, va a quedarse para la *sesión de la tarde*, ensaya una que otra carrereta y, al final, siente sobre sus brazos el forro empapado en sudor de su saco. Ellos, los otros, sin embargo, giran con una luz, con un calor distinto.

Ya, nítidos, los ve. Los precisa, los dibuja. En las filas, en el comedor o en los juegos: palpitante, un solo organismo lleno de ruido y sudor, surge de sus cuerpos unidos. Y él intenta vivir un poco como ellos, doblar para sí, como si fuera un pañuelo, el tapiz de sus gritos. Y se acerca al banco de madera de la galería donde está sentado Ramón López: gordo, anodino, fofo, con barquillo de helado en una mano. Y se pone a imitar sus gestos de niño cándido —casi idiota—, como para remendar la soledad.

Pero, no hay salida, tiene que verlos de lejos. Tiene que ver su inmensa masa, globo de ruidos y colores fulgurantes, que suena con la nostalgia de los lugares adonde no ha estado, con las risas del circo donde estuvo solo. Porque esa inmensa presencia, porque ese ruido de ellos, es la presencia y el ruido, de una carpa grande, tan grande como el mundo, en que él no penetra.

The Rector's Saint's Day

That day arrives, a party in the school: it's like a blast of cold inside him. But he's going there too, right up to their edge. Close to them, but only to think about what they're up to, what they're almost up to, their story. That's why he can't know what their cries, laughter, games are like. And when the Jesuit—fat and out-of-breath—throws caramels from a window, he gets up with the others, bends over like them, even picks up candies in a corner; but then he sees himself entering their joy like someone insolently intruding into another's house, and feels ashamed.

Some play horsey; others, near the baseball field, approach the soft-drink truck: breathless, they fight, they laugh: he'll never know their secret. But he still insists, he's going to stay for the *afternoon session*, he tries some cartwheels, and, when finished, feels the sweat-soaked jacket lining under his arms. They, however, the others, whirl with a light, a different heat.

Now, in sharp outline, he sees them. He defines, draws them. Standing in line, at the dining hall, and at play: palpitating, a single organism full of noise and sweat emerges from their combined bodies. And he's trying to live like them a bit, to fold for himself like a handkerchief the tapestry of their shouts. And he approaches the wooden bench in the gallery where Ramón López—fat, insignificant, flabby, holding an ice-cream cone—is sitting. And he starts imitating his innocent—almost idiotic—boy's gestures, as if to mend the solitude.

But there's no escape, he has to see them from a distance. He has to see their immense mass, a globe of noises and dazzling colors, which sings of nostalgia for places he's never been, with the laughter of the circus he went to alone. Because this immense presence, because this noise of theirs, is the presence and noise of a big tent, as big as the world, which he can't enter.

Ahora ya es de noche. Ha terminado el día del santo del Padre Rector. Desde un pequeño paradero de tranvías —mortecina luz donde nacen chicharras, un solo banco de piedra para un viajero de humo— él, de la mano de sus padres, va entendiendo, lentamente, por la soledad, como el que escala, cautelosamente una ladera nocturna. Y no es que deje de verlos, no: sabe que están allí, en el colegio; sabe que están dentro de una carpa grande, tan grande como el mundo. Y sabe, también, que ellos han de reírse, siempre, con ruido voluptuoso y alucinante, sobre la estéril pantomima de sus gestos.

Él: soledad, títere: lanza su lamentable mímesis, cubierto con el forro empapado en sudor del uniforme de gala del colegio. Ellos: surgiendo, entrando, saliendo, por esa calle siempre prestigiosa, donde los cinematógrafos están cubiertos con la sombra de un gigante familiar.

Eso es así, lo sabe desde entonces, lo sabrá siempre. Y, cuando después de haber tomado el tranvía, apoya su frente en el cristal de la ventanilla, comprende que esas pequeñas luces que ruedan por lo oscuro de la noche, tienen la misteriosa dulzura del frío que se acepta, del frío en que se penetra por secreta vocación.

Now it's night. The Rector's saint's day is over. From a small trolley stop—fading light in which cicadas are born, a single stone bench for a traveler of smoke—he, at his parents' hand, will come to understand, slowly, through solitude, like someone cautiously climbing a nocturnal slope. And it's not that he stops seeing them, no: he knows they're there, in the school; he knows they're inside a big tent, as big as the world. And he also knows that they always have to laugh, with a voluptuous, beguiling noise, at the sterile pantomime of his gestures.

He: solitude, puppet: he hurls his lamentable mimesis, covered in the sweat-soaked lining of the school dress uniform. They: emerging, entering, leaving, through this always high-toned street, where the movie theaters are covered with the shadow of a familial giant.

That's how it is, he knows it now, he'll always know it. And when, on the streetcar, he leans his forehead on the windowpane, he understands that those tiny lights whirling through the darkness of the night have the mysterious sweetness of the cold one accepts, the cold one enters through a secret calling.

En este viejo país de la infancia

Tarde. En este viejo país de la infancia. ¿Qué desdibuja a esos niños que salen del mismo colegio donde estuve? Ellos cruzan la calle que yo cruzaba. Y el parque, ruidoso con el canto de los pájaros. Parece estar más cuidado.

Esta tarde en el viejo país de la infancia. Y mirad: tristes, fúnebres campanadas en la iglesia del pueblo: mañana será el entierro. Hay silencio. Cae el sol. Ruido de las sartenes se pone a freír del uno al otro extremo de la calle. En algunas casas se encienden las luces del portal.

Nada nuevo. Lo que tiene que ocurrir, lo que ocurre siempre. La muchacha, cuyo pelo rubio cae sobre mi mirada como un escándalo, se pinta en la saleta, frente al espejo de la bastonera. Claro está, nadie ha dicho que no hay que usar los objetos del viejo país de la infancia, y la otra, la chica del sweater, abandona el portal con su vacío guiño de pepilla.

Noche cayendo. Calles que empiezan a existir con la sombra —es natural—. Estrellas que tú vistes. Estrellas que entonces no habían nacido. Lacio, rajado emblema de la noche, sobre el parque del pueblo.

En la antiquísima esquina del hotel seguía la conversación de años atrás. El notario dijo: "La vida es como un sueño sobre un pilón de maíz: te quitas una mazorca que te molesta, y te cae otra. La vida..." Lejos, ilumina un relámpago: el mismo de antes; el que no se convierte en rayo; el que casi en un baúl familiar puede guardarse como una cinta.

Se enredan párpados, labios, voces, de la noche. Sembrando de puntos este insecto mayúsculo, sobre el cual un guijarro cruza. De las tijeras de ese espejo de la costurera un rostro grandote, familiar: se pone a reír franco, amistoso.

In This Old Country of Childhood

Evening. In this old country of childhood. What blurs these children leaving the school I attended? They're crossing the street I crossed. And the park, noisy with birdsong, looks more cared-for now.

That evening in childhood's old country. And behold: sad, funereal bells toll in the village church: the burial's tomorrow. Silence. The sun sets. The noise of skillets frying from one end of the street to the other. In some houses the entrance lights go on.

Nothing new. What has to happen, what always happens. The girl whose blond hair falls upon my gaze with a crash is putting on her makeup in the hallway, in front of the umbrella stand's mirror. Of course, nobody's said you can't use the objects of childhood's old country, and the other one, the sweater girl, with her vapid cutie's wink, leaves the doorway behind.

Night falling. Streets that begin to exist with the shadows—as expected. Stars you saw. Stars that hadn't been born then. Faded, cracked emblem of the night above the village park.

In the ancient corner of the hotel the conversation from years back continued. The notary said, "Life's like sleeping on top of a barrel of corn: you remove an ear that's bothering you and another one falls on you. Life…" Far off, a lightning flash, the same one as before, that doesn't become thunder, that can almost be kept like a ribbon in a family trunk.

Eyelids, lips, voices of the night become entangled. This enormous insect, speckled with dots, over which a peasant crosses. From the scissors of this seamstress's mirror, a huge, familiar face: it starts laughing openly, amicably.

¡Ese es el primer automóvil que arranca de esta noche! Algunos guajiros van para el ingenio, la zafra va a comenzar. *(A la manera de marco, pétalos, cedazo, y el rostro amoratado de una novia campesina estallando en el borde de una vieja tarjeta de felicitaciones).* Restos de algunas casas —quemadas por si acaso, como por equivocación—, quedan con la pena de decir adiós. En este viejo país de la infancia.

This is the first automobile to start up tonight! Some peasants are leaving for the sugar mill, the harvest is about to begin. *(In the style of a frame, petals, a sieve, and the purplish face of a peasant bride exploding on the edge of an old congratulatory card.)* The ruins of a few houses—burned down just in case, as if by mistake—remain with farewell's sorrow. In this old country of childhood.

Tu voz

Voz tuya, casi irreal, por el hilo del teléfono. Pero, ¿irreal? No, modulante, tangible soplo que pudiera tocar. Sin embargo, choca con ella mi sueño, mi recuerdo; choca mi sangre, lastrada como sombra.

Esa voz, para mí, es como volver a empezar. Es como abrir de nuevo ese frágil túnel, ese mentiroso y equivoco túnel, con que tropiezo siempre cuando impulsado finjo, que mis pasos han de marchar hacia ti. Es, lo digo, lo redigo, como volver a empezar. Es sentirse con miedo; con prisa y a la vez con cansancio. Temeroso de tocar oscura zona.

Es que, por tu voz (fijo, de nuevo descubriendo, el lugar en que fue; clara sombra o mañana, parque sereno, y altos aquellos, altísimos aleros, que cobijaban nuestros pasos) se han levantado de nuevo los árboles, dioses otoñales de un viejo cuento que había olvidado. Por tu voz, lago inmóvil hiere palabras, nombres que oscuramente entiendo, desde la alucinada flora de sus ondas. Por tu voz, figura o sueño, nítido deletrea su doctrinal de espuma, libre ya de lo oscuro.

Y, por esa, tu voz, también, lejos de ti, recordándola, me he mirado, solo, en la zozobra de una tarde neutra: frío su crepúsculo: capitel desquiciado de sus sueños ausentes. Y, por esa, tu voz, también, lejos de ti, recordándola, al apretarse el dolor de tu ausencia he creado, quizá, entre tantas cosas, una lluvia húmeda de mayo, con reguero de luces en su centro, con nostalgia feroz en sus cristales de ocaso, que fingían trémulas saetas de una tarde sin tiempo.

Pero ahora lo digo, lo redigo, esa tu voz por el hilo de un teléfono, me vuelve a comenzar por un túnel. Enterrado en horrible cabina telefónica —por supuesto de un bar—, palpo el inevitable azar de mi derrota; contemplo, impasible, pero también desesperado, eso de tu ausencia… Y, sometido al dolor, veo, o desdoblo, por el neutro cristal

Your voice

Your voice, almost unreal, through the telephone wire. Unreal? No, modulating, tangible breath I can touch. But my dream, my memory, collide with it, my blood collides, burdened like a shadow.

This voice, for me, is like starting over. It's like once again opening this fragile tunnel, this lying, equivocal tunnel, which I always bump into when, driven, I pretend that my steps have to go towards you. I say it and say it again, it is like starting over, like feeling at once scared, in a hurry, and tired. Fearful of touching a dark zone.

Through your voice (fixed, again discovering the place where it was, bright shadow or morning, a serene park, and those high, so very high eaves that sheltered our steps) the trees have risen again, autumnal gods of an old story I'd forgotten. Through your voice, a motionless lake wounds words, names I hear obscurely, from the hallucinatory flora of its waves. Through your voice, figure or dream clearly deciphers its doctrine of foam, now freed from darkness.

And because of this, your voice also, far from you, remembering it, I've gazed at myself, alone, in the sinking of a neutral evening: its cold columnar dusk unhinged by its absent dreams. And because of this, your voice also, far from you, remembering it, while clutching the pain of your absence, I've created, perhaps, among so many things, a soaking May rain, with a trickle of lights at its center, with a ferocious nostalgia on its sunset mirrors, which feign tremulous arrows of a timeless evening.

But now I say it and say it again, this voice of yours through the telephone wire, sends me back to the beginning through a tunnel. Buried in a horrible telephone booth—in a bar, of course—I fondle the inevitable chance of my defeat, I contemplate, impassive but also

de la cabina, como ellos, los demás —ese que pasa, simula un frío dibujo con la sombra—, convertidos en burlescos duendes, desatan la miniatura de nuestra lejanía, cruelmente iluminada, en el techo, por una famélica franja de estrellada noche.

Y es que, aunque pudiera, otra vez, volver a la tierna pausa de tu cabello; y otra vez, secamente, furiosamente, volver a besar la hiriente sal de sus ondas, ya sé que no es lo mismo. Y aunque pudiera, otra vez, acariciar, o ásperamente revolver mis dedos sobre tu pelo negro, buscando, pesquisando, esa orilla insegura de tu estar en mí, ya sé que no es posible…

Sí, tu voz, hoy, ¿irreal?, recogida en una cabina telefónica, no sólo es el anuncio de tu olvido, es también, con su lejano, aunque tangible eco, esa forma feroz, terrible, de la ausencia, que comienza desatando los recuerdos —¡tan nuestros un día!—, hasta volverlos solos, en nosotros, hincados por esa sombra que hiere con un reverso inevitable. O es también, lo que empieza a constar del vacío, vaciándose en tu ausencia para colocarnos a los dos, aunque estemos frente a frente, con un rostro escondido, con una voz irreal, con una figura, apenas, lamentable, donde ya no se copian nuestros sueños.

desperate, this matter of your absence.... And, crushed by grief, I see, or I split in two, through the booth's neutral glass, like them, the others—this thing that's happening is simulating a cold drawing with shadow—transformed into comical goblins, unleash the miniature of our distance, cruelly illuminated, on the roof, through a famished fringe of a starry night.

And it's that, though I could return once again to the warm pause of your hair; and again, dryly, furiously, kiss once again the cutting salt of its waves, I already know it's not the same. And though I could caress again or roughly run my fingers through your black hair, searching, fishing for that uncertain shore of your being within me, I already know it's not possible.

Yes, your voice, today, unreal? picked up in a telephone booth, not only is the omen of your forgetting, but also, with its distant though tangible echo, that ferocious, terrible form of absence, which begins by unleashing memories—so much our own one day!—until once more they are alone, within us, driven into us by that shadow that bruises with an inevitable reversal. Or it is also that which begins to consist of the void, emptying itself into your absence in order to place both of us, though we are facing each other, with a hidden face, with an unreal voice, with a lamentable figure, barely, where our dreams are no longer copied.

Aquí una canción

La tarde, pálida, confunda los astros. Se mezclan, con los peatones, viejos dioses mágicos: sus rostros, solemnes, barbados: absorben la escasa miel del ocaso con la hojarasca de sus ojos. Se insinúan, a través de lejanos relámpagos, temibles, aunque silenciosos, bramidos.

Grande confusión de esta hora. Ellos se precipitan hacia los ómnibus. Otros peatones de rostros cansados, esperan en discretas esquinas. Mujer grande, absurda, casi vieja, cuyo torcido arrebol mancha sombras pequeñas. Y los caminos; y la noche aquella, sobre el olvido; y los soplos de un parque, en que una estatua se hizo con el aire; y el áspero frotar de la salida de un cine: con leve, aunque inquietante equívoco, cambian sus sinos, sus rostros.

Me acerco a esa desazonante baraúnda, abro su neblina. De pronto, parezco comprender: obsesión, voces ahogadas por las bocinas; enclenque tripulación de fantasmas que, el techo de una marquesina riega por las sombras. ¡Pero, también, me siento como un loco! Palpo, en medio del charco de una acera, cómo el Doncel cae entre una muchedumbre indiferente; o cómo el viejo Adivino presagia un río, sobre ese sótano en que las sombras se inclinan. Ah, no miremos, no, al rostro de ese rey mágico, cuyo ojo, picado por la muerte, siembra, en medio del sueño, una fuente de sombrío terror.

Pero ¡es increíble! En esta hora de los peatones; en esta hora de terribles oficinistas, buscando, con prisa, sus ómnibus, escucho pedazo de una canción: "he de quererte", dice; también murmura, "suave sombra haciéndome tus ojos". Es increíble que bajo el peso de esta tarde, cruce el suave desierto de una canción, cruce el amor como alucinante neblina.

Here's a Song

Evening, pale, blurs the stars. With the pedestrians mingle old magical gods: their faces, solemn, bearded: with the leaf storm of their eyes they absorb sunset's scant honey. Gradually, through distant lightning, they venture fearsome though silent roars.

This hour's great confusion. They hurry toward the buses. Other pedestrians, tired-looking, wait on discreet corners. A big, absurd, nearly old woman, whose twisted blush stains small shadows. And the roads, and that night, above oblivion; and the breaths of a park, in which a statue was made out of air, and the rough friction of a movie theater exit: with a mild though disturbing ambiguity, they change their destinies, their faces.

I approach this restless tumult, open its mist. Suddenly, I seem to understand: obsession, voices drowned out by car horns; sickly crew of phantoms that the roof of a marquee spatters in the shadows. But I also feel like a madman! I can feel, amid a pavement puddle, how the Stripling falls among an indifferent crowd; or how the old Soothsayer foretells an end, above this cellar on which shadows lean. Ah, no, let us not look upon the face of this magical king, whose eye, pierced by death, sows, in the middle of slumber, a source of somber terror.

But how amazing! In this hour of pedestrians, of dreadful office-workers, hurriedly looking for their buses, I hear a snatch of song: "I must love you," it says, murmuring also, "gentle shadow your eyes make for me." It's amazing that beneath the weight of this evening, the soft desert of a song is passing by, love passing by like a marvelous mist.

(Pues ellos machacan sus sombras. Se lanzan, aparatosamente, sobre esos inexistentes ciervos que, un disparatado mapa ha de regar por las calles. Pues ellos se incendian con sus miradas, peces autómatas que un espejo, apenas solitario, ponzoña con su imagen. Gritan, gritan también. Aunque silenciosos, aunque oscuros. Gritan bárbaras X, neblinas. Gritan aparatosas, pero desleídas, pero blancuzcas serpentinas que, mañana, el barrendero Adivino, el barrendero, el Doncel, ha de recoger con la precaución de quien descubre minúsculas ramas de astas).

Ese canto es, como si cruzara el engaño, o el sueño, por los rincones de mi corazón. Es como alucinante rumor que estalla, subrepticiamente, sobre el techo de las calles. (No he dicho que, en esas calles, se abrían inquietantes grietas sobre un muro oscuro; sobre la saleta que una ventana deja ver; sobre el viejo toldo de una borrosa tienda).

Por eso, mi razón, ahora, proclama frente a todos los absurdos, el amor. Se decide, libremente, a aspirar al aire. Se resuelve, violentamente, con pasión, entre rostros humanos, bramidos, impuros jirones de neblina, seco asomar de objetos.

Es increíble este comprender en que me sumerjo. He luchado por estas calles lacias; entre estas figuras desechadas por el sentido; he visto saetas de esos dioses mágicos, cuyos rostros desleídos como naipes rozados por los dedos, componen equívocas figuras sobre espejos mudables; para que así, sencillamente, la antigua y simple canción del amor roce mis labios, con tranquila e ingenua suficiencia.

Pues soy —lo puedo decir ahora— como estos rostros indiferentes que me rodean; como esta baraúnda en que hastiados unos, e inocentes otros —quizás también hasta sencillos y alegres—, baten las calles, con unas palabras, con una pena, con un rito casi ininteligible. Pues estoy, con ese viejo solemne que ha cruzado la esperanza con un gesto trasnochado; con esas manos rústicas de quien, aunque sin comprenderlo, no desdeña lanzar su compasión sobre un viejo mito;

(So now they're crushing their shadows. They're hurling themselves ostentatiously on those non-existent stags that a senseless map has to pour onto the streets. So now with their gazes they're setting fire to robot fish that a barely solitary mirror poisons with its image. They're shouting, shouting too. Though silently, though darkly. Barbarous X's are shouting, mists. Ostentatious, but shrinking, but whitish streamers are shouting which tomorrow, the street sweeper Soothsayer, the street sweeper Stripling, will have to collect with the precaution of someone discovering tiny branches of spears.)

This song is as if deception were crossing, or a dream, through the corners of my heart. It's like an amazing noise surreptitiously exploding over the roof of the streets. (I haven't said that in these streets disturbing cracks opened on a dark wall; on the hallway seen through a window; on the old awning of a faded store.)

Because of this, my reason now proclaims, in the face of everything absurd, love. It freely decides to inhale the air. It resolves itself, violently, with passion, among human faces, roars, impure scraps of mist, dry looming of objects.

It's incredible, this understanding in which I submerge myself. I have struggled through these withered streets; among these figures discarded by meaning; I have seen arrows of those magical gods, whose faces dissolving like cards brushed by fingers compose ambiguous figures on mutable mirrors; so that in this way, simply, the ancient, naïve song of love might brush my lips, with peaceful and ingenuous sufficiency.

Because—I can say it now—I'm like these indifferent faces around me; like this tumult in which some who are bored and others innocent—perhaps even simple and carefree—beat against the streets, with a few words, with grief, with an almost unintelligible ritual. Because I am, with this solemn old man who has passed hope by with

con esas gráciles y jóvenes figuras, cuyo curso inocente se desliza con la paradójica inmovilidad de un espléndido animal que oscila su apariencia dentro de un círculo mágico. Pero mi razón proclama, ahora, frente a todos los absurdos, el amor. Pero mi corazón, sembrado en ti, comprende de nuevo, con ingenuas letras, esa fuerza de tu nombre, de tu deseo.

Ah, quedar, mi amiga en ti, siempre, entre estas infieles figuras, entre esta plebe de heráldicos jirones —calle, tarde, proclaman su furia vencida—, por sólo lo suave de una canción de amor que alguien apenas dijo; por sólo lo suave de una canción de amor que, por un instante, entre el fluir de un reloj —muchedumbre como confuso tejido—, alguien, quizás, me permitió soñar.

a hackneyed gesture; with these uncouth hands of someone who, though without understanding it, does not disdain to hurl his compassion upon an old myth; with these graceful young figures, whose innocent path unfolds with the paradoxical immobility of a splendid animal oscillating his appearance within a magic circle. But my reason now proclaims, in the face of everything absurd, love. But my heart, seeded in you, once again understands, with ingenuous letters, this power of your name, your desire.

Ah, to remain, my dear one, in you, always, among these faithless figures, among these plebeian heraldic tatters—street, evening, proclaim their vanquished fury—solely because of the gentleness of a love song someone barely uttered; solely because of the gentleness of a love song that, for a moment, amid the flowing of a clock—multitude as a confused weave—somebody, perhaps, enabled me to dream.

Amarte en la lluvia

1

¿Qué silenciosas tarjetas, de espeso aire cruzadas, por tus ojos invitan? Lluviosa la tarde de este domingo. Querida, todo lo que el chapotear de esta humedad, quemando resucita.

Las aceras que recorro gimen desiguales historias. Hay apenas olvidados bastiones, con olor a moho, con olor a seca lluvia rociando una madera: texto irreal apenas hablan sus notas: sueño que apenas viví cuando, atrás, tarde tras tarde lo repasé.

Querida. Definir el amor. Eres, ahora, como ese rincón cuyo húmedo sabor apenas comprendo. Me he propuesto el desafío de teñir tus ojos, tus labios, tu cuerpo, con ese jirón viscoso con que un álamo imita a la lluvia.

Para mí deja, ¡oh mi amiga!, el sabio devenir de estas imágenes que flébilmente compongo: un piano desde una sala mezquina; un hombre pequeño que en un balcón no espera nada; caer lacio de gotas churriosas, desde una puerta poco resistente.

2

Lluviosa la tarde de este domingo. Y, ¿no compondré para ti un áspero sortilegio?

¿Solamente tiritar bajo tu recuerdo? ¿No poder cifrar manga, codo, cuerpo, de tu presencia? Sin embargo los ruidos —¿calles solas, ahogadas?—, suspirando componen la seca sombra de una escalera, o con fragmentos reúnen la disipación de un charco helado.

Loving You in the Rain

1

What silent cards, traversed by dense wind, tempt through your eyes? This Sunday evening, rainy. Beloved, all that the pitter-patter of this moisture, burning, brings to life again.

The sidewalks moan their different stories. Barely forgotten bastions, smelling of mildew, smelling of dry rain sprinkling a piece of wood: a text that's unreal the moment its notes speak: a dream I barely lived when, in those days, I went over it evening after evening.

Beloved. To define love. You are now like this corner whose moist taste I barely understand. I have proposed the challenge of dyeing your eyes, your lips, your body, with this sticky shred that is the elm tree's imitation of the rain.

Oh dear one, leave to me the wise becoming of these images I feebly compose: a piano from a wretched living room, a little man who waits for nothing on a balcony; the languid falling of curious drops from a barely-resistant door.

2

This Sunday evening, rainy. And shall I not compose some rough magic for you?

Only shivering under your memory? Unable to summarize sleeve, elbow, body of your presence? But the noises—streets alone and drowned?—compose, sighing, the dry shadow of a staircase, or with fragments reunite the dissipation of a frozen puddle.

Vuelvo la cabeza, veo. Tú, mi amiga, con lo sencillo de ese sol que, ahora, por la humedad comienza a moler el bronce pálido de su luz.

¿Por qué todo se vuelve hacia otras tardes, hacia otros años? Trepado han los techos por la lluvia, con una aterradora claridad.

Pero el amor como la sencillez. Querida, rociar con vastas palabras este inútil camino: en esta lluvia, tu rostro, tu cuerpo, ingenuamente responderá a mis preguntas, como el carbunclo que estalla con el recuerdo de una feria.

Agua goteando sobre sucios cristales. Sumida, en silencio, se té, sobre mi vida.

Húmedos charcos, solos, sostienen la descabezada imagen de un loco erizo. Moho, su olor. El humo chapotea. No sé lo que pondrás pensar. Pero te quiero.

I turn my head, I see. You, dear one, with the simplicity of this sun that now through haze begins to grind its light's pale bronze.

Why does everything return to other evenings, other years? Because of the rain, the roofs have leaned back with terrifying brightness.

But love like simplicity. Beloved, watering this useless road with vast words; in this rain, your face, your body, guileless, will answer my questions, like the carbuncle bursting at the memory of a fair.

Water dripping on dirty windowpanes. I know you, immersed, in silence, in my life.

Damp puddles, alone, sustain the wild image of a crazy porcupine. Mildew, its smell. The smoke is splashing. I don't know what you're going to think about. But I love you.

Ritmos Acribillados

Ahogo, o la sal: tantos otoños asaltan. Pero único este septiembre: coloración surgiendo de la piel de las cosas, que en las sienes, se instala como un mito.

Tartamudeo de rincones, de gritos usados y perdidos. Ahogo, o la sal: tantos otoños asaltan. Y un río de baratos ritos, un río de viejos programas de cine, un río donde una sed sin sentido desalienta a una tarde anacrónica.

Mi amiga, tú, fiel a mi aventura. Mi amiga, fiel. Como no eres el rencor, ni el rechazo, ni la furia, busco, sin metáfora, tu pelo, como un espacio, humano, donde no sea necesario que me esconda.

Pero bate… Sin duda. Bate quemado rostro o historia, una anécdota que ya a nadie preocupa. Bate una brisa estéril, una brisa guardada, ¡y que hay que ver para qué puede servir una brisa guardada! (Brazos rotos, de ausentes atrapados en espejos. Fauna de antiguos circos arados por el tiempo. Risas que sólo los muertos esconden.)

Mi amiga, tú, ritmos acribillados. Mi amiga, esas palabras que, como tatuajes o medallas, se han colocado sobre mochas estatuas. Pero hemos visto tantas noches; pues hemos visto una sola, la noche, agujereada o tránsfuga, difícil, y sin embargo, su unidad cedía, en nuestras manos, algo tan antiguo como la rosa seca que sirve de señal a un libro.

Bate…sin duda. Es el otoño. Ahogo, o la sal…Mi amiga —ritmos acribillados junto a mí. Y decimos: el corazón, el silencio, las nubes, el recuerdo, los ojos en la noche, el amor inmortal, la primavera; pero un viento seco de cristal ajado, o un viejo polvo de la ausencia, o un sonido de rota victoria raspando la herida —petrificada— de todos los objetos, nos envuelve, nos cruza, a nosotros, vacilantes —quizás—, ante la nada.

Riddled Rhythms

I'm stifling, or the salt: assault of so many autumns. But this September's different from all others: a coloring emerging from the skin of things, installing itself in one's temples like a myth.

Stammering of corners, of lost, worn-out cries. I'm stifling, or the salt: assault of so many autumns. And a river of cheap rites, a river of old movie programs, a river where a meaningless thirst disheartens an anachronistic evening.

My dear, you, faithful to my adventure. My dear, faithful. Since you are neither rancor nor rejection nor fury, I seek, without metaphor, your hair, like a human space, where I don't need to hide.

But it beats…of course. A burned face or story beats, an anecdote no longer of interest to anyone. A sterile, guarded breeze beats, and it remains to be seen what use a guarded breeze is! (Broken arms of absent ones trapped in mirrors. Fauna of ancient circuses ploughed by time. Laughter only the dead can hear.)

My dear, you, riddled rhythms. My dear one, these words that, like tattoos or medals, have been fastened to mutilated statues. But we've seen so many nights; then a single one, night, perforated or traitorous, difficult, and yet, its unity surrendered, in our hands, something as old as the dried rose used as a bookmark.

It beats…of course. It's autumn…I'm stifling, or the salt…My dear—riddled rhythms by my side. And we said: heart, silence, clouds, memory, eyes in the night, immortal love, spring; but a dry wind of faded glass, or an old dust of absence, or a sound of a broken victrola scratching the—petrified—wound of all objects, wraps us round, passes over us, ourselves, vacillating—perhaps—before nothingness.

Mi amiga, tú, quererte. Pero ritmos acribillados junto a nuestras sombras, junto a nuestras noches, junto a nuestros cuerpos fundidos, como soles grabados sobre una inmemorial arena de rostros anacrónicos.

Ahogo, o la sal: tantos otoños asaltan. Pero único este septiembre: coloración surgiendo de la piel de las cosas que, en las sienes, se instala como un mito. Y tú, yo, inventándonos, amándonos, bajo el liso desquiciamiento de la nada; bajo la rugosa, inmóvil, insistencia, de viejos objetos apenas olvidados.

My dear, you, loving you. But riddled rhythms next to our shadows, our nights, our fused bodies, like suns engraved on an immemorial arena of anachronistic faces.

I'm stifling, or the salt: assault of so many autumns. But this September's different from all others: tinting, emerging from the skin of things, installing itself in one's temples like a myth. And you, I, inventing each other, loving each other, beneath the smooth disturbance of nothingness; beneath the rough, immobile insistence of old, barely forgotten things.

Lo inútil

¿Cómo puede llenarse esta mañana de extraños restos, de huesos de un naufragio, de absurdos ecos? Y, ¿cuál reverso tala los pensamientos, los sentidos? Mi mirada, mitad aberrada, me contempla estúpidamente sentado sobre una ola irreal.

Es que —¿en qué espacio de mi cuerpo, de mi vida?— han existido seres cortos, seres a medias. Ellos han trastrocado los días, ebrios de un escaso, aunque diabólico resquemor. (Su conducta, ¿para qué decirlo?, ha sido la de girar ingenuamente mis imágenes, con torcida y sorprendente crueldad).

Un recuerdo cercano —de ayer, precisamente— me los vuelve a traer. Ellos —era la tarde. ¡Y qué espléndida fue la tarde de ayer!— llegaron con los viejos disfraces de ser dioses. Tempraneros, oscuros. También meditativos. También crepusculares. Riñeron por fabulosos corales submarinos. Treparon por ramajes irisados por una extraña luz. ¡Ah, cuán pura y clara fue su melancólica metáfora! Y, también, cruel la mentira de su trastrocada aparición como ingenuos reyes fabulosos. Pues al mover sus cabezas, guiñar sus ojos, o girar sus manos, dejaban caer sus mantos de opereta, sólo ofreciendo el triste espectáculo de sus pechos hundidos por la nada.

Como hoy al referirme a esos lamentables dioses, a veces, cuando pienso en ellos —seres cortos, a medias—, empiezo a darme cuenta de mi escaso rumor, de mi mirada inútil, de mis labios apenas.

De modo que hoy la tierra, el mar, el cielo, como una mentira. De modo que hoy extraños restos, huesos de un naufragio, absurdos ecos —la luz, también irreal, talando rostros—. Y todo esto ¿para qué? —¿Para qué, Dios mío, esta mentira? Ah cielos ficticios. Ah seres cortos, aberrantes, apenas guiñando una ilusión. Ah dibujos grotescos

Uselessness

How to fill this morning of strange remains, of a castaway's bones, of absurd echoes? And what reversal fells thoughts, feelings? My gaze, half in error, contemplates me stupidly seated on an unreal wave.

Because—in what space of my body, my life?—short beings, partial beings have existed. They've inverted the days, drunk on a scant albeit diabolical resentment. (Their behavior, why speak of it? has been to cause my images to whirl innocently, with twisted and surprising cruelty.)

A recent memory—from yesterday, precisely—brings them back to me. They—it was evening. And how splendid yesterday evening was!—arrived with their old disguises as gods. Early risers, dark. Meditative too. Crepuscular too. They were quarreling over fabulous undersea corals. They climbed up branches made iridescent by a strange light. Ah, how pure and bright was their melancholy metaphor! And cruel also the lie of their inverted apparition as innocent fabulous kings. Since by moving their heads, winking their eyes, or rotating their hands, they let fall their operetta cloaks, offering only the sad spectacle of their breasts sunk by nothingness.

Just like today when I make reference to these lamentable gods, sometimes when I think about them—short, partial beings—I begin to be aware of my slight murmur, my useless gaze, my lips, barely.

Such that today land, sea, and sky, like a lie. Such that today strange remnants, a castaway's bones, absurd echoes—light, also unreal, felling faces—And all for what?—Why, my God, this lie? Ah, fictitious skies. Ah, short, aberrant beings, barely winking an illusion. Ah, grotesque drawings of dreams in which life can barely fit. Let me tell you, that's really cruel.

de sueños en que apenas puede caber la vida. Los aseguro, esto es bastante cruel.

Es que tierra, mar, cielo, están forrados con una lamentable carpa. Es que ningún sueño ha existido, ni podrá existir. Es que esta mañana es sólo una máquina absurda de prodigios.

Because land, sea, sky, are lined with a lamentable tent. Because no dream has existed, nor can exist. Because this morning is just an absurd machine of wonders.

Es la noche

Tiene escasos rótulos la noche. El se revuelve por una lámina.

Ciudad, nombres de las piedras: parpado escaso: gris, estrellas. Ese ciempiés minúsculo que duerme en la azotea.

A sus lechos bajan los bañistas, a sus lechos bajan los boxeadores de celuloide, a sus lechos los gentlemen forrados con una piel anacrónica. También, del fondo de una garganta, surge, como un relámpago, la voz de una victrola.

Viejos, niños, enfermos, hieráticos asesinos: mitología de una borrosa marquesina. Pues alguien entra, sale, se diluye, por la puerta de una farmacia antigua.

Cercana la noche. Y el amor, y el dolor, y la muerte… pero, en un garage el viejo sereno escurre, por sus dedos, una baraja grasosa. La soledad es un consejo que nadie escucha.

Y las correspondencias que un tic-tac surgiere. Que una voz, a medias, condena.

Pero las palabras, espesas, no le saltan. Lo ahogan. Su mirada.

Por lo que ahora contrae el rostro. Se retira.

El se ha movido por una lámina. Es la noche.

It's Nighttime

Night has scarce signs. He's turning round in an engraving.

City, names of stones: scarce eyelid: gray, stars. This minuscule centipede sleeping on the rooftop.

The bathers descend to their beds, the celluloid boxers descend to their beds, the gentlemen lined with an anachronistic fur descend to their beds. Also, from the depths of a throat, wells up, like lightning, the voice of a victrola.

Old people, children, the sick, hieratic assassins: mythology of a faded marquee. Then someone enters, exits, becomes diluted, through the door of an old pharmacy.

Night is near. And love, pain, death…but in a garage the old watchman riffles a greasy deck of cards. Solitude is advice nobody listens to.

And the correspondences a tick-tock suggests. That a voice, partially, condemns.

But the thick words don't leap from him. They drown him. His gaze.

So that now he screws up his face. He goes away.

He's moved through an engraving. It's nighttime.

Después de algunos años

La comida está servida. ¡Al menos está caliente! Noche. ¡Cómo llueve! Voy a acercarme, a comprender. Al fin, no soy tan joven. ¿Ya no soy joven?

Un aire gastado. Un aire barato. Un aire de usada lluvia, de usada noche. Un aire de usados gestos humanos. Noche. Llueve. Adentro hay humedad. La comida está servida. Puedo tener hambre.

Porque seco, inmediato, el placer se extiende —ya no puedo imaginar lo que, como ilusión, simulaba el paso artificial hacia una inmemorial estatua— y, no deja de estar bien el humo de esta comida caliente. Parece como perdonar...Claro que a veces me quejo, pero tienen olor las cosas, y eso es estupendo.

También me podrán convidar unos amigos que brindan frente a la luna. Me podrá convidar un parque, una noche de cine, unos refrescos. No hay más nada.

Quisimos ser eternamente jóvenes. Quisimos hacernos un alma. Nos parecía que lo seco, lacio, pobre, podría acompañarnos, como una voluptuosidad. ¿Importa haberse equivocado?

¡Al menos está caliente! Humo por las cazuelas. No está mal.

Quizás no llegamos a traicionarnos del todo. Lo que pasa es que...

Y ahora, como hay buena sombra, me fijo en un reloj. Dibujo mi ambiente. Me vuelvo grabado: con la insignificancia triste, también secreta, de una lámina en un libro viejo, recorto mi figura: mármoles artificiales en una mancha de tinta. ¿Habrá una sensualidad irónica?

After Several Years

Supper's ready. At least it's hot! Night. It's really raining hard! I'm going to come closer to myself, to understand. All told, I'm not so young. Am I no longer young?

Stale air. Cheap air. Air of used-up rain, used-up night. Air of used-up human gestures. Night. It's raining. Inside it's humid. Supper's ready. I might be hungry.

Because, dry and immediate, pleasure extends itself—I can't imagine what, as an illusion, the artificial step towards an immemorial statue simulated—and the steam from this hot food continues to be good. It seems like forgiving...Of course I complain sometimes, but things have an odor, and that's wonderful.

Some friends drinking each other's health beside the moon might also tempt me. A park, a night at the movies, some soft drinks might also invite me. There's nothing else.

We wanted to be young eternally. We wanted to make ourselves a soul. It seemed to us that dryness, languidness, poverty, might accompany us, like voluptuousness. Does it matter that we were wrong?

At least it's hot. Steam from the pots. Not bad.

Perhaps we didn't manage to betray ourselves completely. What's happening is...

And now, since there's a nice shadow, I stare at a clock. I draw my ambience. I'm engraved again: with the sad insignificance, secret too, of an engraving in an old book, I sketch my figure: artificial marbles in an ink spot. Could there be an ironic sensuality?

Al menos la comida está caliente. Judit, mi hija, lucha con un oso que es un tren, con un tren que es un tintero —la vida no se acaba y, al detenerme en el grabado irónico que, por un momento, he hecho de mi figura, me conforma la noche, la lluvia.

A veces, la resignación es como un sueño.

At least dinner's hot. Judit, my daughter, is fighting with a bear that's a train, with a train that's an inkwell—life doesn't end and, as I linger on the ironic engraving that, for a moment, I've made of my figure, night, rain shape me.

Resignation is like a dream sometimes.

from

Fantasma juega el juego / Phantom Plays the Game

(1978)

Homenaje a Senghor

El Archivero se agacha sobre aguas exóticas. Se desnuda una gran presencia en el rollo que despliega su mano (En el rollo, sobre el drama del exiliado, ha dicho Cortázar: "Es el drama de la gente que se ve obligada a abandonar su país por la sencilla razón de que si se queda está expuesto a los peores vejámenes e incluso a la muerte").

La carne, paradójicamente intacta, de una gacela calcinada, había sido, junto al monóculo de Saint-John Perse, abandonada en la selva tercermundista.

Cartas espirituosas de abismos, cartas de bosques, cartas de desiertos o razas que traerían *el corazón del universo*, levantaban el vértigo en el alma del lector. Ahí los primitivos explotados. Ahí lucían, bajo la ponchera del sol, sus más alucinantes atributos. Era una estremecedora fiesta del texto.

Pues hay escombros, abismos enloquecedores del vencido. El vencido ha de alzar su rostro cuando los ritmos Aimé Césaire afiebren la noche, la noche iconoclasta. Sagrado espíritu del desierto, o sagrado espíritu del Orinoco. Belle époque, o bello texto de los pueblos liberados. Y así el Archivero saltará, por un instante, desde su asiento, con un fusil en mano. Acotará él, al margen del texto, en la noche calurosa de Caracas, un discurso sobre la amarga soledad del destierro. Pues el Archivero escupirá, con un verbo del esperanto surrealista, a La Esperanza. Escupirá, ya que la noche de los alacranes, la noche de los pavo reales, la noche de los africanos, o la noche de la muerte resucitada, resultará leve brisa fresca, sobe su frente de erudito tercermundista.

Homage to Senghor

The Archivist leans over exotic waters. He strips naked a great presence in the scroll his hand unfurls (In the scroll, with regard to the exile's drama, Cortázar said: "It's the drama of people who find themselves obliged to abandon their country for the simple reason that if they stay, they will be exposed to the worst humiliations, even death").

The flesh, paradoxically intact, of a charred gazelle, had been, along with Saint-John Perse's monocle, abandoned in the Third-Worldist jungle.

Spirited letters from abysses, letters from forests, letters from deserts or races that bring *the heart of the universe*, aroused vertigo in the reader's soul. Here are the exploited primitives. Here they display, beneath the sun's punch bowl, their most astonishing attributes. It was a disturbing textual fiesta.

For there's rubbish, maddening abysses of the conquered. The conquered must lift up his gaze when Aimé Césaire rhythms make the night feverish, the iconoclastic night. Holy spirit of the desert, or sacred spirit of the Orinoco. Belle époque, or beautiful text of liberated peoples. And so the Archivist will, for a moment, leap from his chair, rifle in hand. He will note in the margin of the text, in the hot Caracas night, a discourse on the bitter solitude of exile. Then the Archivist, with a word from the Surrealist Esperanto, will spit on Hope. He will spit, now that the night of scorpions, the night of peacocks, the night of Africans, or the night of resuscitated death, will become a light cool breeze on his erudite Third Worldist brow.

Nonsense

Es el cuento de las palabras en un vaso donde se derrite un Alka-Seltzer. Es el cuento del que ha llegado a un valle donde estaba la muerte.

¡Oh, no!, no digo eso, me confundo. Cuando niño, en un cuento, llegó no a un valle —aunque ahora, en un valle, está la muerte—, sino a un mediodía, donde estaba la muerte. Son las palabras en un vaso. En ese cuento hay una esquina sin reloj, donde reside un boticario estúpido. Y todo resumiéndose en un niño cojo. Todo en una algarabía siniestra, pero muda.

Es el cuento del que cansado, sin persignarse y sin recoger ningún eco, ha llegado a donde estaba la muerte. Un Alka-Seltzer estirándose en un vaso. Un cuento con la sombría algarabía de los que siempre, idiotas, quedan indemnes.

En un valle está la muerte. Cuando niño, aunque no en un valle, también llegó la muerte. Cuando niño miraba, y ahora mira. Palabras derritiéndose en un vaso. En ese cuento hay una esquina sin reloj, y en esa esquina reside un boticario estúpido.

Nonsense

It's the story of words in a glass in which an Alka-Seltzer is dissolving. It's the story of someone who reached a valley where death was.

Oh no! I'm not saying that, I'm confused. When he was a boy, in a story, he didn't reach a valley—though now, in the valley, death is there—but a midday, where death was. These are the words in a glass. In this story there's a corner without a clock, where a stupid druggist dwells. And everything summed up in a lame boy. Everything in a sinister, mute hullabaloo.

It's the story of someone who, tired, without crossing himself or picking up an echo, has reached where death was. An Alka-Seltzer stretching out in a glass. A story with the somber hullabaloo of those who always, idiots, remain unharmed.

Death is in a valley. When he was a boy, though not in a valley, death also arrived. When he was a boy he gazed, and now he's gazing. Words dissolving in a glass. In this story there's a corner without a clock, and on this corner lives a stupid druggist.

Teórico diluvio

Lo anecdótico, ahora sin sombra. Maniquí *art-nouveau* sobre la arena o —tristeza hermética— formas paseando los recuerdos.

Se observa, sobre ese polvo de arroz que cubría a una máscara, viejas muñecas con los olores de una incalificable melancolía. Es el teórico diluvio que las ondas de la banda municipal comienza, mientras la vieja dama se interna por el parque soñado.

Theoretical Flood

The anachronistic, now without a shadow. *Art nouveau* mannequin on the sand or—hermetic sadness—forms parading their memories.

One observes, on this rice dust covering a mask, old dolls with smells of an indescribable melancholy. It's the theoretical flood that the waves of the municipal band are beginning, as the old lady penetrates the dreamed-of forest.

Por una grieta

De este destartalo, por donde vamos recorriendo una galería de mohosas estampas, el bostezo es la grieta. Pero un recuerdo arqueológico—el viejo ruiseñor de Keats— promete abrir, sobre el texto, lo sofisticado de una nítida ventana.

Sería entonces que, abroquelada por ese recuerdo, figuraría, desde un interior gesto anacrónico, la seña inmemorial, la seña inmemorial, la seña que podemos contemplar, grabada sobre un costado de la estatua del poeta.

Y con esto, una magnífica oportunidad de cruzar, pues pasaríamos por entre charcos, para así lograr salvar la imagen del híbrido diluvio que esta inútil grieta parece abrir.

Through a Fissure

Of this wreck, where we walk through a gallery of moldy prints, the yawn is the fissure. But an archaeological memory—Keats's old nightingale—promises to open that which within the text is sophisticated about a precise window.

Then, shielded by this memory, there would figure, from an anachronistic inner gesture, the immemorial sign, the sign we may contemplate, carved on a flank of the poet's statue.

And along with this, a magnificent opportunity to cross, since we would be walking among puddles, in order thereby to succeed in saving the image of the hybrid flood that this useless fissure seems to open.

El viejo Maldoror

Como una boca desdentada: del otoño era la mañana una abertura gris. Labios había que al vacío trituraban.

El viejo y carcomido Maldoror se limpiaba los dientes mientras simulaba, frente al espejo del lavabo, el gesto estereotipado del tiburón textual.

Pues en gorgoritos lanzaba sus labios, pero sólo alcanzaba las descascaradas parcelas de un suntuoso y anacrónico grabado, grabado de folletinesco monstruo marino. O dicho de otra manera: con rotas, estériles, enclenques metamorfosis, intentaba saltar —como con velocípedo intenta un payaso saltar— por entre las distintas pieles que cubren a una legión de estatuas; y esto mientras inauguraba, la ventana del baño, el lúgubre vacío de la luz de la mañana. Como podría comprobarse allí era, mimetizando el rostro de su angustia, Maldoror un inútil saltarín. De escasos movimientos horrendos animales por su rostro trepaban, llevados todos por la equívoca voluntad de hacer triunfar un imposible reto, pues las manos del héroe querrían figurar garras, o saltar como cóndores sus ojos, o pretender sus sueños la aristocracia de unos actos agudos, pero las formas que, escasamente, la voluntad de Maldoror levantaba, sólo, y en lastimera condición, regar lograban la pequeña acuarela de unos ingenuos monstruos.

La estampa del héroe es, pues, el kilo de una ripiosa mentira, simulando, en imagen reflejada, el engaño de unos trasnochados ojos de águila, o la fábula grotesca de unas inexistentes mejillas de bronce. O es esta estampa alegoría de farsa. O alegoría de movimiento que vanamente gestos heroicos intenta, hasta llegar a traducir el congelado espacio de una fiera canija. Ya que, ¡ay!, para siempre el viejo Maldoror, infiel reflejo de una momento olvidado, en su espejo sólo logrará detener la lamentable superficie de ése, diluido, inútil texto de su hazaña.

Old Maldoror

Like a toothless mouth: a gray opening was that autumn morning. Its lips munched on the void.

Old, moth-eaten Maldoror was cleaning his teeth while simulating, in the sink's mirror, the stereotyped gesture of the textual shark.

Then from his lips he hurled roulades, but he only reached the peeled particles of a sumptuous, anachronistic engraving, an engraving of a melodramatic sea monster. Or said otherwise: with broken, sterile, sickly metamorphoses, he tried to leap—like a clown trying to leap with a velocipede—between the various skins covering a legion of statues; this while the bathroom window inaugurated the lugubrious void of morning light. As could be seen there, Maldoror, mimicking the face of his anguish, was a pointless leaper. With slight horrid movements animals crept up his face, all driven by the ambiguous will to make a triumph out of an impossible challenge, since the hero's hands wished to feign claws, or his eyes to leap like condors, or his dreams to attempt the aristocracy of a few clever actions, but the forms that, barely, Maldoror's will alone erected, and in pitiful condition, managed to sprinkle the small watercolor of some innocent monsters.

The hero's portrait, then, is a couple of pounds worth of verbose lies, simulating, in a reflected image, the deception of a few haggard eagle eyes, or the grotesque fable of some nonexistent bronze cheeks. Or this portrait is a farcical allegory. Or an allegory of movement that vainly tries out heroic gestures, until achieving the translation of a puny beast's congealed space. Now, alas! forever will old Maldoror, faithless reflection of a forgotten moment, in his mirror alone manage to hold back the wretched surface of this diluted, useless text of his exploits.

Con una advertencia

Casi irreconocibles signos estas noches trazando. Adefesios mudos. Cambiando. Cambiándome siempre.

Casi invisible, pues, entre espacios diminutos. Y, también revolviéndome sin revolver, grotescamente solitario, o lo que no me sueña del sueño de una unidad.

Así confieso estar, siempre, un poco fuera de mis testimonios. Confieso no comprender bien.

With a Warning

These nights tracing almost unrecognizable signs. Mute motleys. Changing. Always changing myself.

Almost invisible, then, among minute spaces. And tossing and turning without turning as well, grotesquely solitary, or something I can't place in the dream of a unity.

So I confess to being, always, a little outside my testimonies. I confess I don't understand that much.

Texto martiano

Desde una concha electrónica, con la joven quinceañera, Martí desciende bailando. Giran, ahí con el recordatorio alegórico, el punzó descolorido, o el blanco, o el azul desteñido: colores del prisma albino.

Desde una concha electrónica, de mirar y recordar todo el tiempo disponible. ¡Tenemos, todos, el tiempo!

Desde una concha electrónica se aplaude con el silencio. Un punzó descolorido se iza por los rincones. Hay pinos. Y en el sillón del portal el que su vejez desliza.

Desde una concha electrónica ha vuelto la noche albina. Martí ya deja la danza y vuelve a Fundar la Patria. Hay huesos. Hay un parque inexistente. Hay un banco desteñido. Al muerto acuesta Martí. A dormir acuesta al muerto sobre la noche del banco. No se oye. Y un punzó descolorido en el parque inexistente.

Martían Text

From an electronic shell Martí descends dancing with the young debutante. They whirl, there, with the allegorical obituary, the discolored scarlet, or the white, or the faded blue: colors of the albino prism.

From an electronic shell, looking and recalling all available time. We, all of us, have time!

From an electronic shell, applause with silence. Martí leaves the dance now and goes back to Founding the Nation. There are bones. There's a nonexistent park. There's a faded bench. Martí puts the dead man to bed. He puts the dead man to sleep on the bench's night. Inaudible. And a discolored scarlet in the nonexistent park.

Buscándome el vacío

Porque me han seguido los manchones. Porque he comprobado, piezas superponiendo o rostros de esta mañana, que están los desvaídos azules de unas ventanas.

Todo eso quería decir abeto, o el aire; querría decir cielo, o estoy cansado. Aunque como encogiéndose, ensanchándose líneas más del texto, o menos alcanzar nube tamaño de diminuto cisne, ¿dónde estaría mi centro? Pues también debo insistir puse mi mano en un bolsillo y tacto ligero de un vacío logré, aunque realmente no sabía dónde estaba mi mano. ¿Y entonces se trataría de si sólo soy el médium o el ventrílocuo de un texto que no es mío? Por lo que no logro saber cuál es mi nada. Y así, pues, debo volver. Y así me enredo, me insisto, me repito en el no logro tocar, ya que hasta ahora no sé si manchón es mi cuerpo; así como, lo que toco, tampoco puedo llegar a saber si es una sombra.

Seeking My Void

Because the stains have followed me. Because I've confirmed, superimposing this morning's pieces or faces, that they're the pale blue of some windows.

All of this meant fir, or the air; it could have meant sky, or I'm tired. Although like shrinking, stretching more lines from the text, or less reaching for a cloud the size of a tiny swan, where would my center be? Because I must also emphasize that I put my hand in a pocket and barely touched a void, although really I didn't know where my hand was. Would it then be a question of whether I'm just the medium or the ventriloquist of a text not mine? Because I can't figure out what my nothingness is. So, then, I must go back. And I get tangled up, insist, repeat the I can't touch, since I still don't know if the stain is my body; I still can't figure out if what I touch is a shadow.

Ilusión venida a menos

Para el texto estoy persiguiendo abetos y árboles encantados para el texto, como también para el texto la sutil e irónica sonrisa de un congelado vacío. Pero esto, esta labor, sólo llegaría a ser tangible si lograra alcanzar, yo, eso que es superficie de una sibilina astucia verbal.

Pero, en verdad, no he tomado en cuenta mi cansancio. Por lo que, bien considerada mi actual situación, no me dirigiré hacia mi escritorio, ya que seguiré moviéndome con el rocío real, por entre estos abetos y árboles reales, que he encontrado en el paseo de esta tarde. Así pues, se trata de que como estoy cansado y aunque la melancolía del texto posible me sigue persiguiendo, dudo mucho poder alcanzar, con la palabra, eso como leves chispas, eso en que consiste una ilusión venida a menos.

Illusion Come to Naught

For the text I'm pursuing firs and enchanted trees for the text, as also for the text the subtle, ironical smile of a frozen void. But this, this work, would only become tangible if I were able, I, to reach the surface of a sibylline verbal cunning.

But, truth be told, I haven't taken my weariness into account. Because of which, given my present situation, I won't head for my desk, I'll keep traveling with the real dew, among the real firs and trees I've come upon in this evening's walk. So it's about how, since I'm tired, and although the melancholy of the possible text keeps pursuing me, I seriously doubt that I can reach, with words, this that is like light sparks, this that an illusion come to naught consists of.

Letra para el doctor Fantasma

El doctor Fantasma rebatía sus orígenes: frente a hojitas de jazmín buscaba círculos —intersección— donde puntos ceros cortan los sintagmas de los recuerdos infantiles.

El doctor Fantasma, imagen frente al espejo, al mediodía escuchaba el ruido de una sierra: era cuando su cuerpo se desgarraba en grumos; era cuando su especular consunción embestía un híbrido espacio (¿Así que era su espejo ese ruido —¿casual?— de la sierra al mediodía).

El doctor Fantasma era el ciudadano de una patria albina. Rastreaba sus equívocos de transparente snob, por lo que había que verlo allí, gallardo como el disfrazado reverso de un Wilde químicamente puro, trazando las diminutas peripecias de una microscópica pradera mallarmeana.

Llevaba a su cuerpo por frígidos avatares de delicias, aquélla, su teoría espiritual, para que así él, el transparente, meciera piezas somáticas dentro de objetadas alquímicas sensaciones, de tal manera que sus fríos, su caliente, sus pedos, surgieran y se dilataran por dentro de una cenestésica pradera metafísica. O sea —dicho de otra forma— que él, artista doctor Fantasma, sus recetas doctor Bachelard destilaran pedrerías anacrónicas o vidrieras de lujoso fin de siglo, así fuera en la calle donde la no transparencia o el calor pudiera reconciliarse, hasta convertirse en médiums ahorcados eso de una trasnochada fauna de personajes surrealistas.

Por ello esta letra dice: ¡Oh modelo, parámetro, oh estructura! La letra dice que, sincrónicamente, te perfilaste lujoso, doctor Fantasma, pues tus dedos no tocaron los abismos, sino que oscuro, adelgazado continuamente remendaste las siempre fieles superficies —texto de heladas letras—, hasta que el rasguño de la palabra fue convirtiendo tu inútil cuerpo en un tatuaje de signos exquisitamente ininteligibles.

A Reading for Doctor Phantom

Doctor Phantom rejected his origins: face to face with jasmine leaves he sought circles—intersection—where points zero cut off the syntagmas of childhood memories.

Doctor Phantom, image before the mirror, at midday listened to the noise of a saw: it was when his body shed itself in clumps; it was when his specular consumption assaulted a hybrid space. (Was his mirror that—fortuitous?—noise of the saw at noon?)

Doctor Phantom was the citizen of an albino country. He dredged through his transparently snobbish wordplay, so that you had to see him there, elegant as the disguised reverse of a chemically pure Wilde, tracing the diminutive adventures of a microscopic Mallarméan meadow.

It brought his body through cold avatars of delights—"it" being his spiritual theory, so that he, the transparent one, could hammer somatic parts into presented alchemical sensations, in such a way that their colds, their heat, their farts, would well up and dilate within a synesthetic metaphysical meadow. Or—said otherwise—that he, the artist Doctor Phantom, his Doctor Bachelard recipes should distill anachronistic precious stones or stained-glass windows from the luxurious *fin de siècle*, even if it were in the street where non-transparency or heat could be reconciled, changing that type of outmoded fauna of Surrealist characters into hanged fortunetellers.

Because of that, this reading says: Oh model, parameter, oh structure! The reading says that, synchronically, you gave yourself a luxurious profile, Doctor Phantom, since your fingers did not touch the abysses, but, obscure and continually slimmed down, you continually patched up the ever-faithful surfaces—a text of frozen letters—until the scratching of the word went on converting your useless body into a tattoo of exquisitely unintelligible signs.

No me explico

¿Será tan literario que traza sombras o cúpulas sobre espacio minuciosamente alquímico? ¿Será tan literario que anticipa sus miradas?

Me explico: hace varios días que ejecuta sus ejercicios: una caminata diaria (cuarenta cuadras diarias, para mayor precisión).

Es lo que dice Duchamp: "Gráficamente, esta carretera tenderá hacia la línea pura geométrica sin grosor (encuentro de dos planos me parece el único medio pictórico de llegar a una pureza").

Es decir, un grabado: mechón de azufre sobre un parque abandonado. Hay gatos con una increíble textura de pares: pares de resultados: la anécdota que cuenta un vecino cojo, la nariz Cleopatra de una vieja. Quisiera él, el doctor Fantasma, consultarlo con Juarroz, ya que sin puentes se quedan los espacios.

Se trata de que quiere, él, inventar, literariamente, un secreto alquímico. O, quizá mejor, se trata de que quiere acabar de atornillar el sueño en su cabeza.

Pero no me explico.

I'm Not Making Myself Clear

Will he be so literary as to trace shadows or domes on a meticulously alchemical space? Will he be so literary as to anticipate its gazes?

Let me be clear: he's been doing his exercises for several days: a daily walk (precisely forty blocks daily).

This is what Duchamp says: "Graphically, this road will tend towards the pure geometric line without thickness (the meeting of two planes seems to me the only pictorial means of attaining a purity)."

That is to say, an engraving: a sulfur lock of hair in an abandoned park. There are cats with an incredible texture of pairs: pairs of results: the anecdote told by a lame neighbor, an old lady's Cleopatra nose. He, Doctor Phantom, would like to consult with Juarroz on the matter, since the spaces remain without bridges.

It's about his wanting to invent, literarily, an alchemical secret. Or, better perhaps, it's about his wanting to have done with fastening his dream inside his head.

But I'm not making myself clear.

Arañazo mediúmnico

Cuchillo, filo, faro. ¿Qué más? Y el decorado, filigrana, de una caja de bombones Art Deco.

¿Qué es eso?

Borde donde reaparece el... Viejo asunto —todo eso— de la nada. Y en el texto (imposible texto) lo que, con hirsuta fidelidad, bien pudiera perderse.

Pero, confieso que yo tampoco entiendo.

Mediumistic Scratching

Knife, edge, beacon. What else? And the decoration, filigree, of an Art Deco candy box.

What's this?

The reappearance at a border of... Old matter—all this—of nothingness. And in the text (impossible text) something that with hirsute fidelity could well be lost.

But I confess I don't understand either.

El extraño rigor

Con requerido rigor computarizó el paisaje: la cosa estuvo programada con todos los hierros, alambres, tornillos, etc. ¡Ni una sola imagen sin colocar! ¡Perfecta la acuarela! Por lo que al final, terminada su faena, no cupo duda de que en lo simultáneo del reverso, él no dejó de sacar del horno lo que antes había puesto a calentar: ese juego de sus tantas piezas, perennemente frías.

Strange Rigor

With requisite rigor he computerized the landscape: the whole thing was programmed, all the chains, wires, screws, etc. Not one image missing! The watercolor—perfect! So that at the end, his task completed, there was no doubt that in the simultaneity of the reverse, he didn't forget to remove from the oven the thing he was reheating: that game with all its—perennially cold—pieces.

¿Qué es?

Que como si en lo que antes fue mi esperanza me durmiera, es hecho cierto (O digo, al menos, así algo que se le parece). En lo que es vuelta de todo. Vuelta aun de propia vida.

Pues, como extraño monstruosillo la imagen se revuelca; girando: lamentablemente sobre los mismos ojos del desvelo.

Y es que nunca acabo de saber la simetría o no del tal cosa. Tal situación..., si es ya la muerte o si, estático por toda chiquita eternidad, mi aburrido libreto repite y repite, mecánicamente, su ininteligible saludo.

What Is It?

That it's as if my sleeping in that which what was once my hope should be a fact (or at least I'm saying something close to it). In that which is the return of everything. The return even of my life.

Then, like a strange little monster, the image rolls around; whirling; lamentably on the same insomniac eyes.

I never end up knowing the symmetry or not of such a thing. What a situation…if it's already death or if, static for all tiny eternity, my boring libretto repeats and repeats, mechanically, its unintelligible greeting.

Colosal olvido

Colosal olvido que ya ni me pertenece, como piedra —¿fulminado?—, y más allá, por supuesto, de cualquier resto de la mirada.

(En los álamos despegos: sus raras cenizas).

Mientras desciendo: sin vocación, ni rumor; tras lo poco —enjuto— de este viento enfermizo.

Se oye el ruido del avión que, sin duda, ahora pasa, no muy lejos de aquí.

Colossal Oblivion

Colossal oblivion that now no longer belongs to me, stone-like—lightning-struck?—and of course, beyond whatever remains of the gaze.

(In the indifferent elms: their strange ashes.)

As I descend: without vocation or noise; behind what little there is—and thin—of this unhealthy wind.

The noise of the airplane is heard which doubtless is passing now, not very far from here.

Anticipando la pedrada

Seco, seco. Feo, feo. Sin otro diente que perder. ¿Ya tan viejo? O ingenuamente comprueba que faltan espejos, torres; hasta comprueba que faltan estatuas.

Después, el sueño de clavetear vendaval de muertos, casi a diestra y siniestra.

Pero sobreviene el miedo.

Pero hay un bastón (y ¿qué hace aquí el bastón?, ¿no es anacrónico?)

Así que la Pregunta es: ¿en qué momento tendrá que echarse a cuestas su soledad?

Anticipating the Stoning

Dry, dry. Ugly, ugly. Without another tooth to lose. So old already? Or he ingenuously confirms that mirrors, towers are missing; he even confirms that statues are missing.

Afterwards, the dream of nailing down a gale of dead men, almost to the right and left.

But fear happens.

But there's a walking stick (and what's the walking stick doing here? isn't it anachronistic?).

And so the Question is: at what moment will he have to shoulder his solitude?

from

Bicoca A Piqué / A Cushy Deal Down the Drain

(1989)

1

Oda a un Ruiseñor

Sólo el tartamudeo de aquella noche. ¿Cómo es lo suave de una noche? Una luz que ahora trato de imitar. Luz que ahora, con *verdosos fulgores*, quisiera copiar. Pero las *sendas* de esa Oda han quedado demasiado traicionadas por el tiempo. (Tiempo que no hay espacio donde bien pudiera reconstruirse).

1

Ode to a Nightingale

Only the stammering of that night. What is the tenderness of a night? A light I'm now trying to imitate. A light that now, with *verdurous glooms*, I'd like to copy. But the *winding mossy ways* of this Ode have been far too betrayed by time. (A time without space for it to be properly reconstructed.)

8

Lo que oculta un Motel

La maraña o la rama de lo que desenreda en un paisaje. Una luz como el desorden pero apenas. He visto en el Trompe-l'oeil, entre apagado medallón de hojas de plátano lo absurdo de una escurridiza conversación que ya, definitivamente, el Tiempo desfiguró. Pero esto es sólo el telón de un más opaco, aunque último mundo. Un mundo donde, extrañamente, las alegorías tienen toda la brusca inmediatez de unas viandas acabadas de tragar. Un artificio (aunque también naturaleza) muy raro, sin embargo: pausas (árboles) y puntos (quemadas luces) que en esta tarde de Otoño se extienden con la compulsión de lo que, al aparecer, desaparece. ¡Muy raro!, pues, lo que oculta este Motel.

8

What a Motel Hides

Thicket or branch of what comes untangled in a landscape. A light like disorder, but barely. I saw in the trompe-l'oeil, in between the muted medallion of banana leaves, the absurdity of an elusive conversation that already, definitively, Time had defaced. But that's only the curtain of a more opaque though final world. A world where, strangely, allegories have all the brusque immediacy of some freshly swallowed viands. A very odd artifice (though also nature), however: pauses (trees) and spots (burned-out lights) that in this Autumn evening extend themselves with the compulsiveness of something that, when it appears, disappears. Very odd, then, what this Motel hides!

17

Manuscrito para la cajita

Para la cajita. Pudiera decirse que la Transparencia (como, en la pared de la cajita, la foto de aquel pobre diablo que sólo en disfrazase pensó) cubierta de telarañas. Pero esto, ni mucho menos, es una cajita surrealista. Es —semejante al chabacano dibujo de una hamaca pobre— cómo la cosa que traduce a una voz en el ocaso. O más: lo que pudiera parecer más complicado: 1, un discurso que serviría para decir al olvido; o 2, lo desdibujado, en la colisión de un tiempo de mediodía de allá, ________ (HAY, EN EL MANUSCRITO, UN ESPACIO BORRADO) cuando ________ (HAY EN EL MANUSCRITO, TAMBIÉN UN ESPACIO EN BLANCO), aquel niño que fui, tomaba el jugo de naranja.

17

Manuscript for the Box

For the box. It could be said to be Transparency (like the photo, on the wall of the box, of that poor fellow who had only wanted to disguise himself) covered with spider webs. But this is nothing less than a surrealist box. It's like—as is perhaps the ordinary drawing of a meager hammock—the thing that translates a voice at sunset. Or, still more complicated: 1, a speech that would adequately speak oblivion; or 2, something blurred, in the collision of a noon from over there. ____________ (THERE IS AN ERASURE IN THE MANUSCRIPT) when ____________ (THERE IS A BLANK SPACE IN THE MANUSCRIPT) that boy I was drank the orange juice.

21

Las Tablas de Armand Schwerner

Traduzco, para aplicar a *La Desarzonada*: .... que significa lo intraducible: +++++++++, que significa lo perdido; (¿ ?), que significa una posible manera de interpretar; [ ], que es la aclaración del Traductor; Θ, que significa lo confuso.

21

The Tablets of Armand Schwerner

I translate, to apply to *The Unhorsed Woman*: .... which means the untranslatable: +++++++, which means the lost; (?), which means a possible way of interpreting; [   ], which is the Translator's clarification; ⊖, which means confusion.

22

La voz en el texto en blanco

¡Tan nítido!: ahora es el blanco cartón de la cuadrícula. Lo blanco de los cuadrados contiguo y... ¡qué bien lo emblemático del agua! Pero junto a ello, murmurando en el primer cuadrado, y proliferando por los cuadrados contiguos, hay una voz intraducible. Una voz que, increíblemente, reflejase el discurso de un violeta a pique. Lo que+++++++ apenas........., como lo paradójico la voz: que se acerca-alejándose la voz: sale de un cuadrado para [de esa manera, casi inmediatamente] volver a entrar en otro.

22

The Voice in the Blank Text

So clear: now it's the grid's white cardboard. Whiteness of the contiguous squares and...how good the emblematic quality of water! But next to it, murmuring in the first square, and proliferating through the contiguous squares, is an untranslatable voice. A voice that, incredibly, should reflect the speech of a violet going down the drain. What+++++++ hardly......., like the paradoxical; the voice which approaches as it withdraws: it leaves a square to enter (in this way, almost immediately) another again.

26

No, vano discurso no es vacío

Blando, pasa: ¿sueño de evaporación desde fijo período de destino? Van por el canal las algas, flotando las cajitas desechadas. Como dado, dativo..., donde la humedad podría ser... ¿cuál rumbo, cuál discurso? Pero en este mocho canal se puede decir nada de lo que..., imprudente (no existe, ni existió); como tampoco de esa agua que, sin ninguna duda, nada más —seco— sabido ha ni ha podido, relatar.

26

No, Vain Speech Is Not Empty

Softly, it passes: a dream of evaporation from a fixed period of destiny? Through the canal drift the seaweed, the discarded boxes floating. As if given, dative…where moisture could be…what direction, what speech? But in this mutilated canal nothing can be said about… imprudent (it doesn't exist nor has it existed); nor about this water which, without any doubt, nothing more—dry—has not known how to nor been able to relate.

28

Con tiza en el espejo

¿Si con tiza me abrigo en el espejo? signos..., unos cuantos signos de más. También hasta unas crucecitas, o florecitas amarillas (pobretonamente pintadas, por supuesto). Esta tarde lo trazo todo en mi espejo mental. En ese espejo mental (pobretón también) que, oxidando con negros punticos algunos ángulos de mi pensamiento, a veces involuntariamente se despliega, como fingiendo la pátina de una libreta antiquísima.

28

With Chalk on the Mirror

What if I bundle up with chalk in the mirror? signs...a few signs too many. Also even a few little crosses, or little yellow flowers (wretchedly painted, of course). This evening I'm tracing everything in my mental mirror. In this mental mirror (also wretched) that, rusting with little black dots a few angles of my thought, sometimes involuntarily unfolds, as if faking the patina of a very old notebook.

32

Recordando a Ponge

¿Qué sitio —Mito— orgánico para que surjan las cosas inorgánicas? Pues voz vegetal, roce de pezuñas, o el paso de unas aves, para que en verdad aparezcan las cosas. Una tijera, por ejemplo, saldría de un matojo, de unas venas, o simplemente como resultado de una extraña solidificación del agua. Por lo que habría que colocarle al garabato material de unos raíles, la orgánica memoria de ese gato que bien supo, en su momento, cruzar por el opaco espesor de una tarde.

32

Remembering Ponge

Which organic site—Myth—for inorganic things to emerge? Well, a vegetal voice, friction of hooves, or a few birds passing, so that things appear in truth. A scissors, for example, would come out of a bush, from some veins, or simply as the result of a strange solidification of water. Because of this it would have to be placed with the material scribble of some rails, the organic memory of that cat which well knew, in its moment, how to cross the opaque thickness of an evening.

37

Junto al campo de golf

Esos dos viejos golfistas (¿o son tres golfistas, montados en el carrito añil?) En el campo de los antílopes, en esta tarde antediluviana, cuando -con los mandados regreso del Winn Dixie. Sosa, tan sosa es la banderita amarilla que ahora ya no se la ve. Pudiera saltar, pero necesariamente camino de prisa como si, absurdamente, fuera a bordar las pesquisas —¿qué pesquisas?— de ese camino levantado —¿cuándo levantado?— sobre lo resbaladizo —¿por qué resbaladizo?— de una quincallería plástica. ¡Vaya Novela de Caballería!

37

By the Golf Course

Those two old golfers (or are they three of them in the purple cart?). In the field of antelopes, in this antediluvian evening, when I return after running errands at the Winn-Dixie. Dull, so dull is the little yellow flag that it's disappeared from sight. I could jump, but of necessity I walk quickly as if, absurdly, I were to perform these investigations—what investigations?—on this raised path—when was it raised?—over the slipperiness—why slippery?—of a plastic hardware store. That's some Novel of Chivalry!

42

Testamento

Con despanzurrada carroza. Con tripas al viento de la colombina. Con oxidado, viejo bastidor. Con colchón sin ch (no sé lo que me digo), como en muerte. Todo eso al fin, destartalado creo que sí, que al final creo que está bien: lo coloquen junto a (a lo estatua-arlequín) esa piscina, o luz neón, de ese mocho Motel sin ton ni son.

42

Testament

With a squashed carriage. With guts in the wind of the columbine. With a rusted old stretcher. With a mattress without an "attr" (I don't know what I'm saying), as in death. All this at the end, decrepit I'm pretty sure, that in the end I think it's fine: they'll place him (like a Harlequin-statue) next to the swimming pool, or the neon light, of that squat Motel without rhyme or reason.

43

Revisando la visión

Por blanca cal de ese muro del Motel. Del Motel la sonrisa sin gato de la luz neón. Con, bajo ese tubo, la evocación del quirófano en la sombrilla playera. Por lo que como suerte —muerte— bastante escaso el rastrilleo de la piscina sin agua, a la vera de la sombrilla. Pasar, repasar. Soñar, soñar. Ese momento —a veces en el crepúsculo— petimetre donde para broma de la fotografía del Motel, ritualmente es como si se quemara la mismísima esquina de una sucia tarjeta postal, supuestamente en blanco.

43

Revising the Vision

Through this Motel wall's white lime. Of the Motel, the neon light's grin without a cat. With, beneath this tube, the evocation of the operating room in the beach umbrella. So that, like fate –death—quite infrequent, the dragging of the waterless swimming pool, at the edge of the umbrella. Passing, back and forth. Dreaming, dreaming. This foppish moment—sometimes in twilight –where, as a joke on the photograph of the Motel, ritually it's as if the very same corner of a dirty postcard, supposedly blank, were being burned.

55

Caluroso el día

Una zona de explosión zonza: el día que estúpidamente disiente. Sólo componen, los sucios cartuchos de papel sobre el sofá abandonado en el terreno baldío, un no-presagio. Es lo hecho, o es lo no-hecho, para no decir más. Pero es que, también, con la mirada basta para mantenernos. Soy (aunque no sé lo que esto pueda significar) una mirada.

55

Warm Day

A zone of inane explosion: the day that stupidly dissents. The dirty paper cartridges on the abandoned mattress in the vacant lot merely compose a non-omen. It's what's done, or it's what's not been done, nothing more to say. But it's also that our gaze is enough to keep us going. I am a gaze (though I don't know what that could mean).

59

Un mandala

Como que se encendió en un circo, pues tiene el esplendor falso de una luz neón. Me muerdo las uñas para ello, situado en la misma diagonal donde el pasado, por el lado de una madrugada, fracasó. Así que, también, me limpiaré de cualquier conjuro, pues sólo el viento, ya híbrido, deberá recorrerse.

59

A mandala

As if she lit herself in a circus, since she has the false splendor of a neon light. I bite my nails for her, located in the same diagonal where the past, through the side of a dawn, failed. And so I shall also cleanse myself of any spell, since only the wind, already hybrid, should pass through.

from

Vílis / Bileville

(1998)

DIARIO DEL CONSTRUCTOR DE CAJITAS — No me importa lo que los plásticos, o sea lo que los pintores y escultores piensan de mí. Ya sé que ellos no pueden entender mi propósito de lograr una marquetería olfativa. Ellos no entienden nada, y como no entienden nada, están diciendo que mis estudios sobre la desodorización, y sobre los caramelos asépticos, son puro disparate. ¡Al diablo con ellos! Aunque se me crea un loco, yo soy el único artista importante de mi generación. Por lo pronto, para la construcción de mis cajitas estoy haciendo lo único que a estos tarados pintores y escultores nunca se les ocurriría hacer, o sea, estudiar los olores. Hay el olor (aunque esto resulte casi inconfesable) de una mierda que podría calificarse como proustiana. Hay el olor de lo que no tiene olor pero que, en su desodorización, machaca como si fuera el tintineo obsesivo de una música minimalista. Hay como el olor restregado (olor como con un color sucio) que emana de los gestos. (¡sí, óiganlo bien, de los gestos!) de una pareja que conozco. Hay el olor, sin olor, de una vida que casi no es vida. Y, por último, están esos olores, procedentes de una difícil vena plástica, y que son, por ejemplo, ese olor, como con rincón, de una luneta de cine de barrio en un mediodía de la década del 40 (y, precisamente, sobre este rincón de luneta estoy trabajando actualmente), o el olor de la luz de neón (¡sí, pintores, de la luz neón!) sobre la piscina sin agua de un Motel de color cotorra. Así que con eso ando, y aunque lo pintores y los escultores no sepan cómo trabajar con los olores, para mí, eso también es lo plástico.

DIARY OF THE BOX BUILDER—I don't care what other visual artists, painters and sculptors in particular, think of me. I know they can't understand my quest to achieve an olfactory marquetry. They understand nothing, and since they understand nothing, they say that my studies of deodorization and aseptic candies are a total joke. To hell with them! They think I'm a nutcase, but I'm the only important artist of my generation. For now, in order to build my boxes I'm doing the one thing that would never occur to those moronic painters and sculptors: studying smells. There's the smell (though I almost don't want to admit it) of a shit that could be described as Proustian. There's the smell of something that has no smell but which, in its deodorization, crushes as if it were the obsessive tinkling of minimalist music. There's something like the well-scrubbed smell (a smell like a dirty color) that emanates from the gestures (yes, listen up, gestures!) of a couple I know. There's the smell, odorless, of a life that almost isn't a life. And finally, there are those smells, originating in a difficult plastic streak, and which are, for example, that smell like a corner of a stall in a neighborhood movie theater at noon in the 1940s (and it's precisely that corner of a stall that I'm working on now), or the smell of the neon light (yes, painters, the neon light!) on the waterless swimming pool of a parrot-colored Motel. So that's what I'm up to, and although painters and sculptors don't know how to work with smells, this for me is also visual art.

Aunque lo parece no se trata, precisamente, de un tren de lavado chino, sino de un prostíbulo. Este prostíbulo está en el Prado de Vilis, y él llega allí a través de un laberinto de callejuelas.

Llega con una muchachita que es casi Lolita y casi china.

La Lolita china, después de acostarse en una cama del prostíbulo, luce como embalsamada. La colcha que la cubre es como la sábana que se le pone a una momia.

Lolita, reducida de tamaño, tal parece un pan de color chocolate. En su misma cama hay una niña que también parece embalsamada. El Coronel Manrique se acerca a la niña, y observa que ésta tiene ojos de animal, los ojos de un pájaro.

Quizá la Lolita y la niña, como dos buenas lesbianas, acaben haciendo el amor, pero esto, para el Coronel Manrique, sería contemplar un acto en frío. El se siente asqueado.

Although it appears to be, this isn't about a Chinese laundry train, but a brothel. This brothel is on Bileville's Prado, and he arrives there through a labyrinth of alleyways.

He arrives with a girl who's almost Lolita and almost Chinese.

The Chinese Lolita, lying in a bed in the brothel, appears embalmed. The bedspread covering her is like the sheet placed over a mummy.

Lolita, shrunken, looks just like chocolate-colored bread. In her bed, there's a little girl who also appears embalmed. Colonel Manrique approaches the girl and observes that she has the eyes of an animal, the eyes of a bird.

Perhaps Lolita and the girl, like two good lesbians, will end up making love, but that, for Colonel Manrique, would be coldly contemplating an act. He feels nauseated.

DIARIO DEL CONSTRUCTOR DE CAJITAS — Me preocupan cosas muy difíciles de expresar, cosas que no sé cómo decir. Por ejemplo, quisiera construir mi propio corazón en tamaño diminuto, pero lo difícil no es esto, sino que también quisiera que esa disminución de mi propio corazón tuviese una semejanza con lo que se pudiese llamar un estuchito de pesadillas. Pero ¿cómo lograr esto? Pues ¿qué cosa puede ser un estuchito de pesadillas? Y si lograra dar pie con bola, ¿cómo lograr que el estuchito se pareciese a mi corazón? Sin embargo, lograr cosas como éstas es lo único que creo que vale la pena. No me interesa construir una cajita realista. Todo realismo me deja indiferente. Pero eso sí, aunque estoy convencido de que todo realismo es una estilización innecesaria, requiero que mis objetos sean precisos. Si digo estuchito de pesadillas tiene que ser estuchito de pesadillas, no me conformo con vaguedades neblinosas. Y quizá, también, por rechazar las vaguedades, es que me siento totalmente identificado con esto que, en una carta, escribió Henry Miller: "Y cuando un pintor también escribe, yo generalmente disfruto de su escritura más que la de los escritores. ¡No me preguntes por qué! *Las Cartas a Theo* de Van Gogh, por ejemplo, significan tanto para mí como las novelas de Dostoievski." *O sea, para terminar, no me interesa la estilización realista, pero cuando hablo de objetos precisos me refiero a ese tipo de objetividad que Clarice Lispector visualiza en una frase:* «Era un perro extraño y objetivo». *Un perro así es el que me interesa meter en la cajita.*

DIARY OF THE BOX BUILDER—I'm worried about things that are very difficult to express, things I don't know how to say. For example, I wanted to build my own heart in miniature, but that wasn't the hard part, I also wanted this miniature of my heart to look like what could be called a little container of nightmares. But how to achieve this? Well, what kind of thing could a little container of nightmares be? And were I to manage to get it right, how to make the little container look like my heart? Achieving things like this, however, is the only thing I consider worth the trouble. I'm not interested in building a realist box. All realism leaves me cold. But one thing's for sure, although I'm convinced that all realism is an unnecessary stylization, I require my objects to be precise. If I say little container of nightmares, it has to be a little container of nightmares, I won't accept misty vagueness. And maybe also, if I reject vagueness, it's because I identify completely with what Henry Miller wrote in a letter: "When a painter also writes, I generally enjoy his writing more than other writers. Don't ask me why! Van Gogh's *Letters to Theo*, for example, means as much to me as Dostoevsky's novels." *In other words, to conclude, I'm not interested in realist stylization, but when I speak about precise objects, I refer to the type of objectivity that Clarice Lispector visualizes in a sentence:* "It was a strange and objective dog." *A dog like that is what I'd be interested in putting in the box.*

Lorenzo García Vega, al llegar a Vilis, hizo lo mismo que hacen todos los viejos: se puso a recordar a Jagüey Grande, su pueblo natal. Lorenzo dijo: —Felito era un niño que conocí. Estábamos en Jagüey, era en una peregrinación, y nos bajamos de una carretera. Entonces se me ocurrió que *cuando se cambia un diamante, éste aumenta de tamaño.*

Pero ¿qué querría decir Lorenzo? Ese viejo es casi genial, pero cuando cae en el autismo no se entiende ni él mismo. Es una lástima.

Lorenzo García Vega, when he reached Bileville, did what all old people do: he started remembering Jagüey Grande, his native town. Lorenzo said: "Felito was a boy I knew. We were in Jagüey, it was on a pilgrimage, and we got off a cart. Then it occurred to me that *when you exchange a diamond, it increases in size.*"

But what did Lorenzo mean? This old guy is almost a genius, but when he descends into autism even he can't understand himself. It's a shame.

¡Qué de cosas suceden en Vilis! Soy bag boy en el Super Mercado, en el Publix, y el poeta Roberto Fernández Retamar me ha pedido el carrito con que le llevo los mandados a los clientes. «Te lo presto hasta las cuatro», le dije, mientras el carrito se convertía en ese móvil en que montan a los enfermos, en los hospitales. Retamar salió mandado con él, pero ahí, no sé cómo, me iluminé. Me iluminé, por lo que supe que el Poeta no iba a regresar con el carro. Lo supe, y me puse a gritar y a correr. Entonces Retamar, que me vio correr, y me oyó gritar, empujó el carrito todo lo que pudo, para no dármelo. Sin embargo, yo corrí más que él, así que le pude quitar el carro. Se lo quité y, entonces vi cómo Retamar regresaba a un patio donde tenía su auto. Es triste eso. Todos queríamos a Retamar, pero él no era amigo de nadie.

The things that happen in Bileville! I'm a bag boy in the Supermarket, the Publix, and the poet Roberto Fernández Retamar asked me for the shopping cart I use to bring deliveries to the customers. "I'll lend it to you until four o'clock," I told him, as the shopping cart changed into the mobile bed they put sick people on in hospitals. Retamar left with it and a delivery, but then, mysteriously, I was enlightened. I was enlightened, and that's how I knew the Poet wouldn't return with the cart. Then Retamar, who saw me running and heard me yelling, pushed the cart as fast as he could so as not to let me have it. But I ran faster than he, and was able to take the cart away from him. I took it away, and then I saw Retamar go back to a courtyard where his car was parked. It's all quite sad. We all liked Retamar, but he was nobody's friend.

HAY UNA ULTIMA CANCION—Retirado, confidencialmente, me dijo el viejo camarero que antes, en los grandes banquetes, con sólo probar el hielo de sus hieleras respectivas, podía él cantar las canciones de los países de aquellos clientes que estaban sentados a la mesa. «Por ejemplo» —me dijo, «llegué a una perfección tal que, en inolvidable ocasión y después de probar el hielo de la mesa de unos bolivianos, al instante empecé a cantar el Himno Nacional de Bolivia. ¡Qué éxito fue aquello, Lorenzo!». Sin embargo, siguió diciéndome el camarero, sucedió que una vez, por probar infructuosamente, varias veces, el hielo de la hielera de unos argentinos (argentinos que, además, habían llegado tarde al banquete), le fue imposible, a él, cantar ningún tango. Y esto, terminó diciéndome el camarero, fue desastroso para él, ya que por la depresión que le produjo su fracaso con el hielo de los argentinos, no le quedó más remedio que jubilarse.

Pero nunca he sabido el porqué de que el viejo camarero me contara todo esto. Es muy posible que él esté completamente loco.

ONE LAST SONG—Taking me aside in confidence, the old waiter told me that before, during the large banquets, just by tasting the ice in their trays, he could sing the songs of the countries of those customers seated at the table. "For example," he said, "I reached such perfection that, on an unforgettable occasion and after tasting the ice on the table of some Bolivians, right away I began singing the Bolivian National Anthem. What a success it was, Lorenzo!" But, he went on, it so happened that once, after fruitlessly tasting, several times, the ice from the tray of some Argentines (Argentines, moreover, who had arrived late at the banquet), it was impossible for him to sing any tangos. And that, the waiter finished, was disastrous for him, since because of the depression caused by his failure with the Argentines' ice, all he had left was to retire.

But I never knew why the old waiter told me this. It's quite possible he was completely mad.

Y, para terminar, llego a Cuba. Me paseo, en cueros en pelotas, por los salones del Capitolio.

También me encuentro con Lezama, y me reconcilio con Cintio (quien, por cierto, me pide prestados $200 pesos).

Por las calles de La Habana hay enormes edificios blancos.

Edificios espectrales que parecen como hechos con yeso.

Entro en un café. El café es un lugar largo, y a lo largo de las paredes, puestas en venta, están las lápidas.

También, en el café, hay viejas cubanas de la vieja burguesía, muertas desde hace bastante tiempo.

Me digo, pues, que dentro de una semana regresaré a Vilis, pero que ya tengo ganas de regresar a Vilis, lugar donde, sea como sea, tengo mi habitación.

Y observación final para comemierdas que pudieran escandalizarse:

— Y es que Cintio nunca le ha pedido prestado nada a nadie, y mucho menos $200 pesos a mí, pero la literatura es literatura, y nada más. Menos mal...

And, to conclude, I've arrived in Cuba. I stroll, stark naked, through the rooms of the Capitol.

I also meet Lezama, and I reconcile with Cintio (who, by the way, asks me to loan him 200 pesos).

In the streets of Havana are enormous white buildings.

Spectral buildings that look like they're made of plaster.

I enter a café. The café is a large space, and along the walls, on sale, are tombstones.

Also in the café are old Cuban women from the former bourgeoisie, dead for quite some time.

I tell myself, then, that within a week I'll return to Bileville, but I already want to return to Bileville, the place where, whatever it may be, I have my room.

And a final observation for ass-kissers who might get offended:

– And the fact is that Cintio's never asked anybody to loan him anything, much less 200 pesos from me, but literature is literature, and that's all. Just as well…

from

Caminandito hasta estar sentado / A Little Walk Until Sitting Down

(1999)

Otro intento autista

Comencé, o creí comenzar con una visión: la figura sentada como frente a un mar blanco. La figura miraba para un lado. La figura se levantaba, se iba. ¿Era el retrato de un fantasma? Pero, después supuse que no debería responder más a esa figura.

Era –me dije– otra cosa. Era intentar lo semejante a una traducción. Sí, se trataría como si me hubiese propuesto una traducción. Mi brazo dormido y, a medias, yo más despierto que nunca.

Pero entonces... de verdad entonces... cuando con la traducción intenté la pequeñísima construcción de mi pirámide (pues de una pequeñísima, sin duda, pirámide se trataba), he ahí que, sin duda, estaba trabajando en otra cosa...: absolutamente distinta la otra cosa.

Otra cosa, absolutamente distinta de aquello que me había propuesto.

Pues, he ahí que resultaba tan absurdo el resultado. Pues era que se propusiera la escritura como... ¿cómo qué? (es absurdo formularlo), ¿como llevándola a cabo sobre pianos blancos? Y donde entonces, del otro lado de la ventana, colillas húmedas habría y, la grotesca semejanza de un papel donde pintados unos... como... como lamentables, inservibles, nada menos que flacos gatos.

Por lo que, con lo que tengo dicho, cada vez le tengo más miedo a las denuncias si es que, con ellas, lo que verdaderamente significaría *hacer*, sólo sería, ¡fíjense bien!, revelar.

¿Revelar qué? ¿Revelar el verdadero estado de mis sentimientos?

O como si, paradójicamente me atreviera a señalar que, cada vez, voy siendo más la figura sentada frente a un mar blanco conque comencé, en la primera línea de este texto.

Propongo, entonces, lo que quiere decir un mar interior blanco. ¿Un mar interior blanco es alguna pregunta?

Another Autistic Attempt

I began, or thought I began, with a vision: the figure seated as if facing a white sea. The figure was looking off to one side. The figure got up, went away. Was it the portrait of a phantom? But afterwards, I supposed I shouldn't respond to that figure any more.

It was—I said to myself—something else. It was attempting something similar to translation. Yes, it was something like my having proposed a translation. My arm had gone to sleep and I, the rest of me, was more awake than ever.

But then…really then…when with the translation I attempted the teeny-tiny construction of my pyramid (because it concerned a doubtless teeny-tiny pyramid), here I was, doubtless, working on something else…completely different, that something else.

Something else, completely different from what I'd proposed.

So the fact was that the result ended up absurd. So the fact was that it proposed writing as…as what? (formulating it is absurd) as bringing it to conclusion on white pianos? And where, then, from the other side of the window, there would be damp cigarette butts and the grotesque semblance of a paper on which there were painted a few, something like…like lamentable, useless, nothing other than skinny cats.

Because of this, what with what I admit to having said, every time I'm more afraid of denunciations if it's the case that, with them, what would truly mean *making* would only be—pay close attention!—revealing.

Revealing what? Revealing the true state of my feelings?

Or as if paradoxically I would venture to point out that each time, I am becoming more and more the figure seated facing a white sea at the very beginning of this text.

I therefore propose what a white interior sea might mean. Is a white interior sea some kind of question?

Palabra alguna

De pronto, con esa colcha raída que tenía en mis manos me pregunté, sin saber por qué, sobre una borrosa infancia.

¿Una borrosa infancia, deletreada desde esa colcha raída? ¿Había habido un andén?

O, quizá, preguntarme si, en algún momento, hubo alguna luz mocha.

¿Luz mocha?

Quizá lejano, muy lejano en el tiempo, quizá sobre unos raíles, lo semejante a un trampolín. Pero, pensándolo bien, ¿no podría ser un fingido trampolín?

Aunque, después, yo estaría seco. Seco estaría: entrando, saliendo, por donde ya no había puertas. O, lo que es lo mismo, lo semejante al círculo mocho de una luz opaca. Pero ¿qué puede ser de lo que estoy hablando? ¿De un círculo mocho estoy hablando? Pero ¿una luz opaca para qué? O, ¿quién, precisamente, en un andén que quizá no existió, pudo necesitar, dentro de un circulo opaco, una luz mocha?

Pero entonces, planteado así, quizá no hubiera nada.

O, entonces, quizá, por el momento, con rígida mandíbula, no habría por qué llegar a masticar palabra alguna.

Y esto porque… Y esto, ya que es cierto que lo que digo, o lo que no digo, no es, hasta ahora, palabra alguna.

Any Kind of Word

Suddenly, holding that frayed bedspread, I asked myself, for some reason, about a blurred childhood.

A blurred childhood, derived from this frayed bedspread? Had there been a platform?

Or asking myself if maybe there'd once been a kind of thick light.

Thick light?

Maybe distant, very distant in time, maybe on some rails, something like a trampoline. Or, giving it some thought, maybe a feigned trampoline?

Although, afterwards, I'd be dry. Dry I'd be: entering, exiting, where there were no longer doors. Or, much the same, something like the thick circle of an opaque light. But what can I be talking about? Am I talking about a thick circle? What's the point of the opaque light? Or who, precisely, on a maybe nonexistent platform, could need a thick light within an opaque circle?

Put thus, maybe there'd be nothing.

Or maybe, then, for the moment, jaw set, there'd be no reason for mouthing any kind of word. Because…

And this, now that it's certain that what I'm saying, or not saying, is not, until now, any kind of word.

Cursor descontrolado

El como endiablado cursor moviéndose, rewind. Un parpadeo hacia atrás, febril, como una película. Si hubiera seguido con el mimo ritmo que tenía, habría logrado aquellas escenas silentes de mi infancia en que Tom Mix corría en su caballo.

Pues llueve de una manera brutal y, por supuesto, el parabrisas está haciendo todo lo que puede hacer.

Me imagino que soy yo el que está en el volante: el cursor, el rewind junto al parabrisas devorando mi pasado, hasta recorrer todas las millas.

Pero nada más que en un instante coloca, ¡es lamentable!, entre tanta lluvia como está cayendo, su garra el Tigre de lo Invisible. ¡Es lamentable!

Ya que sólo esto le ha bastado al Tigre –tocar con ferocidad instantánea–, para que el cursor se convierta, junto al parabrisas inútilmente disparado, en lo que, trebejo como tareco, sólo sirve para mostrarse con ese zumbido, móvil-inmóvil, de lo que nunca volverá a dar pie con bola...

Uncontrolled Cursor

The cursor, as if demonic, moving, rewind. A backward blinking, febrile, like a movie. If it had continued at the same pace, it would have arrived at those silent scenes of my childhood when Tom Mix raced along on his horse.

Now it was raining terrifically and, of course, the screen was doing everything it could.

I imagine I'm the one who's at the wheel: the cursor, the rewind, the screen devouring my past, until it covers all the miles.

But in a flash—it's pathetic!—amidst all that rainfall, the claws of the Tiger of the Invisible grasp it. It's pathetic!

Since this alone sufficed for the Tiger—with instantaneous ferocity—to change the cursor, next to the pointlessly switched-on screen, in which, a junky gadget, it only displays itself, with that buzzing, mobile-immobile, of something that will never again hit the nail on the head.

No lo encontré

Por supuesto.

Cuando iba en canal, hasta abajo, en una yagua.

A lo lejos un potrero –fue en otra vida–, simulaba: o un cuchillo que, al final, estrella de la tarde.

Por única vez, en aquella ocasión, el agua (¿el agua era mi cuerpo?)

Sombra –¿una bruja de cartón?– hubiera podido ser dedal, medida, o como un cucuyo: unas risas como metal, a un lado: sosteniendo un pedazo.

Pedazo: tela, o murciélago (ya no puedo precisar la diferencia).

Pero no llegué, del todo, a agarrar aquel momento.

Recogí lo semejante a un fetiche hilito: creo que lo guardé, en el bolsillo.

Hubo una fragua, o lo semejante a una fragua, en un rincón que fingió una máscara.

Pero no hubo tal campana. (Ahora, sí, lejano, el ruido de una locomotora).

Tampoco pude agarrar aquello.

Entonces fue –¿qué tiempo después?– cuando me acerqué a un pozo.

Al acercarme al pozo me metí dentro de un cuento.

Nunca he podido saber la manera en que me contaron aquel cuento.

Miré, fijamente, todo aquello. El pozo como para que, lo que nunca fue, no se perdiera.

Nunca.

I Didn't Find It

Of course.

When I was floating on a canal, downstream, on a royal palm.

At a distance a pasture (in another life) was pretending: or a knife which, in the end, shatters the evening.

For the one and only time, on that occasion, water (was water my body?).

Shadow—a cardboard witch?—could have become a thimble, a measure, or something like a firefly: some laughter like metal, to one side: supporting a piece.

Piece: canvas, or bat (I can no longer tell the difference).

But I didn't manage, at all, to grasp that moment.

I picked up something like a fetish piece of thread: I think I kept it in my pocket.

There was a forge, or something like a forge, in a corner that was pretending to be a mask.

But there was no such bell. (Now, yes, far off, the noise of a locomotive.)

I couldn't grasp that either.

It was then—how long after? —I approached a well.

When I approached the well, I put myself inside a story.

I've never known how they told me that story.

I gazed intently at all this. The well in such a way as to, which never happened, not get lost.

Ever.

O sea, nunca llegué adonde, por ninguna razón, pudiera haber llegado.

Desgarrón, entonces, o como un manchón caliente: acorraló todas las señales.

Los ojos de aquella vez, entonces, se perdieron.

O, yo hubiera querido tener aquello, lo que no fue ni sería.

Mirada fija, sin duda, para entrar en el pozo.

O tiempo pobre: la pomada amarillenta que se metía dentro de una cajita.

Y así poder, por un momento, haber agarrado lo que, definitivamente, nunca se pudiera haber agarrado.

Which is to say, I never got to where, for no reason, I could have.

Agony, then, or like a big hot stain: it cornered all signals.

So the eyes of that time got lost.

Or, I would have wanted to have that, which didn't happen, nor would it.

An intent gaze, no doubt, to enter the well.

Or a poor time: the yellowing pomade that placed itself inside a box.

And thus to be able for a moment to have grasped what, definitively, should never have been grasped.

Canción

Para Alessandra Molina

Y el sótano se hunde dando un paso.
William Blake

Para una canción, tal como el murciélago de un cuento.

Es triste y gris todo. Se está cayendo la luna, aunque todavía es de día.

Sí, se está cayendo la luna.

Efectivamente, efectivamente, es así, ¡oh!

En una ocasión, ciertos enanos corrieron y se agitaron, deslizándose por un sendero.

Ahora, esto que acabo de decir ya..., yo..., ni sé lo que pueda significar.

Ya..., yo...

Miren, miren, los muy respetables: ustedes: en un lado de una competición era llevada, en un receptáculo, mi sangre.

Era llevada.

Era llevada, me consta que fue así. Ese relato se titulaba: EN EL BAÑO de POMPEYA. Tal como lo digo ahora.

Pues quisiera no tener más pesar que ese pesar que implicaría el poder llegar a ser un fantasma.

Un fantasma, tra la la, un fantasma, tra la, lo aseguro.

Quisiera acabar de ser un fantasma, lo aseguro.

Y entonces se sabría, como ya he dicho, que mi sangre, toda, estaría en un receptáculo.

Song

for Alessandra Molina

And the Cellar goes down with a step.
William Blake

For a song, just like the bat in a story.

Everything's sad and gray. The moon is falling, though it's still day.

Yes, the moon is falling.

Indeed, indeed, that's how it is, oh!

Once, certain dwarfs ran and got agitated sliding down a path.

Now, what I've just said is already…I…I don't even know what that might mean.

Already…I…

Look, look, you highly respectable people: all of you: on one side of a competition my blood, in a receptacle, was brought.

Brought.

It was brought, I swear that's how it was. This story was called: IN THE BATH OF POMPEII. Just like I'm saying now.

So I'd like to have no regrets other than the regret that would imply ending up as a phantom.

A phantom, tra la la, a phantom, tra la, of that I'm sure.

I'd like to end up as a phantom, of that I'm sure.

And then it would be known, as I've already said, that my blood, all of it, would be in a receptacle.

¿En un triángulo? No, no precisamente en un triángulo.

He dicho en un receptáculo.

En Pompeya. Tal como el murciélago de un cuento. Tal como lo preguntaría ésta, la Canción, si cantarla supiera.

Si cantarla supiera

In a triangle? No, not exactly a triangle.

In a receptacle, I said.

In Pompeii. Just like the bat in a story. Just like this, the Song, would proclaim, if I knew how to sing it.

If I knew how to sing it.

El salvador de las pestañas

¿Una oruga deslizándose?,
¿sobre una caligrafía?
Sospecho que estoy literaturizando.

Al cagar,
se le detuvo la mirada,
cegado por un espejo de baratija.

¿La conciencia es el pitazo de una locomotora?
La oigo, todas las noches,
sentado frente a un patio seco.

Feliz con el monstruo que vi,
en la película de la tele.
¡Yo era el monstruo!

Un espantapájaros en una película silente,
visto a las doce de la noche.
¡Regresé a la infancia!

¿Espantapájaros frente a una gasolinera?
Lo vi en un cartel.
Me hizo bien.

¿De dónde vino ese cucuyo?
Una puerta se abrió,
¿pero qué más pudo ser?

Pasa una motoneta,
por la calle, o dentro de mí,
durante el sueño nocturno.

The Rescuer of Eyelashes

A caterpillar sliding?
on calligraphy?
I suspect I'm being literary.

While shitting,
he averted his gaze,
blinded by a cheap mirror.

Is consciousness a locomotive whistle?
I hear it, every night,
seated in front of a dry courtyard.

Happy with the monster I saw,
in the TV movie.
I was the monster!

A scarecrow in a silent movie,
seen at twelve at night.
I regressed to childhood!

Scarecrow in front of a gas station?
I saw it on a poster.
It did me good.

Where'd that firefly come from?
A door opened,
but what else could it be?

A motorscooter passes,
down the street, or inside me,
during my nocturnal slumber.

¿Una naranja sobre la tarde?
No, no hay lectura superpuesta,
sólo, caminandito, una hilera de patos.

¿Inventar un polvo de telaraña?
No. Ayer, inútilmente, quise inventar un sauce.
Mejor, entonces, mirar para los celajes.

El recuerdo de un cine devastado,
la alucinación con la devastación de un Hotel,
pero sin ninguna flor de loto, ni sin ninguna nieve.

¡Lo que pudiera pensar sobre mí mismo!,
pero sólo el almacén amarillo.
El mismo lugar, donde estuvo la colchoneta vieja.

No hay ninguna manguera que riegue mi cerebro.
Como si hubiera un carrusel perdido,
en una noche dentro de mí.

Cuento con muchas manchas, sin duda
manchas frente a una gasolinera
manchas en un tramo del canal.

Al ver ese canal en la oscuridad:
entonces es cuando la historia empieza de verdad:
una historia, por cierto, donde no se verá a nadie.

Puedo imaginar, después de tomar un somnífero:
cómo un fantasma pudiera ahorcarse.
Pero esto, al despertar, se me olvida.

Me siento hasta espiritual,
cuando, desde la terraza,
oigo el ruido de una sierra.

An orange upon the evening?
No, there's no superimposed reading,
just, taking a little walk, a row of ducks.

Inventing cobweb dust?
No. Yesterday, uselessly, I wanted to invent a willow.
Better, then, to look at the sunset clouds.

The memory of a devastated movie theater,
hallucinating the devastation of a Hotel,
but with no lotus flower, nor even any snow.

The things I could think about myself!
but only the yellow warehouse.
The same place where the old mattress was.

There's no hose that can water my brain.
As if there were a lost carousel
in a night within me.

I've counted a lot of stains, no doubt
stains in front of a gas station
stains in a stretch of the canal.

Upon seeing this canal in the darkness:
that's when the story really begins:
a story, of course, where nobody will be seen.

I can imagine, after taking a sleeping pill:
how a phantom could strangle itself.
But when I wake up, I forget this.

I even feel spiritual
when, from the terrace,
I hear the noise of a saw.

Una guagua sucia y amarilla.
al transportar a unos niños borrosos.
Hace pensar en un viaje hacia nada.

Hay cosas con las que no he soñado:
la cama, por ejemplo,
en que me encontrarán muerto.

La basura postal de cada día, en el buzón.
El buen destino que dios me ha dado.
El viejo que soy.

Arriba unos pájaros negros, sobre el tendido.
Abajo unos patos negros, caminandito en la arena.
No creo que esté pidiendo más.

Así que me metería debajo de la cama.
Me metería, por ejemplo,
si todavía esperara una respuesta.

¿Flores de cerezo? ¿Dónde?
Almacenes, solares yermos.
Una mancha siempre se puede encontrar.

Me alucina oír el pronóstico del tiempo.
Me obsede contarme un cuento,
en el momento en que tomo agua.

El cuidad con la próstata,
los parciales que bien me cuidan.
¡El viejo que soy!

A dirty yellow bus,
as it transports some blurred children.
It makes one think of a trip to nowhere.

There are things I haven't dreamed about:
the bed, for example,
in which they'll find me dead.

The everyday junk mail, in the mailbox.
The fine destiny god's given me
The old man that I am.

Above, some black birds, on the wires.
Below, some black ducks, taking a little walk on the pavement.
I don't think I'm asking for more.

And so I'd put myself under the bed.
I'd put myself, for example,
if I could still hope for an answer.

Cherry blossoms? Where?
Warehouses, vacant lots.
A stain can always be found.

I'm amazed listing to the weather forecast.
I'm obsessed with telling myself a story,
at the moment I'm drinking water.

Care of the prostate,
the tests that take good care of me.
Old man that I am!

¿Cuál es la ceniza que guarda mi corazón?
Se va pareciendo a unas latas,
mientras que, las latas, se van pareciendo a unas manchas.

Un rictus inmóvil,
¿qué duda cabe?
lo fabrica la noche.

¿Desnudo irreal?
O finge un desnudo,
o sueña con una dirección.

¡Qué raro!
Sólo al oír el pitazo de la locomotora,
estar perdido.

Ya petrificados,
nombres que fueron,
¿quién podré ser yo?

Lo cerca, entonces, una estrella
cuando, orinando –apocado–
al lado de una esquina.

En mi mente,
pretendí alcanzar,
lo que miro.

Invisible tirándome,
mirándome,
en nada que mirar.

What is the ash my heart keeps?
It's beginning to look like some cans,
while the cans are beginning to look like some stains.

An immobile rictus,
how to doubt it?
the night fashions it.

Unreal nude?
Either it's pretending to be a nude
or it's dreaming of an address.

How odd!
Merely hearing the locomotive whistle,
getting lost.

Already petrified,
the names that used to be,
who might I be?

A star then surrounds him
when—timid—pissing
near a corner.

In my mind,
I aspired to reach
what I look at.

Invisible, hurling myself,
looking at myself.
With nothing to look at.

from

Palíndromo en otra cerradura: Homenaje a Duchamp / Palindrome in Another Lock: Homage to Duchamp

(1999)

27

Cápsulas (Energía Duchamp)

1

¿Dónde está la energía del crecimiento de mis uñas? Increíblemente, había que remontarse a mi infancia, rescatarla en la sombra de una cocina que ya no existe. También la energía del crecimiento de mis uñas se manifestó en un patio, mientras con una tijerita las cortaba. Procesos de alquimia interior (aseguro que, bajo condiciones favorables, podría reducirlo todo).

2

En la casa, desde hace tiempo, nadie toca el timbre de la puerta. Ese sonido del timbre, extendiéndose por dentro de la casa, tiene que tener una energía. ¿Se ha ausentado esa energía? Si no es así ¿dónde puede estar escondida?

3

Ha dejado de fumar. Pero tiene que haber quedado almacenada, en alguna parte, la Energía contenida en los cigarros que fumó. Así que si llegara a encontrar esa Energía, bien podría utilizarla para construir un sofisticado, pequeño cuerpo astral. Un pequeño cuerpo astral, como de tocador.

4

También la orina contiene la Energía, pero esto es Proceso arduo de contar. Es la orina que contiene miedo (sólo ésta conduce la energía), y puede venir (aunque no necesariamente) acompañada por escalofríos. La orina, ésta del miedo, procede de una de esas fiebres infantiles que marcan al sujeto para siempre.

27

Capsules (Duchamp Energy)

1

Where's the energy of the growth of my nails? Incredibly, I had to return to my childhood, rescue it in the shadow of a kitchen that no longer exists. The energy of the growth of my nails was also displayed in a courtyard, while I was cutting them with a nail-scissors. Processes of interior alchemy (I assure you that, under favorable conditions, I could reduce all of it).

2

In the house, for some time, nobody's rung the doorbell. This doorbell sound, spreading inside the house, must have an energy. Has this energy gone away? If that's not the case, where could it be hidden?

3

He stopped smoking. But he must have, somewhere, stored up the Energy contained in the cigarettes he smoked. So if he manages to encounter an energy, he could well use it to construct a small, sophisticated astral body. A small astral body, like a boudoir's.

4

Piss also contains Energy, but this is a Process arduous in the telling. It's the piss that contains fear (that alone conducts energy), and (though not necessarily) can be accompanied by tremors. Piss, the one from fear, proceeds from one of those childhood fevers that mark the subject forever.

5

Hay quien caga pensando en una monja judía y excéntrica, que escondida en un convento se dedicaba a examinar las heces fecales de sus discípulas (eso puede encontrarse en una novela, cuyo título y autor se le ha olvidado al cagante). La presencia del Personaje monja en la meditación del que caga, no hay duda de que ha conllevado una buena porción de Energía.

6

La Energía está en todas partes. A veces se confunde con la Vanidad o, hasta puede ser que sea la misma Vanidad. En cuanto a Saber, nadie sabe nada de nada.

7

Duchamp no conoció a los huérfanos que cantaban los números de la Lotería, pero eso existió. La energía se metamorfoseó por entre distintas venas del aburrimiento. En un momento sabía el número ganador, el Premio Gordo. Se hacía un pequeño silencio-espacio para el aburrimiento. La energía de un pequeño cuadradito se abría sobre un mar municipal.

8

Hay quien caga haciendo ejercicios de Atención con una monja judía excéntrica. La monja le ensena a sus discípulas el cagar sin dejar huellas (en el concento no se necesitaban rollos de papel higiénico).

9

Si no era silente, era casi silente. Era una película de hace miles de años. Vista en un cine llamado Valentino, en el film aparecía un carro de línea impulsado por una palanca que un hombre manejaba. ¿Qué pasó? Debe de haberse producido una cómica situación. En la noche del cine, al lado del que era niño en aquella época, estalló una inolvidable, fantástica risa. Esa risa pudo ser drásticamente humana. Pero ahora, considerada después de tantos años, se puede saber que esa risa era, también, la Energía.

5

There's someone who shits while thinking about an eccentric Jewish nun, who, hidden in a convent, devoted herself to examining the fecal leavings of her disciples (this can be found in a novel whose title and author the shitter has forgotten). There is no doubt that the presence of the Character, the nun, in the meditation of the one who shits has conveyed a goodly amount of Energy.

6

Energy is everywhere. Sometimes it's confused with Vanity, or it could even be Vanity itself. As for Knowledge, nobody knows anything about anything.

7

Duchamp didn't know the orphans who sang out the numbers, but that did exist. Energy metamorphosed through various veins of boredom. In a moment it knew the winning number, the Grand Prize. It made a little silence—a space for boredom. The energy of a tiny little canvas opened onto a municipal sea.

8

There's someone who shits while doing exercises of Attention with an eccentric Jewish nun. The nun shows her disciples how to shit without leaving traces (in the convent they didn't need toilet paper).

9

If it wasn't silent, it was almost silent. It was a movie from thousands of years ago. Seen in a movie house named Valentino, in the film there was a handcar propelled by a lever operated by a man. What happened? A funny situation must have occurred. In the night of the theater, next to the one who was then a boy, an unforgettable, fantastic laugh burst forth. This laugh could have been drastically human. But now, considered so many years later, it is apparent that this laugh was also Energy.

10

Comenzó, la energía de las lágrimas, cuando se echó a llorar el niño al oír la música *Cuatro milpas tan sólo quedaron*. Se complicó esto, además, cuando a través de un tubo de alquimia interior, las lágrimas de la música de las cuatro milpas se derramó sobre el primer velorio que el niño alcanzó a ver. La Energía es asunto bastante complicado. Nadie sabe cómo resolverla bien.

11

Los gestos demostrativos, decía Duchamp. En la noche, fieras contracciones de mis piernas no sólo son Indicador de mi genética diabetes, sino como comunicador que se petrifica en la Energía desprendida de un pasado difícil de resolver. Por supuesto es casi imposible decir más. Siento emplear imágenes que pueden estar periclitadas. Siento decir lo que no debería decir. Pero esta Energía de mis piernas diabéticas está ahí...., conectándome con lo que ya no está.

12

Las miradas duras, decía Duchamp. Las conozco. Muchas de ellas, con su Energía elevaron el termómetro de los niños cuando episodios lamentables, que ya no hay por qué evocar. Miradas duras entre sensaciones (¿en cuáles cenestesias se han infiltrado esas sensaciones?), entre sombras (tragadas, algunas, por el hueco negro), y con algo así como ese garabato ortopédico en que se ha podido convertir el pasado. En fin, todo eso ha quedado en la floración petrificada, en la más o menos sana señal. Diremos en ésa que se enciende en la fría habitación, cuyo suelo está cubierto por el agua sucia y por las hojas podridas. Es un horror.

10

The energy of tears began when the boy started crying upon hearing the song "Four Plots of Land Were All That's Left." This was also complicated when, by means of a tube of internal alchemy, the tears of the song about the four plots of land spilled out over the first wake the boy saw. Energy is a rather complicated business. Nobody knows how to deal with it.

11

Demonstrative gestures, said Duchamp, at night, ferocious contractions of my legs are not only an Indicator of my genetic diabetes, but are like a communicator that petrifies into the Energy detached from a past that's difficult to deal with. Of course it's almost impossible to say more. I feel I'm using images that could be outdated. I feel I'm saying what shouldn't be said. But this Energy of my diabetic legs is there…connecting me to what no longer is.

12

Hard looks, said Duchamp. I know them. Many of them elevated with their Energy the thermometer of children during lamentable episodes, which there's no longer any reason to call up. Hard looks between sensations (into which synesthesias have these sensations infiltrated?), between shadows (swallowed, some of them, by the black hole), and with something like this orthopedic scribble into which the past changed. In the end, all this has remained in petrified flowering, in the more or less healthy symptom. About this, let's say that it's lighting up in the cold room, whose floor is covered in dirty water and rotting leaves. It's awful.

13

Energía extraña, espectral, cuando la electricidad (la luz blanca) se transforma en el agua estancada de una abandonada habitación.

14

Sigue Duchamp con los brazos. Nos interesa entablillar, para siempre aquellos brazos que en su horrible Colegio de Belén, los cagones jesuitas nos obligaban a tenerlos cruzados. "Por la cuarta baldosa y con los brazos cruzados", decían los mierdosos. La sucia sexualidad, toda, de los adolescentes, con el sudor pegándose a las camisas de los que íbamos por la cuarta baldosa. Espectáculo, para vomitar tres veces seguidas. Pero en aquellos brazos (y los más jodido en su posición de brazos cruzados), increíblemente se aposentaba la Energía. Una energía que aunque no debiera de haber sido la Energía, no dejaba, sin embargo, de ser la Energía.

15

La masturbación fue una gran conquista de aquellos años inolvidables. La fina masturbación –alquímica– de los años de la adolescencia. ¿Cómo se puede negar la neta superficie de aquella convulsividad? Además, para los que quieran estudiar el asunto más detenidamente, están los grandes espacios que, a veces, la gran masturbación contenía. Esto habría que compendiarlo en una cápsula, habría que hacer una receta. Por ej., lo interesante fue cierta noche de masturbación en que, tratando de imaginar un paroxismo de lo sexual, el telescopio de la imagen fue lamido por una rala telaraña, casi de moneda gótica. Se diría que la masturbación como la Poesía, es un sistema de conocimiento.

16

Se sacaba los mocos. O sea, un hecho ordinario, corriente, pero cuando se lo evoca, es como si hubiera sucedido bajo la fría luz de una bombilla. Mantiene, la Energía disuelta, una impar conservación: es una repetición para amargados.

13

Strange spectral energy, when electricity (white light) is transformed into the stagnant water of an abandoned room.

14

Duchamp continues with his arms. We're interested in forever putting in splints those arms that, in their horrid Colegio de Belén, the shit-for-brains Jesuits forced us to keep crossed. "Off to the tiled room with your arms crossed," the shitheads said. The filthy sexuality, all of it, of the adolescents, with sweat sticking to the shirts of the ones who went to the tiled room. A spectacle to inspire vomiting thrice over, but in those arms (and most fucked-up of all, in their crossed-arm position), incredibly, Energy is lodged. An energy which, though it shouldn't have been Energy, did not, however, cease to be Energy.

15

Masturbation was a great conquest of those unforgettable years. The subtle—alchemical—masturbation of the years of adolescence. How can the net surface of that convulsiveness be denied? As well, for those wishing to study the matter more thoroughly, there are the large spaces that great masturbation contained. This would have to be condensed in a capsule; a recipe would have to be devised. E.g., the interesting thing was a certain night of masturbation in which, trying to imagine a sexual paroxysm, the image's telescope was licked by a sparse cobweb, almost a Gothic coin. It could be said that masturbation, like Poetry, is a system of knowledge.

16

He picked the snot from his nose. An ordinary, commonplace action, but when evoked, it's as if it happened under the cold glare of a light bulb. The Energy having been dissolved, it maintains a unique conservation: it's a repetition for embittered people.

17

Además, lo más importante, el ridículo de ser joven. ¿Qué significaba una cuchillita de afeitar? La luz neón; puesta sobre el sillón de la adolescencia la tabla de madera, con los libros de texto. A veces, cuando en ciertas noches brillaba la demasiado luz neón, entonces el pelo crecía horriblemente, sobre una esquina de la tabla. Es que la Energía se descubría sola –era corporal–pues había desniveles entre los poros, o las piernas alteraban los ruidos incipientes que nadie hubiera podido oír.

18

Energía estética. Energía petrificada y por tanto, condenable. Al estamparse sobre el color sepia de un viejo sofá, después de salir disparado por efecto de la tos, se convertía en serpiente de gargajo.

19

También el ronquido en New York, convertido en mar. Tenía este ronquido, como telón de fondo, un tren que iba por arriba, al lado de las azoteas de la barriada.

20

el desvanecimiento, decía Duchamp. Aquel alcohol utilizado para restregarse la sien. La abuela la usó. Literariamente, esta energía congelada ha quedado como uno de los objetos que se exhiben en el poético fondo de un pozo.

21

¡Filosofía de la energía: cuantos más niños canten, más muertos estaremos!

17

Besides, the most important thing: the ridiculousness of being young. What did a little razor blade mean? Neon light; the wooden table, with textbooks, arranged on adolescence's easy chair. Sometimes, when on certain nights the too-bright neon light shone, hair then grew horribly, on a corner of the board. Energy was revealed to be alone—it was corporeal—since there was unevenness among the pores, or the legs modified the incipient noises that nobody could have heard.

18

Aesthetic Energy. Petrified and hence condemnable Energy. While imprinting itself on the sepia color of an old sofa, after leaving in a shot due to coughing, it turned into a serpent of phlegm.

19

Also snoring in New York, changed into a sea. He had that snore as a backdrop, a train passing overhead, next to the neighborhood rooftops.

20

Vanishing, said Duchamp. That alcohol used for rubbing foreheads. Grandmother used it. Literarily, that frozen energy has remained as one of the objects exhibited in the poetic depths of a well.

21

Philosophy of energy: the more children sing, the deader we'll be!

33

Noli me Tangere

Vuelta noche oscura, en la piscina
el Hipopótamo mascando la sangre del vientre derramada.
Pero, mientras lentamente sorbe la sangre, su rostro fotográfico
es el silente, autista deseo *de una certificada ternura.*

CAPA DE UNA EMOCIÓN

1. Una luz neón/heredera/de otra luz neón.
2. Lo anterior no es inaplicable, ya que tuve que ver con todas esas categorías que tienen su origen en lo relacionado con un bombillo.
3. *Como cuando una fresa, reducida a la letra F.*

RESULTA ABSOLUTAMENTE NECESARIO CONSTRUIR LA AUTISTA

Baratijas para mi Autoinvento

(1) Me he leído sentado, día a día, frente a un sol mocho / pero sin alegría, pues es cierto que todos los delirios acaban siendo de medio pelo.

(2) O que la única inmortalidad sea repetir / repetir por ejemplo, el hecho de ir a un Super Mercado, para conducir un carrito.

(3) O, dicho de otro modo, estar mirando a un solo mocho es acostumbrarse a colgar palabras en un perchero oxidado / pero así tampoco cuando llegan las lluvias: no me sucede nada: me tizno mal con la lluvia.

(4) Sin embargo, lo único positivo es que, con los años que llevo, me he hecho un extraño maduro.

33

Noli me Tangere

Dark night returned, in the swimming pool
the Hippopotamus chewing blood, spilled from its entrails.
But, as it slowly sips the blood, its photographic face
is the silent, autistic desire *for a certified tenderness.*

LAYER OF AN EMOTION

1. A neon light / inheritor / of another neon light
2. What precedes is not inexplicable, since it had to do with all those categories originating in what's related to a light bulb.
3. *Like when a strawberry's reduced to the letter S.*

IT BECOMES ABSOLUTELY NECESSARY TO
CONSTRUCT THE AUTISTIC

Little Cards for My Self-Invention

(1) Day by day, I've set about sitting in front of a thick sun / but without joy, since it's true that all deliriums end up second-rate.

(2) Or that the sole immortality be to repeat / to repeat, for instance, the fact of going to a Super Market to push a shopping cart.

(3) Or, said otherwise, to be looking at a thick sun is to get used to hanging words on a rusty coat rack / but no more like that when the rains come: nothing happens to me: I have a hard time getting dirty from the rain.

(4) The one positive thing, however, is that with the years I carry I've made myself into a mature stranger.

(5) O sea, que ni vi nada, ni llegué a ninguna parte, pero así la Farsa se cumplió.
(6) Se cumplió, fue creciendo / depositando boberías, o fragmentos, en la alcancía en que no creo del todo.
(7) Pues el asunto es que, con un muchito (entienda el que pueda) de lo que como sabe a descontado, me he ido haciendo el Héroe.
(8) Intento unas Confesiones, no como las de San Agustín, sino como las de Rrose Sélavy.
(9) Pues de verdad, como se dice, me he vuelto un Héroe / cubierto con los ya viejos, trapos de aquel actor que hizo de Sabio Antiguo.

Otros restos de mi Confesión

1. Ese Salmo, el Salmo que se vuelve mudo.
2. En lo que conozco un venado no es símbolo, sino la figurita que se mete dentro la cajita.
3. Cuando una luz de pasadizo. Una luz de pasadizo, aunque en realidad es una luz de afuera (esto que estoy diciendo, entiéndase como se pueda) / Esa luz va yendo un color ramplón, color ramplón que libera por lo mocho (¿cómo esto se puede entender?).
4. Pues hubo un tiempo / ahora puedo asegurarlo, en que los fantasmas no llegaban a asustar tanto. / Hasta (hay que decir lo último que nos ocurra) en ciertos momentos se morían, como kilitos dentro de una alcancía.
5. Había un silencio que no era el que debía ser / Había estatuas que orinaban. Pero eso, semejante a lo olvidado, ya se ha vuelto Retórica.)
6. Me voy a poner en un rincón, a ver si aparezco en la Gran fotografía (aunque debo contar conque –ya me ha pasado– lo mejor en el último momento, no salgo.)

(5) In other words, that I neither saw anything, nor arrived anywhere, but in this way the Farce was completed.
(6) It was completed, went on growing / depositing idiocies, or fragments, in the cashbox in which I do not believe at all.
(7) Since it's the case that, with a little too much (understand it who will) of something that tastes kind of like something excluded, I've gone about playing the Hero.
(8) I'm attempting some Confessions, not like St. Augustine's, but like Rrose Sélavy's.
(9) Since really, as they say, I've become a Hero / covered with the already old rags of that actor who played an Ancient Sage.

Other Remains of My Confession

1. That Psalm, the Psalm that falls mute.
2. As far as I know, a deer is not a symbol, but the little figure that puts itself in the box.
3. During an alleyway light. An alleyway light, though in reality it's a light from outside (this that I'm saying, let understand it who will). / This light brings with it a coarse color, a coarse color which liberates by its thickness (how can this be understood?).
4. There was a time / now I can guarantee it, when phantoms didn't manage to cause such a fright, / Even (we have to say the last thing that occurs to us) at certain moments they died, like extra kilos inside a cash box
5. There was a silence that was not what it should have been. / There were statues pissing. (But that, like the forgotten, has already become Rhetoric.)
6. I'm going to stand in a corner and see if I appear in the Big photograph (though I have to count on—it's already happened to me—perhaps at the last moment, not leaving).

34

Fuente, Jicotea

En realidad se trataba de una fuente muy pequeña, la cual sólo contenía una jicotea.

Refiriéndose al color, el color era lo húmedo. Algo así. Digo, a veces, sólo no era más que lo último húmedo.

(Había más peripecias que contar, pero sería andar demasiado. Hay que fijarse que se trata de un relato que se pierde).

Ahora, por ejemplo, cuando viéndolo todo desde ausencia de paisaje difícilmente clasificable.

Ahora que me mantengo. Sentado, me mantengo en una terraza albina. Cuando, entonces, parece que vino aquello. Entonces cuando es alisar, frontalmente, la fotografía de lo húmedo que fue un espacio con fuente, la cual sólo contenía una jicotea.

34

Fountain, Tortoise

In reality, it was about a small fountain, which only contained a tortoise.

With regard to the color, it was the color of moisture. Something like that. I mean, sometimes, only it wasn't more than the last moisture.

(There were more wanderings to tell, but that would be going too far. You have to understand, it's about a tale that gets lost.)

Now, for example, when seeing everything from the absence of a landscape that's difficult to classify.

Now that I'm hanging on. I'm hanging on, seated on an albino terrace. When, then, it seems that that one came. So when it's directly polishing the photograph of the moisture that was a space with a fountain, which only contained a tortoise.

35

Historia de corbata postiza

Esto, todo, semejante a historia de corbata postiza. Pero ¿hablo de qué? ¿De qué embuste, o metáfora, o enredo de imágenes digo, cuando quiero decir de corbata postiza?

No sé, no sé bien, se parece a... (todo se parece a..., cuando se trata de una historia que se escapa).

Por eso quizá por ser historia que se escapa, se puede decir que es historia de...

Nadie sabe, de verdad, de verdad, lo que pudiera contener una corbata postiza./ Tampoco sabré nunca lo que pueda asemejársele.

Es como cuando, algunas noches, los árboles se desconsideran pero realmente nadie sabe lo que se está diciendo cuando alguien dice que, algunas noches, los árboles se desconsideran.

El hacinamiento es un hecho tremebundo / demasiado hondo./ Los restos, en verdad, caen por todos los lados.

O que no hay manera de ser sincero, sea cualquiera la capa que se intente.

O cosas que se acaban de decir, de las cuales nunca, nadie, tiene la menor idea. Hay que ser cuando alguien, vallejeanamente, puede decir: ¡Hay que ser!

35

The Story of a Clip-On Tie

This, all of it, resembling a story of a clip-on tie. But what am I talking about? What lie, or metaphor, or tangle of images am I talking about, when what I want to say is: clip-on tie?

I don't know, I don't really know, it looks like… (everything looks like…when it's all about a story that's escaping).

Because of that, perhaps because it's a story that's escaping, it could be said that it's a story of…

Nobody really, really knows what a clip-on tie could contain. / Nor will I ever know what could resemble it.

It's like when, on some nights, the trees disregard each other but really nobody knows what's being said when somebody says that, on some nights, the trees disregard each other.

Piling up is a terrifying thing / too deep / The remains, in truth, fall all over the place.

Or that there's no way to be sincere, whatever the layer that's attempted.

Or things that end up being said, of which nobody ever has the slightest idea. It has to be when somebody, in the style of César Vallejo, can say: *One must be!*

36

Un fragmento del Libro perdido de los Origenistas

Fue cuando rielaba una astuta Luna sobre el cielo de la noble Habana. ¡Atiza!, había tatuados dólmenes en toda la extensión de la Avenida del Puerto. La banda, en el Prado comenzó los primeros acordes del Himno Fundacional. Fue ahí, en la noche cruzada, cuando atravesamos y gatos sin cabeza, famélicos por lo demás. Estos gatos, a la manera Rimbaud, se restregaron en la hierba. Más tarde, al lado de ellos, el súbito de una cerca irreal parecía cortada por una cuchilla; por lo que esto, sin duda, auguraba el advenimiento de esos cupidos iluminativos de la Nación.

Así, también, en lo Imaginario es Drajón, o Drujón, el apellido respectivo de tres Papas. A uno de estos Papas le conocemos con el nombre: Inocencio. Inocencio Drujón, pues.

(Hay, también, en el *Libro perdido de los origenistas*, una canción onírica que el Sueño le dictó al autor en la siesta: que transcurrió durante un 31 de diciembre. La Canción se llama *Los pantalones del diablo*, pues así la tituló el Inconsciente)

LOS PANTALONES DEL DIABLO

Raro, de una noche dinosauria,
el acento clavicordio.
Raíz larvaria el Cometa,
Quién lo traza?
Entonces, cuando desintegra fama,
el occipucio del Muro.
Tamarindo retrechero es una tabernero mudo.
La ínsipa tropa—metástasis—perdura,
En su carmelitana insidia,
¿Quién se cuida, majadero,
del rubí que lo devora?

36

An Excerpt from the Lost Book of the Origenistas

It was when a cunning Moon shimmered over the noble Havana sky. Gosh! there were tattooed dolmens all the way down the Avenida del Puerto. The band on the Prado began the opening chords of the Foundational Hymn. It was there, in the crossed night, that we crossed the path of a lot of headless cats, and starving to boot. These cats, à la Rimbaud, were scrubbing themselves in the grass. Later, next to them, the suddenness of an unreal fence that seemed cut by a cleaver, and as a result this doubtless augured the advent of those light-giving cupids of the Nation.

And so, as well, in the Imaginary, Dragón or Drujón is the respective surname of three Popes. We know one of these Popes by the name: Innocent. Innocent Drujón, then.

(There's also, in the *Lost Book of the Origenistas*, an oneiric song that Slumber dictated to the author during his siesta: which took place during a 31st of December. The Song is called "The Devil's Trousers," since that's the title the Unconscious gave it.)

THE DEVIL'S TROUSERS

Strange, from a dinosaurian night,
the clavichordian accent.
Root would wash the Comet.
Who traces it?
So then, when fame disintegrates,
the Wall's occiput.
A tricky tamarind is a mute bartender
The insipid flock—metastasis—endures,
In its Carmelite snare.
Fool, who looks after
the ruby that devours you?

42

Rubén Darío Park

Es un parque que como si no acabara de ser, sin embargo es el parque que alucina al Personaje. Hay un redondel de cemento con cosas como éstas: bancos; tres diminutas carabelas de lata, enarbolando los títulos respectivos de 3 obras de Darío; y en el centro, con un yeso que simula una helénica bata, la estatua de Rubén Darío que mira los celajes.

A lo lejos, una larga fila de enanos rusos, acabados de salir de un automóvil, también miran los celajes. Son los dueños de Sweetwater.

Esto parece que como si no acabara de ser. Esto es la reducción de algo que, estando a su lado, lo contiene: otro parque –por supuesto, de mayores dimensiones– cuyo nombre es Rubén Darío Park, y que también es como si no acabara de ser.

Además, parque—reducción, y Rubén Darío Park que lo contiene, ambos están contenidos en un poblado mayor que, cuando se mira mejor, resulta ser una ciénaga. Es el lugar donde vive el Personaje.

El Personaje dice: "el parque que me alucina es lo que no acaba de ser".

Es por la tarde. son lamentables los bancos, y el Personaje se sienta sobre uno de esos bancos. Es lamentable la estatua de Darío, y el Personaje la contempla hasta darse gusto.

Un redondel de cemento, Yerba magra rodea a este redondel de cemento.

La yerba negra cubre, también, a la sucia arena de esa ciénaga que está un poco más allá.

El orgullo
el soberano azote del viento
lo que pudiera analizarse
tal como se analizarían polvos
depositados en un sobre

Hay un cuerno debajo de la casa
todo lo que pudiera analizarse, sería,
insertarme dentro de una tradición
tal como inserto está el cuerno

42

Rubén Darío Park

It's a park that even if it doesn't end up being one, is, however, the park that amazes the Character. There's a cement circle with things like these: benches, three tiny tin caravels sporting the titles of 3 of Darío's works and, in the center, a plaster cast simulating a Hellenic tunic, the statue of Rubén Darío gazing at the sunset clouds.

In the distance, a long line of Russian dwarfs, freshly emerged from an automobile, are also gazing at the sunset clouds. They are the rulers of Sweetwater.

This seems like it'll never end up being. This is the reduction of something that, being at its side, contains it: another park—of larger dimension, of course—whose name is Rubén Darío Park, and which also is like it'll never end up being.

Besides, park-reduction and Rubén Darío Park which contains it, are both contained in a larger settlement which, looked at more closely, ends up a swamp. It's the place where the Character lives.

The Character says: "The park that amazes me is the one that doesn't end up being."

It's evening, the benches are deplorable, and the Character sits on one of those benches. The statue of Darío is deplorable, and the Character studies it until he enjoys it.

A cement circle. Sparse grass surrounds this cement circle.

The black grass also covers the dirty sand of that swamp that's a little further on.

Pride	
the wind's sovereign lash	There's a horn under the house
what could be analyzed	everything that could be analyzed, would be,
just as one would analyze dust	to insert myself into a tradition
deposited in an envelope	just as the horn is inserted

Sigue mirando el Personaje, la túnica de yeso de Rubén Darío, pero ahora no es que se dé gusto, sino que se ha alucinado. Saca, entonces, de su bolsillo un cuaderno, un lápiz.

Con el lápiz, escribe en el cuaderno la siguiente lista:

un animal con cuerpo
un animal goliardo
el pelo en el cuerpo
una pierna de Darío
un mechón de pelo

La caída de la tarde se convierte en un escenario, pero el Personaje, desentendiéndose de esa conversión, termina durmiéndose después de haber recitado varias veces la lista que acaba de escribir.

Sueña, al dormirse, el Personaje. Sueña que recién Rubén Darío está extremadamente disgustado, ya que cree que alguien lo ha comparado con un animal.

"¿Por qué, en un instante, sueño semejante cosa, se pregunta el Personaje dormido, y al preguntarse se despierta. No sabe ni puede saber, así que, a la manera de un alucinado, de nuevo se pone a recitar la lista de palabras.

– Partes del cuerpo, un animal con cuerpo, un animal goliardo – dice el Personaje en voz alta, mientras el sudor le resbala por el cuerpo.

De pronto la tarde cayendo sobre el parque, cayendo sobre la ciénaga, se ha vuelto horrible. Rubén Darío se ha convertido en un yeso increíblemente irreal.

A lo lejos, en el lugar donde se vio la larga fila de enanos rusos, hora se ve a tres jesuitas, con sus brillantes sotanas / Un recuerdo de Buñuel, por supuesto/

Por lo que, como el Personaje piensa que alguna inteligibilidad tiene que haber, sorpresivamente se pone, él, a recitar otra lista de palabras. Una lista que, una vez, el francés Jean-Pierre Brisset dijo.

The Character continues to look at Rubén Darío's plaster tunic, but now he isn't enjoying it; rather, he's become amazed. He then takes a notebook and pencil from his pocket.

With the pencil, he writes the following lines in the notebook:

an animal with a body
a goliard animal
hair on the body
a leg of Darío
a lock of hair

Evening's descent changes into a stage, but the Character, knowing nothing of this conversion, sleeps after reciting several times the list he'd just finished writing.

While he sleeps, the Character dreams. He dreams that Rubén Darío is utterly disgusted, since he thinks someone's compared him to an animal.

"Why am I suddenly dreaming such a thing," the Character asks himself, and as he asks himself, he awakens. He does not nor can he know, so, like a lunatic, he starts reciting the list of words.

"Parts of the body, an animal with a body, a goliard animal," the Character recites aloud, as sweat rolls down his body.

Suddenly, the evening falling on the park, falling on the swamp, has become horrible. Rubén Darío has changed into an incredibly unreal plaster.

In the distance, in the place where the long line of Russian dwarfs was seen, now three Jesuits appear, with their shining cassocks. / A memory of Buñuel, of course.

Because of this, since the Character thinks that there must be some intelligibility, he unexpectedly begins reciting another list of words. A list that the Frenchman Jean-Pierre Brisset once said.

La lista de Brisset comenzaba así:

Les dents la bouche
Les dents la bouchent
l'aidant la bouche

Lo que había dicho el francés eran 9 frases. 9 frases que jugaban con diente y boca.

Existen en la palabra numerosas Leyes, desconocidas hasta el momento, añadía Brisset.

"Hay que comprender bien el exterior del libro de la vida oculto en la palabra y sellado con siete sellos", añadía Brisset.

Fue entonces que se vio a Rubén Darío, y a un Interlocutor, salido de la nada. El Interlocutor parecía ingenuo, ya que sólo quería aprender sobre las partes del cuerpo.

–¿Tienes una pierna? –le preguntó Interlocutor a Darío

–¿Tienes un codo? –volvió a preguntarle Interlocutor a Darío.

Y, llegado el momento de saber sobre el pelo, sorpresivamente el Interlocutor formuló su pregunta de esta manera: "–¿Tienes un mechón?"

Fue el momento en que se hizo visible todo el Eje-Centro que debe sostener este relato. A Rubén Darío no le gustaba que le preguntaran por su mechón, ya que consideraba que esto era compararlo con un animal.

El Eje-Centro. Y Brisset había dicho: "Luego se preguntó: este eje, sabes que esto (ce exe, sais que ce?) = este eje, ¿sabes qué es? (ce point, sais-tu quoi c'est?), lo que se convirtió en" sexo (sexe) -¿Sabes qué es? ese eje es, sexo es, ese exceso (Sais que c'est? Ce exe est, sexe est, ce excès): Ese exceso (ce excès) es el sexo.

(Había una gran fiesta, con goliardos. Se ponía en duda el lugar donde podría estar Darío. ¿Estaría en un café? ¿o acaso estaría en la escuela? al final se supo que Darío también estaba con los goliardos, en el escenario).

Brisset's list began as follows:

Les dents la bouche
Les dents la bouchent
l'aidant la bouche

What the Frenchman said were 9 phrases. 9 phrases playing with teeth and mouth.

There exist in the word numerous Laws, unknown until this moment, added Brisset.

"The exterior of the book of life hidden in the word and sealed with seven seals must be well understood," added Brisset.

It was then that Rubén Darío, become an Interlocutor, was seen emerging from nothingness. The Interlocutor seemed ingenuous, since he only wanted to learn about the parts of the body.

"Do you have a leg?" the Interlocutor asked Darío.

"Do you have a tail?" the Interlocutor again asked Darío.

And when it came time to learn about the hair, the Interlocutor unexpectedly formulated his question as follows: "Do you have a lock of hair?"

This was the moment in which the Axis-Center that has to support this story became completely visible. Rubén Darío didn't like being asked about his lock of hair, since he thought this meant comparing him to an animal.

The Axis-Center! (And Brisset had said: "Then he asked himself: this axis, do you know what (ce exe, sais que ce) = this axis, do you know what it is? (ce point, sais-tu quoi c'est?), which turned into sex (sexe)—Do you know what it is? this axis is, it's sex, this excess (Sais que c'est? Ce exe est, sexe est, ce excès); This excess (ce excès) is sex."

(There was a big party, with goliards. The place where Darío could be was sought. Could he be in a café? or could he be, by chance, in school? in the end it was learned that Darío was also with the goliards, on stage.)

Después, las sombras de la noche cubrieron al Rubén Darío Park.

El Personaje quedó como una pieza. Se enfrió, sorprendido por la repentina noche de la ciénaga.

–Les dents, la bouche, todo eso que masticaba Jean-Pierre Brisset –absu rdamente se dijo el Personaje, mientras una rana saltaba por el camino de piedrecitas por donde él iba caminando.

Caminando. Siguió caminando. Se oyó un trueno, y "es como una fibra de mi inconsciente", se dijo él. Cayó un rayo, por el lado sur del Rubén Darío Park.

Por lo que agilizó el paso. Gotas de lluvia empezaron a caer.

Se dijo, él , sin saber por qué, que se sentía como una bienhechora convicción, pero esto fue cuanto, al aumentar la fuerza de la lluvia, él ya iba corriendo.

Iba corriendo, corría más. Mientras, un delirio le hacía gritar esa lista que había inventado, sentado en el banco.

–¡Partes del cuerpo!—gritó, mientras el agua le caía en la boca.

–¿Tienes un mechón de pelo?—volvió a gritar, mientras la lluvia lo invadía todo.

Pero, repentinamente, como por arte de birlibirloque, cesó de llover.

Él, pensando en la existencia de ese diminuto milagro que, al convertirse en objeto, pudiera meterse dentro de una cajita, traspasó la salida del Rubén Darío Park.

Salió del parque como si no hubiese pasado nada, como si se hubiese convertido en un paseante sereno.

Atravesó, entonces, una callejuela llena de trailers (O las paredes de los trailers estaban hechas con el mismo yeso de la estatua de Darío, o él sufría una alucinación).

Y así hasta que, por último, una moto que iba por la misma acera por donde él iba caminando, le rozó la sombra. Por lo que llegó él a pensar que, aunque no se acoplara del todo a la Gramática Lógica de Brisset, alguna relación debía tener con ella ese Darío que, desde un escenario goliardo, protestaba por un mechón de pelo.

Afterwards, the shadows of night covered Rubén Darío Park.

The Character was utterly amazed. He got cold, surprised by the sudden night of the swamp.

–.Les dents, la bouche, everything that Jean-Pierre Brisset mouthed—absurdly the Character said to himself, while a frog leapt on the pebbled path down which he was walking.

Walking. He kept on walking. He heard thunder, and "it's like a fiber of my Unconscious," he said to himself. Lightning flashed on the southern side of Rubén Darío Park.

So he picked up his pace. Drops of rain began falling.

He said to himself, without knowing why, that he felt something like a benevolent conviction, but that was when, as the rain increased in strength, he was already running.

He was running, and ran some more. Meanwhile, a fit of delirium impelled him to shout out that list he had made up while seated on the bench.

– Parts of the body! he shouted, as the water fell into his mouth.

– Do you have a lock of hair? he shouted again, as the rain invaded everything.

But suddenly, as if by magic, it stopped raining.

Thinking on the existence of this tiny miracle which, by changing into an object, could have put itself inside a box, he exited Rubén Darío Park.

Left the park as if nothing had happened, as if he had become a peaceful stroller.

He then crossed a side street filled with trailers. (Either the walls of the trailers were made out of the same plaster as Darío's statue, or he was hallucinating.)

And so on, until at the end, a motorcycle going down the same sidewalk on which he walked grazed his shadow. Because of this, he thought that, although not at all connected to Brisset's Logical Grammar, there had to be some relation between it and that Darío who fussed over a lock of hair from a goliard stage.

Poems from Antología
(1999)

Pianola por el mediodía

¿Es un abismo? ¿Qué es lo que puede haber en un abismo? ¿Piezas? Esa estrella de papel que adorna a una caja de galletas, no tiene por qué parecerse a aquel sitio pobre, llamado Pereira, donde dormía mi abuelo.

Sin embargo, yo vigilaría, durante el sueño diurno de este mediodía, al niño siniestro –sus ojos alucinados– que amenaza con el palo que tiene en su mano (¿habrá un cero?).

Pero ¿cómo puede parecerse la estrella de papel en la caja de galletas, al sitio que se llamaba Pereira? ¿Es que hay alucinación?

Sin embargo, no cabe duda de que el sitio de la estrella de papel en la caja de galletas, es el mismo sitio –un sitio de tierra– que se llamaba Pereira. El sitio donde dormía mi abuelo.

Mientras ¿en un útero? El niño, sin duda, pudiera seguir amenazando con el palo.

¿Será que me va a entrar una gripe?

Y los ojos marcan un rostro egipcio (pero ¿de qué ojos estoy hablando?), mientras puede que se esté al borde de lo siniestro.

O sea, para decirlo en pocas palabas: pudiera ser que con la pianola de este mediodía de hoy, la estrella de papel en la caja de galletas, también nos condujera a una cajita donde no tendría nada de raro que se encontrara un abismo. Uno no entiende nada, pero esas cosas pasan.

Pianola at Noon

In an abyss? What could there be in an abyss? Rooms? This paper star decorating a cookie jar need not resemble Pereira, that poor place where my grandfather slept.

But during this midday's diurnal slumber, I would keep an eye on that sinister child—his hallucinatory eyes—threatening with a stick (would there be a zero?).

But how can the paper star on the cookie jar resemble the place called Pereira? Does this involve a hallucination?

But there's no doubt that the place of the paper star on the cookie jar is that place—a place made of earth—called Pereira. The place where my grandfather slept.

Meanwhile, in a uterus? Doubtless the boy might still be gesturing menacingly with a stick.

Might I be coming down with the flu?

And eyes frame an Egyptian face (what eyes am I talking about?); it could be that one's on the brink of something sinister.

Or, put briefly: it could be that like this noonday pianola, the paper star on the cookie jar will lead us to a box where finding an abyss would not be strange. You understand nothing, but these things happen.

¿Se puede saber qué quiere decir esto?

Esto ¿de qué pedazos? Esto con leguas de películas, películas vistas hace tantos años

El refrigerador en la cocina;
los pequeños saltos del silencio;
los pequeños saltos de unos ruidos;
lo que ya no puede ser como noche a grito pelado, sino como noche taponada.

Recuerdo un velocípedo del tiempo de mi infancia.
Me incliné sobre hojas de sombra (las guardé estando en un cine, hace muchos años).
Sillas, en fin, que ya eran, desde el tiempo de mis abuelos, petrificados, disueltos placeres.

Lo que estoy diciendo, como cualquiera lo puede ver, cada vez se parece a nada.
Muchas veces, ya lo he dicho: cuando llega la noche, la noche está fuera; no la veo.

Por lo que, detenido sobre un rincón de mi pecho como el que, claudicante, se pusiera a respirar los fragmentos de esa insípida luz neón colgada de una pared de ÉLVIRA, el blancuzco motel de medio pelo.

Might One Know What This Means?

This, pieces of what? This, these miles of films, films seen so long ago.

The refrigerator in the kitchen:
the little leaps of silence;
the little leaps of noises;
this, no longer night with its ruckus, but a plugged-up night.

I remember a velocipede from childhood.
I leaned over leaves of shadow (I kept them while I was in a movie theater, long years ago).
Seats, in short, that already in my grandparents' time were pleasures that had turned to stone and dissolved.

What I'm saying, as anyone can see, looks like nothing every time.
As I've said many times before: when night falls, night is outside; I don't see it.

Because of which, detained on a corner of my chest like the one who, surrendering, started breathing the fragments of that insipid neon light hung from a wall of ELVIRA, that pallid, unimportant motel.

No es mirar la rama

No, no, no, pero no es mirar la rama del árbol que está frente a la ventana de mi cuarto, para encontrarle un sentido. No, eso no puede ser. No, yo no puedo contar con eso.

O que me persiguiera a través de algunas sombras. De algunas sombras… Pero no, no, tampoco yo puedo contar con eso.

Yo, entre tantas cosas, no me puedo poner a cacarear. Yo no puedo tener voz. Lo he intentado, pero sería ridículo. La cosa no consiste en que yo pueda tener voz.

¿Si masticara ruinas? Pero tampoco me puedo sostener masticando ruinas.

No, no me podría sostener hablando de las ruinas.

No.

¿Es que sólo debería ser el que percibiera el pinchazo de un mosquito? Pensándolo bien… Quizás…

El pinchazo de un mosquito, o comprender el perfil absurdo que me pudiera otorgar la contemplación, indefinida, de la raya de mi pantalón. Sí, quizás eso no estaría mal.

Acordándome, entonces, que una vez fue, una pianola, el paraíso. ¿Una pianola, el paraíso? Sí, quizás ese juego idiota no sería mal, si lo jugara. Jugar un juego idiota de una pianola que fuera el paraíso (pero jugarlo, sólo jugarlo), no tomarlo en serio), no estaría mal.

Pues el caso es que yo debo quedarme sentado, sin ningún sustentáculo.

It's Not About Looking at the Branch

No, no, no, it's not at all about looking at the branch of the tree that faces my window to find a meaning in it. No, that can't be. No, I can't depend on that.

Or that it follow me through several shadows. Several shadows… But no, I can't depend on that either.

I can't brag while all this is going on. I have no voice. I've tried, but it would be laughable. It's not about my being able to have a voice.

If I were to chew on ruins? But I can't sustain myself by chewing on ruins.

No, I couldn't sustain myself by talking about ruins.

No.

So should I then be the only one to notice a mosquito bite? Upon reflection… Maybe…

A mosquito bite, or an understanding of the absurd profile that the indefinite contemplation of the crease in my pants could bestow on me. Yes, perhaps that wouldn't be a bad thing.

Recalling, then, that once a pianola was paradise. A pianola, paradise? Yes, perhaps this idiotic game wouldn't be a bad thing, were I to play it. Playing an idiotic game of a pianola that was paradise (but playing it, just playing it, not taking it seriously), wouldn't be a bad thing.

So the thing is that I should stay seated, without any support.

Pues, repito, yo no tengo por qué apoyarme en mirar la rama del árbol, frente a mi ventana, para entonces buscarle un sentido.

Pues, repito, yo no tengo por qué hablar de las ruinas.

No, no, no tengo por qué. No tengo. Yo sólo debo quedarme sentado, repito.

So, to repeat, I've got nothing on which to support myself while looking at the branch of the tree that faces my window, in order thereby to find a meaning in it.

So, to repeat, I don't have to speak of ruins.

No, no, no, I don't have to. I don't. Like I said, I just have to stay seated.

El cuento que me repito

Es así, o parece que es así: yo estoy como listo para dibujar el cuento de aquel personaje a quien le faltan algunos dientes de arriba, y también algunos dientes de abajo.

O sea, me miro con una luz viejísima, que el tiempo ha manchado bastante;

o sea, hace muchos años, que vi el deshilachado abriguito de una niña (¿había una noche con hielo?, pero ¿cómo fue que inventé eso?);

o sea, una pieza del horrible museo de Historia Natural, en el Instituto donde estudié el bachillerato;

o sea, una metáfora que ya no podría volver a imaginarla, la cual estaba montada sobre una pianola cubierta por el polvo.

Queda –eso debo señalarlo– lo verde de los matojos, y esto como residuo sublimado de aquel colchón roto que, antes, tantas veces vi, tirado en un solar yermo.

Pues, se me han olvidado las asignaturas que estudié, y hasta los quebrados que me enseñaron en la infancia, ya no sé lo que puedan ser; razón por la cual –me estoy sospechando eso–, en cualquier momento se me va a olvidar mi vida.

Así que, entonces, hay un cuento que, inútilmente, a veces me cuento, y esto, siempre, antes de que se me aparezca el ramillete de una luz neón. Aunque, lo que no logro saber es si ese ramillete, alguna vez, de verdad, lo llegué a tener frente a mis ojos.

The Tale I Repeat to Myself

It's like that, or it seems like that: I'm about ready to sketch the tale of that character who's missing some upper teeth and also some lower teeth.

That is, I look at myself with an old time-stained light.

that is, it was years ago when I saw a girl's frayed coat (was it an icy night? how did I come to invent this?);

that is, a piece from the horrible museum of Natural History, in the Institute where I attended high school;

that is, a metaphor I can no longer go back to and imagine, mounted on a dust-covered pianola.

There remains—I emphasize—the green of the bushes, a sublimated residue of that torn mattress I used to see so often, dumped in a vacant lot.

I've forgotten the subjects I studied, and even the fractions they taught me in childhood, I don't know what they are, the reason why—I suspect—at any minute I'll forget my life.

So there's a story that, pointlessly, I sometimes tell myself, always, before there appears to me the cluster of a neon light. Though what I can't quite untangle is whether I reached the point of having this cluster, at some point, and in reality, before my eyes.

Textilandia Albina

(2004)

Para / for Rogelio Saunders

Una incruenta, aunque usual, ejecución

Teodoro, te doro, te adoro todo el circo, con truhanes, aunque pensándolo bien, quizá con un vulgar picadillo celeste. (?)
¿Qué es una docena de dragones, sino un mismito, respetable, cuento chino? Cuento chino más detestable en este momento: a esta detestable hora del mediodía, como que hay un reloj increíblemente viejo sobre una esquina que, ya hace años, se abolió.

«Todas las perras piezas están desnudas», dijo. Esta es una afirmación vulgar, y hasta licenciosa, lanzada como está, lanzada ahora, en el momento estúpidamente impropio.

Por lo que así con todas las tripas afuera, de la misma manera como está mi lengua, y como están mis palabras. Y lo que no deja de corresponder, por cierto, a este estar bajo una muñeca sin ojos que, hace ya mucho tiempo, no dejó de convertirse, toda entera, o encuera como efectivamente estaban, en un destartalado cilindro de un color igual al de la Luna.

A Bloodless, Though Commonplace, Execution

Theodore, thee I tore, thee I adore the whole circus, with
mountebanks, though giving it some thought, perhaps with common
celestial mincemeat. (?)
What are a dozen dragons, if not a respectable
cock-and-bull story? The most detestable cock-and-bull story
at this moment: at this detestable noonday hour,
as if there's an incredibly old clock on a
corner that, years ago, abolished itself?

"All the sonofabitching pieces are naked," he said. This
Is a vulgar, even licentious affirmation, hurled
as it is, hurled now, in the stupidly inappropriate
moment.

And so, just like this, with all my guts hanging out, like
my tongue, and my words.
And which still, naturally, corresponds
to this moment of being beneath an eyeless doll that,
for quite some time now, hasn't ceased changing itself, wholly
and completely, or nakedly, as indeed it was, into a
decrepit cylinder of a color like the Moon's.

Necesidad de lo práctico

Listo, dentro.
Disponer de una ratonera,
dentro de nosotros.

Para que cace –caiga–
lo negativo que viene de afuera,
uniéndose a lo negativo que nos viene de dentro.

The Need for the Practical

Ready, inside.
Disposing of a mousetrap,
inside us.

So it can hunt—cause to fall –
the negativity coming from without,
joining the negativity coming from within us.

¿Nada más que una mata?

Una mata. Una mata rubia.
Podada.

La mata se escondió, bajo unos meses.
Nadie la vio, por supuesto.

Increíblemente, después, se escondió en mi cuarto.
A los amigos les escribí varias cartas, hablándoles de
este asunto.

Entonces, parece que, por última vez, la mata apareció
en la pantalla de la TV.
Por última vez pero, por supuesto, cuando la pantalla
no estaba encendida.

La vida ofrece variables.

Just a Bush?

A bush. A light-colored bush.
Pruned.

The bush hid, beneath months.
Nobody saw it, of course.

Incredibly, afterwards, it hid in my room.
I wrote several letters about this
to my friends.

It seems that, for the last time, the bush appeared
on the TV screen.
For the last time, but, naturally, when the screen
was off.

Life offers variables.

Inodora canción

Con tanta zoncera como la que hoy cruza por las nubes,
resulta que el bobo es más bobo que nunca.

Una venda luce rara, si se la pega a un pie.

Añadiéndole una canción que emanaría de un gramófono.
Pero el caso es que, ¿quién diablos, a estas alturas,
se podría empatar con un gramófono?

Por lo que, por mucho que lo piense, no voy a llegar a
ninguna conclusión.
No, no voy a llegar.

Odorless Song

With as much silliness as crosses the clouds today,
it so happens the idiot is more idiotic than ever.

A bandage looks weird, stuck on a foot.

Adding to it a song emanating from a gramophone.
But who the devil, at this stage,
would bother with a gramophone?

As a result, however much I try, I'll reach
no conclusion.
No, I won't reach.

Matraca

Una matraca. La hacía sonar, en Semana Santa, el sacristán Crescencio.

¿Podré, actualmente, ser lo suficiente ingenuo? ¿Podré, diríamos, querer convertirme en aquella vieja matraca? Francamente, no lo creo.

Rattle

A rattle. On Holy Week, the sacristan Crescencio
made it sound.

Can I still be sufficiently innocent?
Can I, let's say, wish to become that old
rattle? Frankly, I don't think so.

Seco, yo

Estoy más seco que... ¿Más seco que qué?
Una luna como una débil pupila. Pero lo inquietante es que no me canso de negarme a verla, aunque sólo sea un segundo.

Dry, Me

I'm drier than… Drier than what?
A moon like a weak pupil. But what's disturbing is that
I'm not tired of refusing to see it, even if only for
a second.

Soy esa nostalgia

La película muda en la que yo debería de haber
participado como actor.
¿Cuántas veces he pensado en eso?

I'm That Nostalgia

The silent film in which I should have
participated as an actor.
How many times have I thought about that?

¿Se trata de una rosa?

La ausencia de una rosa. Empecemos por ese manido tema.

Empecemos.

Después, anotaríamos los desperdicios.
¿Como cuántos desperdicios serían?

No me importaría, dentro de mi lamentable estupidez,
volver hacer otro registro. ¿Qué les parece?

Virgilio Piñera –lo sé de buena tinta teosófica– se
despide de nosotros,
al pasar de un cuerpo astral,
a otro cuerpo astral.

Editarme, entonces, en todos los colores.

Pues, otra vez más, yo no sé ni adonde estoy parado.

Is This About a Rose?

The absence of a rose. Let's begin on that trite note.

Let's begin.

Afterwards, we'll make a note of the detritus.
So how much detritus would that be?

It wouldn't matter to me, given my lamentable stupidity,
to go back and count it up again. What do you think?

Virgilio Piñera—I have it on theosophical authority –
Is bidding us farewell
as he passes from one astral body
to another astral body.

Publish me, then, in all colors.

So, once again, I don't even know where I've stopped.

La Cruz del Sur

Una Comedia Sagrada (al menos, pienso que podría ser así), donde una comadrita desfondada, en el tiempo de la sala de la casa de mi abuela. ¡Ha llovido bastante!

Ha llovido bastante, desde entonces, pero no hay por qué quejarse; al fin y al cabo, uno no ha acabado de morirse del todo.

The Southern Cross

A Sacred Comedy (at least, I think it could be), where there's a bankrupt neighbor woman, back in the days of my grandmother's living room. It's rained a lot!
It's rained a lot since then, but there's no need to complain; all things considered, one hasn't yet stopped dying.

Salto del sapo

Me voy escondiendo / vuelvo a aparecer. ¿Como un buzo?
No lo creo, aunque si quieren que sea como un buzo,
pues bien sí, entonces es como un buzo.
Lo que sí sé es sentirme mal. Nunca me siento bien.
O lo que veo es lo que veo: blanco. Aunque no sé por
qué insisto en que lo que veo es blanco.
Un revólver quizá.
Una discoteca, ¡fíjense!: como a pedir de boca.
Pues ahorita vienen los bomberos.
Y, extraños niños picoteando, vastos termómetros.
O pudiera, quizá, decir que féretro, como para recrear
la visión.
¿Lo que más me gustaría?: pues volver a ver aquel
Hotel (Bristol, se llamaba), donde estuve en mi
infancia.
O, con sólo ver unas hojitas, poder fingir que fuera
(¿quién? yo, por supuesto) un alquimista.
Un alquimista, o hasta me conformaría con ser un
simple maquinista.
Pues no soy un paraguas,
sino lo semejante a un paraguas,
probablemente mortal.
Y dicho y hecho entonces, como lo oyen.
Y así mismo. Entonces así mismo, tal como lo oyen.

The Toad's Leap

I'm hiding / I'm reappearing. Like a diver?
I don't think so, though if you want it to be like a diver,
okay, fine then, it's like a diver.
What I do know is how to feel bad. I never feel well.
Or what I see is what I see: white. Though I don't know
why I insist that what I see is white.
A revolver maybe.
A discotheque, imagine! it all worked out just right.
So now the firemen are coming.
And, strange children gabbling, vast thermometers.
Or I could, perhaps, say: coffin, as if to recreate
vision.
What I'd like most? well, to see again that
Hotel (Bristol was its name), where I stayed when
a child.
Or, just by seeing a few leaves, to be able to pretend
I was (who? me, of course) an alchemist.
An alchemist, or I'd even settle for a
simple machinist.
Well, I'm not an umbrella,
but something like an umbrella,
probably mortal.
So said, so done, as you hear it.
And just so. Just so, just as you hear it.

Nadie sabe lo que es un silogismo

Un día, después que los ángeles nos remienden la cara,
hablaremos sobre el paraíso. Mientras tanto… Había
antes como un extraño, enloquecido silogismo, donde
una palma, digamos, se conjugaba con la noche (¿qué
significaba eso?), pero ya todo (como si se pudiera
hablar, al pasar un tren, sobre un manicomio; pero sin
que, al final, se pudiera hablar sobre el manicomio)
se perdió.
Es espantoso, entonces, cantidad de azogue o
machacado granizo, de lo que casi es un manchón hueco:
vacío grito intraducido.
Pero, lo mejor, por ahora, es no seguir hablando.
Lo mejor es, repito, no seguir hablando.
Pues no hay –o, por lo menos en este momento, no lo
hay–, para seguir hablando, el más mínimo motivo.

Nobody Knows What a Syllogism Is

One day, after the angels have patched up our faces,
we'll talk about paradise. Till then… Before,
there was something like a strange, maddened syllogism, where
a palm tree, let's say, matched itself to the night (what
did that mean?), but everything (as if one could
speak, while a train's passing, about a madhouse, but
without, in the end, being able to speak about a madhouse)
was already lost.
It's frightening, then, the amount of mercury or
crushed hail, of what's almost a hollow stain:
an empty untranslated cry.
But for now, the best thing is not to keep talking.
The best thing, I repeat, is not to keep talking.
Because there isn't—at least at this moment, there
isn't—the slightest motive to go on talking.

Contado por un mudo

Ha sido así.
Ese cartón, solo. ¿Peculiar?
Un frasquito (¿un frasquito se puede parecer a un rasguño?) derramado cuando, precisamente, le pupila hecha, para sólo este instante.
Pues también los palitos de la tendedera, y el sol.
Y, precisamente, cuando arrecife es una palabra que, ahora, sin saber por qué, me resulta delirantemente absurda.
Y esto –nada, ¿cómo diría?– poniendo polvo sobre polvo.
¡Nada!
Entonces yo me pongo, por prescripción facultativa a caminar, al igual que lo hago todos los días.
Desde donde, entonces, he aquí que, ante uno mismo una fachada, la fachada de una casa que ya no debe existir. Una casa donde vivió una tía que ya murió, y que estaba en la calle Benjumeda.
Pero esto, ¿para qué decirlo?, mientras también el miedo vuelve ininteligible lo que, parece, que podría ver pero no veo, sobre los zonzos dados que una sombra (¿dónde está esa sombra?) finge sobre una esquina inevitablemente sucia.
Y ¿qué sentido puede tener todo esto? Y ¿qué sentido puede tener el momento contado por un mudo?

Told by a Mute

It's been like that.
This cardboard, alone. Peculiar?
A little bottle (can a little bottle look like a
scratch?) spilled when, precisely, the eye's
been made, just for this moment.
Okay, also the clothesline stakes, and the sun.
And precisely, at this moment, when for some reason
the word reef seems deliriously
absurd to me.
And this—nothing, how to say it?—placing dust upon
dust.
Nothing!
So, as the doctor prescribes, I begin
to walk, as I do each day.
And there, in front of us a
façade, the façade of a house that should no longer
exist. A house where an aunt lived who's already dead,
in Calle Benjumeda.
But why say this? while fear
also renders unintelligible what, it seems, could be
seen but I don't see, on the stupid dice that a
shadow (where is that shadow?) feigns on an
inevitably dirty corner.
What can all this mean? And what's the meaning of
the moment told by a mute?

Donde estoy

Es sólo una abeja, con un ruido (¿un rabo diminuto?)
casi silencioso. Me aturde, lo confieso (quizá ya no
sé ni cómo reaccionar). Una tarde de domingo, ésta de
que estoy tratando ahora.
Seca.
Una seca tarde de domingo, en realidad, y con débiles
ramificaciones. ¡En fin!
Pero así que ahora, sin saber por qué, divago con una
extraña madeja en que pudiera, mi madre, no estar
muerta.
Mi madre no estaría muerta, sino muy enferma; afectada
por una fiebre mortal, y llevándome a entender que
debo dejarlo todo, e ir hacia ella ahora, en este
mismo momento.
¡Es incomprensible! Como una mano que no fuera la mía,
como una mano que pudiera ser un mapa; como unos ojos
que no fueran los míos.
Una abeja hoy. Una abeja casi muda, casi invisible,
casi inexistente.
Pero, además, esta pesada fábula, tan absurda, que en
este momento ha caído sobre mi cabeza.
Una sirvienta, la sirvienta de una película silente,
ha postergado, y postergado su sesión de trabajo.
La sirvienta pudiera ser que rodara por la escalera de
lo que fue mi casa, en San Rafael 772. ¡Muchos años
viví en esa casa!
La sirvienta está muy nerviosa. Yo no entiendo nada.
La abeja, y este domingo, ¡en fin!, como lo que va a
quedar estancado.
¡Estancado!

Where I Am

It's only a bee, with a buzz (a tiny tail?)
that's almost silent. It stuns me, I confess (or perhaps I no longer
know how to react). A Sunday afternoon, the one
I'm talking about now.
Dry.
A dry Sunday afternoon, in reality, with weak
ramifications. In short!
But now, though I don't know why, I digress to a
strange tangle in which my mother might not be
dead.
Not dead, but very sick, stricken
with a mortal fever, which leads me to understand that
I should drop everything and go to her now, this
very moment.
It's incomprehensible! Like a hand that wasn't mine,
a hand that could be a map; like eyes
that weren't mine.
A bee today. Almost mute, almost invisible,
almost nonexistent.
But also, this weighty fable, so absurd, which in
this moment has fallen on my head.
A maidservant, the maidservant of a silent film,
has postponed and postponed her workday.
It could be the maidservant who rolled down the stairs of
San Rafael 772, which used to be my house. I lived
many years in that house!
The maidservant is very nervous. I don't understand a thing.
The bee, and this Sunday, in short! Like something that will
get into a rut!

Porque, quizá Nada es lo que me espera. Porque también
una pregunta: ¿la luz –no es de día– dónde podrá
estar?
Y también podría haber algunos, algunos que vinieran.
Pero no creo que nadie venga.
Así que esto fue así, hoy domingo. Lo hago constar,
aunque no sé por qué tengo que hacerlo constar.
Y en verdad les digo que, durante todo el día, yo no
he dejado de parecer un bicho raro.

A rut!
Because, perhaps Nothing is what's awaiting me. Because
here's a question too: the light—it isn't daylight—where could it
be?
There could also be some people: some who'd come.
But I don't believe anyone's coming.
So that's the way it was, today, Sunday. I certify it,
though I don't know why I have to certify it.
And I tell you truthfully that all day long, I've
never ceased resembling an odd bird.

Lo que pasó

¿Será el amarillento –aunque ya bastante desvaído– recuerdo de un andén?, ¿será, acaso, como una burbuja?
Ese recuerdo –en la película silente– como romperla con una piedra pudo un niño, y eso cuando recibía, o quizá despedía, a una multitud de antiguos conocidos.
O más bien diremos que un juego de colores, ¡una fruslería!, cuando se acercaban aquellas tropas arcaicas; aquellos oficiales, como soldaditos de plomo, de una película vieja.
¿Desde dónde lo vistes?
Marginal, fílmicamente apartado en un arcón estaba yo, niño entonces, mirando desde un lado.
La película silente que abjuraba…, ¿de qué abjuraba? Quizá había demasiada gente. Quizá los rostros se acercaban con picante obstinación.
¿Estaba, como en amarillo (lo dije antes: ya bastante desvaído), rodeado por mis familiares?
Y, cuando, por aquel entonces, hasta el experimento de una sombra parecía lo suficientemente estable. ¡Había que ver!

What Happened

Could it be the yellowing—though already quite faded –
memory of a platform? could it be, perchance, like a
bubble?
This memory—in the silent film—how a child could
break it with a stone, when he received, or
maybe bid farewell to, a multitude of old acquaintances.
Or should we say rather a game of colors—a
bauble! when those archaic troops approached;
those officers, like little tin soldiers, from an old movie.
From where did you see it?
Marginal, cinematically isolated in a large chest was
I, a boy then, watching from the side.
I forswore the silent film…what did I forswear?
Maybe there were too many people. Maybe the
faces were drawing near with cutting obstinacy.
Was I, as if in yellow (I said it before: already quite
faded), surrounded by my relatives?
Back then, when even the experience of
a shadow appeared stable enough. You had
to see it!

El potaje de un sueño

Esa pausa –¿cartouche que encierra un fracaso?– que
bien ruido puede tener, o bien tener puede el
silencio. Ese entreacto, en fin (y es raro que ahora,
precisamente ahora, pueda yo verlo), donde se trataría
(¿como dentro de un cinematógrafo de la década del
40?) de encontrarle su materia prima.
¡La materia prima de un entreacto!
Miro, es por la mañana, miro por la ventana para
constatar que hay una extraña visión, ¿petrificado
cartouche?, que en sus bordes contiene un agua oscura,
agua lejanísima, pero ¿con cuál relato?
Pues quizá, también sospecho –aunque no sé por qué– lo
semejante a victorianas lámparas –¿espigadas damas,
también junto a esas lámparas?–, con su toque,
ectoplasmático o cremita.
Pero todo esto, a como sea, juntándose, revolviéndose,
para así llegar a ser el potaje de un sueño.
¡Coño!, ¿no será que ya, viejo como estoy y en una
Playa Albina, me estoy empezando a volver loco?

The Stew of a Dream

This pause—cartouche enclosing a failure?—which
might contain a lot of noise, or maybe contain
silence. This entr'acte, in short (and it's odd that now,
precisely now, I can see it), where it's about
(as if inside a movie theater from the
40s?) finding its raw material.
The raw material of an entr'acte!
I look, it's in the morning, I look through the window to
confirm that there's a strange vision—petrified
cartouche?—which on its edges contains dark water,
a distant water, but with what tale?
Well maybe, I also suspect—though I don't know why—something
resembling Victorian lamps—willowy ladies,
and these lamps too?—with its toque,
ectoplasmic or cream-colored.
But all this, whatever it is, blending, whirling,
and so becoming the stew of a dream.
Fuck! could it be that, old as I am and in an
Albino Beach, I'm beginning to go crazy?

Dos poemas / Two Poems
(2004)

Oyendo a Giacinto Scelsi

Ayer por la tarde, con los matojos en verde, y un sol de 90 grados, fue cuando, en esta Playa Albina, me puse a oír un disco de Giacinto Scelsi conteniendo, cerraditas, varias musas.

La música yamaon donde la infeliz vida perdida. ¡Un asco seco! ¿Un abuelo sin luz? Pero ¿qué podrá ser un abuelo sin luz? Hasta que entonces las puertas ya esán abiertas.

Después, la música de Giacinto es anahit, por lo que, entre otras cosas, podría oírla en la pista de autos donde dirijo, vestido de árabe. Hay otro árabe, por descubrir, hasta que, cuando la tarde se oscurece (pero no se oscurece del todo, pues estamos en la hora de verano), aparece esa mujer caballar que pretende blanquear todos los asesinatos cometidos durante la época del tirano Gerardo Machado, en la década del 30.

Una sensación, estamos de acuerdo, con el macabro eslabón de esta música –no oscura–, o tarde de esta hora de verano. Un horrible blanqueamiento.

Hasta que entonces, al final, al oír la música okanagon, resultó que la cama, donde estaba contenida la madre, era una cajita plástica de color crema.

Hecho, lo que se podía ver, como de tierra sucia. O la madre insultando, llena de odio, en esa cama que es una cajita crema. Por lo que, al finalizar el disco, aparecieron tres rabos: 1- titulado el abandono; 2- el cocodrilo del ocultista Saint-Martin; 3- una fea cara. Así que oyendo, pues, finalizar a Giacinto Scelsi ayer –y esto hasta que llegó el momento preciso, el momento en el que hubiera querido (o no sé decirlo bien), desde un cierto ángulo, saber la manera de rajarme la boca.

Listening to Giacinto Scelsi

Yesterday afternoon, with the bushes green, and a 90-degree sun, in this Albino Beach, I put on a record of Giacinto Scelsi containing, enclosed, several muses.

The yamaon music wherein unhappy life lost. A dry nausea! A lightless grandparent! But what could a lightless grandparent be? The doors until then are open.

Afterwards, Giacinto's music is anahit, because of which, among other things, I could hear it on the roadway where I drive, dressed as an Arab. Another Arab awaits until, when afternoon darkens (but it doesn't darken completely; it's summer), a woman on horseback appears who intends to whitewash all the murders committed in the 30s during the era of the tyrant Gerardo Machado.

A sensation, we agree on this, with the macabre link of this—not dark—music or this summer afternoon. A horrible whitewashing.

Until, at the end, listening to the okanagon music, it happened that the bed containing the mother was a plastic cream-colored box.

Made, apparently, of something like dirty earth. Or the mother insulting, hate-filled, in that bed which is a cream-colored box. As a result, when the record was over, three tails appeared: 1—called abandon; 2 –the oculist Saint-Martin's crocodile; 3—an ugly face. So that, listening yesterday to Giacinto Scelsi concluding—until the precise moment, the moment in which I would have liked (I don't know quite how to say it), from a certain angle, to know how to rip open my mouth.

Mantras de Stockhausen

Espesas las bolas del cemento: del comienzo mientras:
se mueve el cristal del timbre. Vista en conjunto.
¿Vista de qué? Vista en conjunto como si fuera el
mazacote de: ¿de qué? El funéreo gris. Las tumbas de
la familia de mi padre.
Golpes del camino. ¿Otra vez el cristal? El temblor de
la mano asegurando el cristal. Pero... Me aseguro,
agarrándome a un piano que vi en mi infancia, con el
paso de un río de letras. ¿Cómo?

Es ese timbre. Nada menos que la botella líquida
(botella también de letras), convertida en timbre.
Fuam-Tu. O mejor FUAM-Tu: se derrama la mano allí,
donde el recuerdo deja de ser.

Vasta, basto. O, que el cristal fílmico –una película
silente– del vaso ¿en qué río se sustenta? Pues una
pluma es una nota, o una pluma-nota es el vacío que
sustituiría al cristal. Pero una vez todo eso fue:
fuimos; negro, negrísimo, por supuesto. Cayendo fue el
cristal o, cuando. ¿La vidriera de la esquina?,
atravesando el lápiz aparentemente de... ¿textura o
espuma? Por lo que el berrido inútil, diminuto, y
hasta un borde que nacía, continuamente deshaciéndose.
Con lo que los sepultureros, que una vez (nadie lo
sabe) cayeron del tren. Era la receta de lo
consuetudinario, de la negra espuma: una vuelta, sin
vuelta, otra vez. Hacía esto repetir, repetir. Otras
tantas onzas, como 13 serían, repitiendo. Repitiendo
los kilos de peso, con mueca, y donde. El piano. ¡Abre
la boca! Hasta que se llega a saber que un pulpo es un

Mantras by Stockhausen

Thick the cement barrels: of the beginning while
the glass of the doorbell moves. Seen as a whole.
What's being seen? Seen as a whole as if it were the
big gloppy pile of: of what? The gray funeral. The graves of
my father's family.
Blows of the pathway. The glass again? The trembling of
the hand that steadies the mirror. But… I steady myself,
I clutch a piano I saw in my childhood, with the
pace of a river of letters. What?

It's this bell. Nothing less than the liquid bottle
(a bottle of letters as well), become a bell.
Fuam-Tu. Better yet, FUAM-Tu: the hand overflows there,
where memory ceases to be.

Course, coarse. Or, that the cinematic glass—a silent
movie—of the goblet, in which river does it sustain itself? Well, a
pen is a note, or a pen-note is the void that would
substitute for the glass. But once all this was:
we were: black, very black, of course. The glass was falling,
or, when. The glassworks on the corner?
crossing the pencil apparently of…texture or
foam? Because of this the useless, diminutive lowing, and
even an edge being born, continually falling apart.
What with the gravediggers, who once (nobody
knows) fell off the train. It was the recipe of the
habitual, of black foam: a return, with no
return, once again. It did this: repeat, repeat. Some
other ounces, there'd be about 13, repeating. Repeating
the weighty kilos, with a grimace, and when. The piano. Open
your mouth! Until you end up knowing that an octopus is a

pañuelo: se deshace. O es mi pelo. Seguramente, mi pelo que fue. Ya caso no me queda pelo. Mi pelo, entonces que no existe. Nadie lo ha inventado. Pudiera ser…, derramándose, terciopelo de abedul cayendo. ¿Cayendo cuántas veces? Varias veces. Varias veces. A la vez que unos zapatos se construyen pero, al mismo tiempo, izándose: vueltos ripios.

Pues con estos mantras, por la puerta, entra el techo. O también la puerta se deshace, al entrar. Las corbatas (si es que hubo corbatas, o si sólo fue silencio).

Una nada tan sólida, como un barril de kilitos; esto venían a ser los mantras.

Con lo que estuve al tanto de que ninguna boca se abriera. Al tanto, lo aseguro. Y después vino ese ruido que nunca se oyó, ni que nadie pudiera asegurar que realmente existe. Una locomotora, sentida desde adentro, no desde afuera. ¿Y con una espuma negra? Pues lo curioso es que la metafísica mocha de aquel, cine viejo, cae, ¿se renueva? Cae, no creo, en verdad, que se renueva. Donde allá lejos. Allá lejos donde, callado, no deja de cantar un perro. O enteros barrios blandos, blandísimos, para descubrir una mañana que nunca existirá. Halando, que nunca existirá. Halando, la casi penúltima. ¿Cuál es la penúltima? Nota de un piano donde un embajador de K. H. se disuelve, antes de que se pudiera llegar a saber si él, realmente, existía y, entonces: fran, tian, ten, fran: cara de ese cine silente que nadie llegó a ver. O lo que, alguien, se hubiera suicidado con una gotas de

handkerchief: it falls apart. Or it's my hair. Surely, my
hair that used to be. I've got almost no hair left. My hair,
ergo, that doesn't exist. Nobody invented it. It
could be…overflowing, velvet of a falling birch.
Falling how many times? Several. Several. At
the same moment as some shoes are being built, but at the same
time, hoisting themselves up: having become debris.

So with these mantras, through the door, the roof enters.
Or the door falls apart as well, upon entering. The
neckties (if there were neckties, or if there were only
silence).

Such a solid nothingness, like a barrel of little kilos; that's
what the mantras came to be.

What with my having kept up with no mouth
opening. I kept up, I assure you. And afterwards this noise
happened that was never heard, nor could anybody be sure that
it really exists. A locomotive, felt from
within, not without. And with a black foam?
Well, the odd thing is that the crumbling metaphysics of that
old movie house is falling, does it renovate itself? It's falling, but in truth,
I don't believe it renovates itself. Way far away. Far away where,
silent, a dog never stops singing. Or entire soft
neighborhoods, really soft, discovering a morning that
will never exist. Hauling, what will never exist. Hauling,
the almost penultimate. Which is the next-to-last? Note of a
piano where an ambassador from K.H. is dissolving, before
one can learn if he really
existed and, then, fran, tian, ten, fran: face of
that silent movie house nobody got to see. Or the one who,
somebody, would have killed himself with a few drops of

cristal. Nada más que con unas gotas de agua. Pues es basto, pero no es nuevo. Pues es agua sin agua. Agua con luz, pero sin luz. Cuando, precisamente ahora, bajo la sombrilla de los mantras, me pongo a conversar en torno a ese hecho de no haber remontado nunca, lo que se dice nunca. Pero: ¡un gesto ligero, como una cuerda!

Pero, en fin, sucede que el silogismo es lo siguiente: el mantra es la campana que repica en el silencio donde no hay campanas. O, lo que es lo mismo: la letra –una letra muy clara– perteneció al muerto que se murió en 1920.

Pues sigue el credo que se enreda, precisamente cuando se sospecha que hay un paquete de pelos, o un dedo mojado, como un trapo –después–, sobre lo que pudiera imaginarse como un horno alquímico. O lo que viene a ser que la mitad de una vibración, seguida por la mitad de otra vibración, sigue siendo, y esto por más que se tratara de cambiar, sólo la mitad de una vibración seguida por la mitad de una vibración. O –si es que esto pudiera explicar algo–, como si fuera el perro silente, surgido del timbre viejo de un cinematógrafo, destartalado.

Pues hay, para seguir navegando sobre el agua que no moja, hojas que se desprenden como sonidos. Pero ¿cuál es el insulto?
¿De qué insulto se trata?
De un insulto tendría que ser.
Pero aquí (así me entiendo un poco) los mantras finalizan. Y, nunca se sabe, bien, qué es lo que podrá pasar debajo de esa agua que no puede ser agua.

glass. With nothing more than a few drops of water. Because it's coarse, but it's not new. Because it's water without water. Water with light, but without light. When, precisely now,
beneath the parasol of the mantras, I start making conversation
around this fact of never, what we call never,
having repaired. But a light gesture, like a
string!

But in the end, it happens that the syllogism is as follows:
the mantra is the bell tolling in the silence where there are no bells. Or what amounts to the same thing: the letter—a very bright letter—belonged to the man who died in 1920.

Then there follows the credo that gets entangled, precisely
when it's suspected that there's a package of hair, or a
wet finger, like a rag—afterwards—on what can
be imagined as an alchemical furnace. Or that which
becomes what half a vibration, followed by
half of another vibration, continues to be, no
matter how it tries to change, only half a
vibration followed by half a vibration. Or—if
this can explain anything—as if it were the
silent dog, emerging from the old doorbell of a
run-down movie theater.

Now, to keep sailing over the water that
doesn't wet, there are leaves that fall away like sounds. But
what's the insult?
What insult is this about?
It'd have to be about an insult.
But here (this way I can understand myself a little) the mantras
come to an end. And one never really knows what could
happen under this water

from

Erogando trizas donde gotas de lo vario pinto / Distributing Scraps when Drops of the Varicolored (2011)

Palabras que repito

Una motocicleta fue, ¡qué raro!, deslizándose con un sobrio paso.

Dicho de otra manera, extravagante un dedo fue, simulando el dibujo –amuleto– de un deforme pájaro.

La noche. Sentado. Sentado estoy.

Desplegando los disponibles gestos.

Un amarillo que a trechos se me escapa –me invento.

Una conversación, la conversación de los vecinos –la conversación que ahora oigo / la que ahora oigo.

De tal manera que por eso ahora, recostado en un taburete, a los inexistentes les invento unas invisibles reliquias, y esto como si sonaran, soñaran, en mis oídos.

Motocicleta con un sobrio paso, repito.

Del todo no estoy en lo que voy diciendo, lo advierto.
Mis palabras, mis palabras habitualmente carecen de entusiasmo.

La flora que displicentemente veo –pero, desde hace mucho, ella se desprendió de una luz, una luz que, por supuesto, se ha extinguido.

Por lo que en cualquier momento, el momento en que esté dispuesto a recibir la visita de un ángel –el ángel a medias destartalado–, también me invitaré a volver a ver a aquel niño *voyeur*. El niño *voyeur* –alucinado– que miraba desde el hueco abierto, en la pared de madera de un devastado cine de Jagüey Grande, aquella película silente que, sin duda, estaba cubierta por el agua negra de una inundación.

Words I Repeat

A motorcycle was—how strange!—sliding forward at a sober clip.

Said otherwise, an extravagant finger was simulating the drawing—an amulet—of a deformed bird.

Night. Seated. I'm seated.

Deploying available gestures.

A yellow that here and there escapes me—I'm inventing.

A conversation, the neighbors' conversation—the conversation I'm hearing now / what I'm hearing now.

In such a way that because of this now, leaning on a stool, I invent for the non-existent ones some invisible relics, as if they were ringing, ringing, in my ears.

I repeat: motorcycle at a sober clip.

Be aware that I'm not completely in what I'm saying.

My words, my words habitually lack enthusiasm.

The flora I offhandedly see—but, for quite a while, they've given off a light, a light that, of course, has gone out.

Because of this, at any moment, the moment in which I'm prepared to receive the visit of an angel—the half-decrepit angel—I will also invite myself to see that *voyeur* child again. The *voyeur* child—stunned –who watched from the open hole, on the wooden wall of a ravaged movie theater in Jagüey Grande, that silent film which, doubtless, was covered by the sewage of a flood.

Penúltimo pecio

Pedazo, lo digo; fue como de frágil luna, el pedazo. La veraniega lluvia también, lluvia vana.

Pues, apenas: dentro del túnel escuchaba una canción. O, quizás, pudiera anotar sobre un silencio. Quizá había un silencio. Un silencio. Pues la canción, ¡qué cosa más rara!, en pedacitos goteaba sus notas.

Pues, para fijar el cuento, antes debo hacerlo girar. Aunque, pensándolo bien... Aunque, pensándolo bien, es inútil intentar el recuerdo de lo que, alguna vez, pudiera haber estado contenido en el pecio.

Ya que también, apenas mirando los pedacitos de esta frágil lluvia que ahora me cerca, puedo entrever el cuento que una vez algo, o alguien, me contó.

(¿Qué resto, invisiblemente posado sobre el mojado polvo negro del patio, parece haber vivido, alguna vez?).

Nostalgia entonces nula, invisible, tal como el imposible rasgo de esa serpiente que, inmóvil, se quedó para siempre, y esto cuando la fijaron sobre el viejísimo cartel de una fea gasolinera.

Pues, entre tantas cosas, el pecio es un reloj que se ha detenido, o es esa luz de una sala que, aunque para siempre perdida, en estos últimos tiempos he logrado –¿con qué fin?, ¿con el fin de conseguir un excéntrico consumo?– inventar o, más o menos, casi inventar.

Penultimate Flotsam

Piece, I'm telling you; it was as if of a fragile moon, the piece. The summer rain also, vain rain.

Then, barely: inside the tunnel I heard a song. Or perhaps, I could take notes on a silence. Perhaps there was a silence. A silence. Then the song, how very odd! its notes dripped in little pieces.

To settle the story, then, beforehand I must make it spin. Although, thinking it over… Although, thinking it over, it's useless attempting to recall what the wreck could ever have held.

And also, barely glancing at the little pieces of this fragile rain that now surrounds me, I can glimpse the story that something, or someone, once told me.

(What remainder, invisibly placed on the wet black dust of the patio, seems to have been lived, at one time?)

A nostalgia therefore null, invisible, just like the impossible features of that serpent which, immobile, remained forever, and that because they stuck it on the ancient sign of an ugly gas station.

Because, among so many things, the shipwreck is a clock that's stopped, or it's that light in a room which, though lost forever, I've recently succeeded—to what end? to the end of obtaining an eccentric consumption?—in inventing, or, more or less, almost inventing.

Un mito de cartón

Confieso que el inodoro está tirado en el borde de la acera / lo que quizás se pueda dictar, cuando por algunas noches aparece la Luna.

¿Para qué? Lo que, aunque insignificante, en realidad pertenece a una mitología, está guardado en una de mis cajitas.

Pues lo que he hecho es que una vez construí lo feo: un pedazo, pobretón, de este puente correspondiente a un canal de esta Playa Albina.

Pero no estoy, por supuesto, para decir más de lo que hasta ahora he dicho / que se levante un altar en el portal de esa tienda donde se venden discos; o que permanezcan encendidas, durante todo este mes de septiembre, las velas que rodean a ese retrato de la Estrella de Cine que está junto al retrato de l Virgen María.

Pues es que que creo, sin ninguna duda,
que a los que vivimos en la Caverna,
esto es lo mejor que nos pueda pasar.

A Cardboard Myth

I confess that the toilet's been tossed onto the edge of the sidewalk / which perhaps can be dictated, when on certain nights the Moon appears.

What for? That which, though insignificant, really belongs to a mythology, is kept in one of my boxes.

Now what I've done is that once I built something ugly: a piece, really wretched, of this bridge corresponding to a canal in this Albino Beach.

But of course, I'm not up to saying more than I've said thus far / let an altar be raised in the doorway of this store where they sell records, or, throughout the entire month of September, may the candles remain lit that surround this portrait of the Movie Star next to the portrait of the Virgin Mary.

Since I believe, beyond a doubt,
that for those of us who live in the Cave,
this is the best that can happen to us.

Termino viendo alguna sombra

Ah, he visto una sombra. La noche entera, he visto. He visto una sombra. Pero también hubo una devastación. La devastación que barrió con aquel cinematógrafo que fue hace mucho tiempo, mucho tiempo.

Pero ¿está ahora, en este hueco, o momento, ese casi insano ruido de un ventilador? (¿De qué ventilador? O ¿en qué casa de una esquina con polvo estuvo ese ventilador? O ¿ese ventilador tuvo que ver con el paso de un tren?).

Así, volveré a decir un poco más alto que no me voy a mover de aquí. Eso: no hay más respuesta que ésta: no me voy a mover de aquí. Un poco más alto, entonces.

Y con una indiferencia tal, que mi cara se ha vuelto de tiza.

Y con un absurdo nocturno, silencio tal, que el asunto –¿qué asunto?– imita, para levar a cabo una mutación después, el mismísimo tamaño de un insecto, o de un lápiz, o de cualquier otro objeto, común y corriente. Pero ¿qué es esto? ¿Qué metamorfosis puede ser ésta? ¿Qué es lo que estoy diciendo?

Y ese ruido. Ese ruido. Esos pasos de unos viejos, lejanos, zapatos sobre la polvosa calle de una tarde de mi infancia; en Jagüey Grande, por supuesto.

¡Tantas cosas desprendidas de mí! Pero, eh, no hay por qué compadecerse, no hay que compadecerme.

De donde me bastaría, para que todo empezara a oler como una risa seca, el que yo pudiera contar con la achicharrada ala de un ángel (¿todavía podré contar con Swedenborg?).

Repito, pues, la noche, que es el silencio. Pues absurdamente imita el tamaño de un lápiz.

Repito: habría una risa de olor tan seco, que no tendría por qué moverme de aquí.

I End Up Seeing Some Shadow

Ah, I've seen a shadow. All night, I've seen. I've seen a shadow. But there was also a devastation. The devastation that swept away that movie theater that happened, a long time, a long time ago.

But, is there now, in this hole, or this moment, this almost insane noise of a fan? What fan? Or, in which house on a dusty corner was this fan? Or did this fan have something to do with a train passing by?

So, I'll again declare a little louder that I'm not going to move from here. That's it: there's no other response than this: I'm not going to move from here.

A little louder, then.

And with such indifference that my face has turned to chalk.

And with an absurd nocturne, a silence such that the matter—which matter?—imitates, to carry out a mutation afterwards, the very same size as an insect, or a pencil, or any other common-or-garden object. But what's this? What metamorphosis can this be? What is it I'm saying?

And this noise. This noise. These steps of some old, distant shoes on the dusty street of an afternoon of my childhood, in Jagüey Grande, of course.

So many things detached from me! But hey, no need to feel sorry, no need to feel sorry for me.

Whence would suffice for me, so that everything would begin to smell like a dry laugh, the one I could tell of with the scorched wing of an angel (will I still be able to count on Swedenborg?).

I repeat, then, night, which is silence. Because it absurdly imitates the size of a pencil.

I repeat: there'd be a laugh with such a dry smell that I wouldn't need to move from here.

Repito, con la achicharrada ala de un ángel. En este hueco, o momento, en que he visto una sombra. ¿Ese casi insano ruido de un ventilador, quizás surgiendo del mundo de los difuntos?

Y es que yo, casi siempre, termino viendo alguna sombra.

I repeat, with the scorched wing of an angel. In this bone, or moment, in which I've seen a shadow. This almost insane noise of a fan, perhaps emerging from the world of the dead.

And almost always, I end up seeing some shadow.

Esto es casi así

Una parda lira. Lirofilia. Quemada alumbre de esta tarde, sin pelo de razón.

¿Qué es esto?

Un fotógrafo me espera, ¿para qué?, cuando hago esa cola para el espectáculo que no entiendo (distraído, además, para colmo, el fantasma, dentro de ese sueño –¿pero cómo, dentro de un sueño, puede estar distraído un fantasma?–, con nueces enterradas).

O sea: Reguero. ¿De qué reguero me omito? Sintiéndome (¿un poco violácea la espuma [¿qué espuma?]?) como para siempre –seguir sin estar listo.

¿Y esto ya casi, trompo mudo en la casi demolida tarde, qué quiere decir?

Y tantas cosas, entonces, que pudieron estar dentro de un baúl violáceo –¿pero es que el baúl era violáceo?–, aunque ya,necesariamente, nada ni nadie podría sugerir…

Por lo que, clamando por mí mismo, al punto estuve de disolverme cuando, sin que otra cosa se me ocurriera, volví a decirme que esto es casi así.

This Is Almost Like That

A grayish-brown lyre. Lyrophilia. Burnt alum of this evening, without an iota of reason.

What's this?

A photographer awaits me, what for? when I get in line for the show I don't understand (distracted, besides, to top it all off, is the phantom, within this dream—but how, within a dream, can a phantom be distracted?—with buried nuts).

In other words: Trickle. From which trickle do I omit myself? Feeling myself (is the form slightly violet [what foam?]?) as if always—following without being ready.

And this now nearly mute whirligig in the demolished evening, what does it mean?

And so many things, then, that could be inside a violet trunk—was the trunk violet?—though by now, necessarily, nothing or nobody could suggest...

Because of which, crying out for myself, I was at the point of dissolution when, without anything else occurring to me, I again said to myself that this is almost that way.

¿Retrato de un lisiado?

En mi barriga hay un autorretrato onírico, pero es imposible sacar ese autorretrato hacia fuera. Choca contra las paredes de mi barriga (cuando lo hace, lo blanco aparece), pero, repito, no lo puedo sacar de mí mismo.

Entonces ¿qué es? ¿Es el retrato de un lisiado?

Pudiera tener, el lisiado, un bárbaro pelo egipcio.

O un arete, con un monstruosillo, pudiera colgar de su oreja.

De sus labios, sin duda, puede salir la tira de un texto-serpiente.

Y, además, hay estilizados, bien dibujados fetos (¿fetos o féretros?), en la novela –noche– del fondo (yo, que a veces en mi paseo llego hasta el pobretón canal, siento el silencio de ese fondo).

Pero, lo inquietante (¿por qué digo que es inquietante?) es que los ojos del lisiado son terriblemente convencionales.

Portrait of a Cripple?

In my stomach there's an oneiric self-portrait, but it's impossible to pull this self-portrait out. It bumps into my stomach walls (when it does this, whiteness appears), but I repeat, I can't pull it out of myself.

So what is it? Is it the portrait of a cripple?

He, the cripple, could have a fantastic Egyptian hairdo.

Or an earring, with a little monster, could be hanging from his ear.

From his lips, no doubt, the strip of a serpent-text could emerge.

And besides, there are stylized, nicely-drawn fetuses (fetuses or fetishes?), in the novel—night—of the depths (I, who sometimes on my walk get as far as the wretched canal, feel the silence of these depths).

But what's disturbing (why do I say it's disturbing?) is that the cripple's eyes are dreadfully conventional.

Todas las noches

Y es que, como si ya fuera un suicida, finge que, para siempre, está cerrando el último acto de su vida. Pero ¿cuándo sucede esto? Pues todas las noches. Pues cuando, todas las noches, so-breviene lo que pudiera convertirse en una obsesión, el paso del tren lejano.

Every Night

As if he were already a suicide, he pretends that, forever, he's closing the final act of his life. But when does that happen? Well, every night. Well, when, every night, there happens what could be changed into an obsession, the passing of the distant train.

Máscara seca

¿Es un mono esa máscara seca? No lo sé. Es ese cuerno, o cavidad, sin ojo (¿la cavidad de un ojo que no contiene ningún ojo?). Y, además, ¿qué son las velas encendidas que iluminan a ese cuerno? Pues una cristalización, entonces; aunque, al final, no sé decir qué clase de cristalización pueda ser ésta. Y aunque, eso sí, también la luz de las velas encendidas es lo petrificado de un amarillo. Ya que oigo, a lo lejos, el ruido del motor de un auto. Lo oigo, pero sólo a lo lejos, muy lejos, pues ese ruido. increíblemente, desde un principio se disolvió. ¿Cómo es eso?

Así como que la luz del día es extremadamente fría, lejana. ¡Cuán fría!, ¡cuán lejana! Como si ella pudiera integrarse a la otra, luz de una farmacia que conocí en mi infancia en una tarde que, por supuesto, fue, pero que invento ahora; y esto, aunque ya cerrada esa farmacia, desde hace muchos años. Pero ¿cómo puedo decir todo esto que estoy diciendo, o, lo que es lo mismo, como puedo colocarme esta máscara, tan seca que no sé cómo nadie se atrevería a tocarla? Repito la pregunta, ¿es un mono esa máscara seca?

Dry Mask

Is this dry mask a monkey? Maybe. It's this horn, or cavity, eyeless (an ocular cavity without an eye?). And also, what are the lit candles that illuminate this horn? Well, a crystallization, then, although, in the end, I don't know how to say what type of crystallization it could be. And although, definitely, the light of the candles is also the petrification of a yellow. Now that I hear, in the distance, the noise of a car motor. I hear it, but only in the distance, the far distance, because this noise, incredibly, from the outset dissolved itself. How come?

Just as daylight is extremely cold, distant. How cold! how distant! As if it could integrate itself into the other one, the light of a drugstore I knew in my childhood on an afternoon which was, of course, but which I now invent, although this drugstore has been closed for many years now. But how can I say all this that I'm saying, or, which comes to the same thing, how can I put on this mask, so dry that I don't know how anybody could dare touch it? So I ask again: is this dry mask a monkey?

Una cabeza

¿Cómo es eso? Es una cabeza que me obsesiona. La cabeza de un híbrido compuesto por un trompo con un agrandado maní (¿que puede ser esto?).

El borde inferior de esta cabeza es un halo de color rojo vino.

Y, en el centro, la cabeza está adornada por una espuela. Una espuela que le sirve de pico a un ave invisible (invisible el ave, pero sin duda de color cremita).

Y el día de hoy es feo, húmedo, cargante, pero yo puedo desentenderme de este día espantoso nada más que por esto: porque yo, aunque obseso, me siento lleno (¿lleno de qué?, ¿lleno cómo?) y con esta cabeza que, como si nada y sin que pueda saber por qué, acaba de plantarse frente a mis ojos.

A Head

How's this? It's a head that's obsessing me. The head of a hybrid of a spinning top and an enlarged peanut (what can it—be?).

The lower edge of this head is a wine-colored halo.

And, at the center, the head is adorned by a spur. A spur that serves as a beak for an invisible bird (the bird's invisible, but doubtless it's cream-colored).

And today is ugly, humid, wearisome, but I can pretend not to notice this horrid day only because of this: because I, though obsessed, feel full (full of what? full how?) and with this head which, quite casually and without knowing why, has just plopped itself before my eyes.

Con un eudiómetro

En la mano, en mi mano (¿no es casi grotesco decir esto?), enarbolaba un eudiómetro.

Me asomé a la ventana: la composición de los gases—extraño amasijo son los pelos del lobo (¿?).

Fue entonces cuando me dije unas palabras—estoy seguro de que me dije unas palabras.

También como que al mirarme en el espejo entendí que no podría tranquilizarme. Es que, entre tantas cosas, maniobrando con el tubo del eudiómetro pude saber que los gases, si se parte de una infortunada lectura, llegarían a descomponer todos los colores de mi habitación.

Y un poco más tarde—ya que no me volví a dormir –, me puse a pensar en lo que podría ser un traductor del esperanto.

Herviría (¿pero qué quiere decir esto?) como la factura de un perfume, me dije.

Por lo que al final, cuando volví a asomarme a la ventana, comprobé que los gases, ya vapuleados por el eudiómetro, se mezclarían con ese silente sonido (¿un silente sonido, idéntico a estas sucias nubes del lugar donde estoy?) que, en cualquier momento, bien puede llegar a ser amenazador.

Pero ¿esto que estoy diciendo tiene algún sentido? ¿Por qué, entonces…?

Pues, ¿qué espejuelos son los que me pongo, para ver cómo me despierto a este lugar donde estoy?

With a Eudiometer

In a hand, in my hand (isn't it almost grotesque to say this?) I brandished a eudiometer.

I leaned out the window: the composition of gases—a strange mixture, those hairs of the wolf (?!).

It was then I said a few words to myself—I'm sure I said a few words to myself.

Also like when I looked at myself in the mirror, I understood that I couldn't calm down. Among so many things, as I fiddled with the eudiometer tube, I was able to find out that gases, if on the basis of an unfortunate reading, would end up decomposing all the colors of my room.

And a little later—since I didn't go back to sleep—I started thinking about what a translator of Esperanto could be.

He would boil (but what does that mean?) like the manufacture of a perfume, I said to myself.

So that in the end, when I went back and leaned out the window, I confirmed that the gases, already beaten by the eudiometer, would blend with this silent sound (a silent sound, identical to those dirty clouds of the place where I am?) which, at any moment could become menacing.

But...does what I'm saying make any sense at all? Why, then...?

So which glasses are the ones I'm putting on, to see how I awaken in this place I'm in?

¿Qué es esto?

¿Qué son los muertos de este domingo? ¿Saben ustedes qué son los muertos de este domingo? ¿Son, quizás, los muertos de una *city* indiferente?

El perdedor arroja, en una escena de una película—década del 40 –, que vi en mi adolescencia cuando mi casa se convirtió en una casa de huéspedes (pues mi casa, en mi adolescencia, se convirtió—y esto, les digo, fue verdad—en una casa de huéspedes), un *boomerang* que a mí por suerte, ahora, ya ha dejado de interesarme.

Es que, además, sobre la mesa del comedor escucho los cabos sueltos de una ventolera, y esto donde antes hubo una estampa, con un ángel pintado por Swedenborg (¿vi esa estampa en mi infancia, en casa de mis abuelos?).

O sea, pasión como quien dice de un pañuelo, procedente del cómic.

O, también, pasión de un clima borrado, ya que debe de haber pertenecido a la disipada noche en que vi la escena de la película década del 40.

Son, pues, como los pies –¿espejos?—de la luna. Son, pues, como el que orina zonceras.

Por lo que me empujo—me empino—hacia un placer de cartón piedra, y esto aunque no sé si, alguna vez, ese placer pudo existir.

Pero, ¿puede alguien explicarme qué enredo, autista, es el que ahora, sin casi darme cuenta, les estoy diciendo a ustedes?

What's This?

Who are this Sunday's dead? Do you know who this Sunday's dead are? Are they, perhaps, the dead of an indifferent city?

The loser tossed, in a scene from a movie—from the 40s—I saw in my adolescence when my house was turned into a boarding-house (since, in my adolescence, my house was turned into—and I'm telling you, it was true—a boarding house), a boomerang, which now, fortunately, has long ceased to interest me.

It's that, besides, on the dining room table, I'm listening to the loose ends of a gust of wind, and this where before there was a print, with an angel painted by Swedenborg (did I see that print in my childhood, in my grandparents' house?).

Or, passion, like what's said about a handkerchief, derived from the comics.

Or else, passion for an effaced climate, since it must have belonged to the dissipated night in which I saw the scene from the movie from the 40s.

They are, then, like the feet—mirrors?—of the moon. They are, then, like the one who pisses trifles.

Which is why I push myself—rear up—towards a pleasure of cardboard stone, though I don't know if, at some point, this pleasure could exist.

But, can anyone explain to me which—autistic—tangle I might be telling you, almost unconsciously?

Un cuento sin espejo

Fue la cortada de un hachazo. O, al revés, fue un hachazo sin ninguna cortada. ¿Lo digo o no lo digo? Nunca sabré si lo cuento o no lo cuento. Nunca sabré si tiene algún sentido contarlo o no contarlo. Yo me he creído que fue en una noche, mientras que se entraba en la nave de aquella pequeña librería que si llegué a conocer. ¿Dónde estaba el comienzo? Era que por quel tiempo yo llegaba, adolescente entonces, al mundo del "Ulíses". ¿Una gran fiesta? Tenía miedo (ya he dicho que yo era, entonces, un adolescente), pero había una gran fiesta, relacionada ella con lo joycista de una "gran próstata" (pero ¿de verdad, se podría decir que se trataba de un "gran próstata?). Entonces—y esto me parece recordarlo mejor—por un lado, por el techo, un pobre, violinista raro, ejecutaba "El barbero de Sevilla." ¿Qué más, en aquel momento del manicomio, se podía pedir?

A Mirrorless Tale

It was the slice of an ax. Or, the other way round, it was an ax without any slice. Am I saying it or am I not saying it? I'll never know if I'm telling it or not telling it. I'll never know if it makes any sense to tell it or not tell it. I believed it happened in one night, as it entered the back area of that little bookstore I did get to know. Where was the beginning? Was it when I arrived, an adolescent then, at the world of *Ulysses*? A big party? I was afraid (I already said that I was an adolescent then), but there was a big party, related to something Joyceian about a "big prostate" (but really, could it be said that it involved a "big prostate"?). Then—and I seem to remember this better—on one side, on the roof, a poor, strange violinist was playing *The Barber of Seville*. What more, in that madhouse moment, could one ask?

Una confesión no viene mal

Yo una vez leí en un tranvía. Se comprueba que este paisaje perteneció a la infancia, cuando se comprueba que el agua llega a tener un color idéntico al fantasma.

Yo me adaptaba a mi camisa de fuerza, manteniéndome en ese color de agua o, más, llegando a ser ese color del agua.

Yo, con mi camisa de fuerza, actuaba con ese color—no veía, ni tenía necesidad de ver pasos por la acera.

Así que, por supuesto, la luna no tenía nada que decir en este asunto. Manteniéndome en el agua, introduciéndome en el agua, sabía que esto conducía a un claro mediodía.

¿Qué clase de claro mediodía?

Sólo puedo decir que ese fantasma que se confunde con el agua es un pedazo, una sección. Un viento que se detuvo junto a mi sombrero.

Pero aunque todo esto, visto desde mi camisa de fuerza, sé que pertenece a mi infancia, sin embargo también sé que disipa, cualquier tecla de esta computadora que estoy manejando, todo vestigio de un tren lejano que pudiera inventar.

No puedo, entonces, hacer nada con lo que perteneció a mi infancia.

Repito: el agua, y el agua se confunde con un fantasma que, ahora que me acerco mejor, veo que aunque mantiene su color de agua, no ha dejado de sobrevenirle un extraño, incomprensible color amarillo que además me deja, dentro de mi camisa de fuerza, más paralizado que nunca.

Pero eso sí, yo he ido perdiendo muchas palabras a la par que mis muelas.

Me voy sintiendo un poquito mejor.

A Confession Would Do the Trick

I once read in a streetcar. It may be confirmed that this landscape belonged to childhood, when it's confirmed that water manages to have a color identical to the phantom.

I adapted to my straitjacket, remaining in this color of water or, more, managing to be that color of water.

I, with my straitjacket, was acting with that color—I didn't see, nor did I need to see, footsteps on the pavement.

So, of course, the moon had nothing to say on the matter. Keeping myself in the water, introducing myself into the water, I knew that this led to a bright noon.

What sort of bright noon?

I can only say that this phantom confused with the water is a piece, a section. A wind that halted next to my hat.

But although all this, seen from my straitjacket, I know belongs to my childhood; I also know that whatever key of this computer I'm on is dissipating every vestige of a distant train I could invent.

I can't, then, do anything with what belonged to my childhood.

To repeat: the water, and the water is confused with a phantom which, now that I'm coming closer, I see that although it maintains its color of water, what continues to happen to it is a strange, incomprehensible yellow color which, besides, leaves me, within my straitjacket, more paralyzed than ever.

But this for sure, I've been losing many words at the same rate as my molars.

I'm feeling a bit better.

De "Gotas de lo vario pinto" (apotegmas visuales)

Partió el tren por la madrugada, cuando el corazón rosado (se le veía por debajo de la ropa) de aquella niña que, con su mano, enarbolaba una botella de sidra.

Un aburrido internauta está dibujando, a la luz de un televisor apagado, la escena de una noche que hasta tiene un poco de amarillo.

Esa escena del internauta tiene algo que ver con un pequeño e insignificante avión que alguien, en el sueño, trata de colocar en 1934.

Pero lo curioso de esto que estoy diciendo es la relación que pudiera tener con esas arenas—arenas como la noche, también con un poco de amarillo—que, una vez, bien pudieron estar en un, ya inexistente, viejo hospital.

La luz: después de haber temblado, ahora recuerda aquel momento en que se metió dentro de un tamaño pequeño, y como para lucir (¿fue en el pasillo de un hotel?) no inmóvil, pero sí lejanísima. ¿1936?

Esa nariz de mármol, que ha surgido después de una afeitada. ¿Hay un chorro amarillo?

"La poesía debe ser seca, como la leña, para que arda bien." Octavio Paz.

Noche, se posa un redondel amarillo—no se sabe cómo, tan lejano.

Inmutable el labio, parece participe de una irracional naturaleza muerta, fijada (¿una pequeña, seca ya, historia de mi infancia?) desde muchos años atrás.

No hay ningún peso, ni lo habrá. Y es en el frío, o sea en el silencio, el punto en que me coloco, en el momento en que puedo ver.

from "Drops of the Varicolored" (Visual Apothegms)

The train left in the morning, at the same time as the rosy heart (visible beneath her clothes) of that girl who brandished in her hand a bottle of cider.

A bored Web-surfer is drawing, by the light of a shut-off TV, the scene of a night that even has a bit of yellow.

This scene with the Web-surfer has something to do with a small, insignificant airplane that someone, in dreams, is trying to locate in 1934.

But what's curious about what I'm saying is the relationship it could have with these sands—sands like night, also with a bit of yellow—which, once, might have been in a now nonexistent old hospital.

The light: having trembled, it now recalls that moment in which it put itself inside a small space, as if to appear (was it in a hotel corridor?) not immobile, but certainly far away. 1936?

This marble nose, which emerged after a shave. Is there a yellow stream?

"Poetry must be dry, like wood, so that it can burn well." Octavio Paz.

At night, a yellow circle alights—it's not known how, so distant.

The lip's immutable, it appears a participant in an irrational still life, fixed (a small, now dry, story of my childhood?) many years back.

There's no weight, nor will there be. And in the cold, or rather the silence, is the point at which I situate myself, in the moment in which I can see.

¿Por qué es como un cielo de tiza, esa figura que desciende de un árbol? La sed as muy clarita, igual que un verde. Me acurruco dentro de un baúl para soñar eso que estoy diciendo. ¿Me acurruco como también lo hice, a la salida de un cine, en 1934? Uno no lo sabe bien, pero hay una anestesia que pudiera orientar.

¡Todo tan lejos, y todo tan cerca! Me acerco, pero sin acercarme.

Lo más que ahora sé es de otra situación, y de otro color: del verde de las hojas que están frente a la ventana de mi cuarto. Son las seis de la tarde.

La botella hacía sombra. Esto fue en el Hotel Vista Alegre, en el Jagüey Grande de mi infancia. Luego, ahora, nadie sabría explicar lo que puede ser el cisma de unas florecitas. ¿El cisma de unas florecitas? Hay una rayita blanca sobre el agua de una piscina. La piscina es roja. ¿Yo sé bien lo que estoy diciendo? Sí, yo sé bien lo que estoy diciendo.

La botella hace sombra. Todavía lo siento.

La sombra de la botella. Una historia con la que siempre cargo. ¿Qué fue? Esa sombra detenida por una pequeña humedad. ¿Por qué, también, me sobreviene—Lionel Barrymore, con ventana abierta en el cine de barrio—una película que ya no recuerdo?

La botella, con su sombra, estaba cerca de una pequeña, y destartalada, y fea fuente. En la fuente estaba una jicotea.

La sombra de la botella, la pequeña humedad, lo detenido en un alucinante retazo oscuro. Y lo que también recuerdo es el olor, ¿y el color de ese olor?

¿Alguna vez podría alucinarme? Siento, mientras escribo estas líneas sobre la sombra de la botella, el silencio de unos lejanos ruidos.

Un gato casi, casi con un sombrero marrón. Además, el gato es cremita. Además, tiene el gato unas rayas: rosadas, pero desteñidas las rayas.

Why is it like a chalky sky, this figure descending from a tree? Thirst is very bright, like greenery. I curl up inside a trunk to dream what I'm saying. Do I curl up like I also did, leaving a movie theater, in 1934? One doesn't really know, but there's a synesthesia that could orient this.

Everything so far away, and everything so close! I'm coming close, but without getting close.

The most I know now is of another place, and another color: of the green of the leaves in front of the window of my room. It's six o'clock in the evening.

The bottle cast a shadow. This was in the Hotel Vista Alegre, in the Jagüey Grande of my childhood. Afterwards, now, nobody would know how to explain what could be the discord of some little flowers. Discord of some little flowers? There's a white stripe on the water of a swimming pool. The swimming pool is red. Do I really know what I'm saying? Yes, I really know what I'm saying.

The bottle cast a shadow. I still feel it.

The shadow of the bottle. A story I carry around. What was it? This shadow held back by a slight dampness. Also, why is it—Lionel Barrymore, with an open window in the neighborhood movie theater—that a film I no longer remember comes to mind?

The bottle, with its shadow, was near a small, decrepit, ugly fountain. In the fountain was a jicotea.

The shadow of the bottle, the slight dampness: what was held within a hallucinatory dark remnant. And what I also remember is the smell—and what about the color of that smell?

Could I sometimes be hallucinating? I feel, as I write these lines about the shadow of the bottle, the silence of some distant noises.

A cat almost, almost with a brown hat. Also, the cat is cream-colored. Also, the cat has some pink stripes, but the stripes are discolored. And

Y, por último, los ojos del gato son los mismos que tenía una abuela. La abuela increíblemente lejana.

Hoy, en medio de un silencio, me acuerdo de eso. Aunque, en realidad, se trata de un recuerdo bastante oscuro.

¿Qué color tiene ese pavor caído de la noche? ¿Un pavor que, después de ponerse chiquito, bien puede asegurarse que no le hace daño a nadie?

¿Hacia dónde iré? Pues hay una serie de viejas fotos que, si las encontrara, estoy seguro me entregarían el sentido de mi pasado, pero... Pero ¿cómo podría ser el color de esas viejas fotos?

Como manchas—pero quizás, esto, lo diga por decir—que tendrían algunas gotas de sangre seca.

Hoy es domingo.

Hay un moño, y un raro muñequito, metidos dentro de un marco viejo.

Ahora recuerdo—como si cayeron líquidos puntos—eso, *poesía muda*, de la que habló Ullán.

Pasa un auto a lo lejos, y me revuelvo con el colorido desconocido—pero ¿qué puede ser un colorido desconocido?—con que están envueltas unas capas de silencio.

Es muy raro esto que estoy diciendo.

Una arena. Una arena quieta y fea. Aunque siempre se le está acabando de echar, a la arena, un jarrito de agua.

Entonces ¿no hay luz? Sí, hay un poco de luz, pero... Pero, a veces, como si la luz (¿fue en 1934?) se fuera a convertir en el polvo de fantasma que había en la botica de mi padre (y ¿en qué lado de la botica yo me inventaba aquel color, carmelita, idéntico al de una tarde?).

Así como que había, también, un timbre. Pero lo mejor es no decir más nada.

lastly, the cat's eyes are the same as one of my grandmothers'. The incredibly distant grandmother.

Today, in the middle of a silence, I remember this. Although it's actually a rather obscure memory.

What color is this fear fallen from night? A fear that, making itself very small, could assure itself that it isn't hurting anyone?

Where will I be going? Because there's a series of old photos which, if I find them, I'll be sure will grant me the secret of my past, but… But what could be the color of these old photos?

Like stains—but perhaps I'm just saying this for saying's sake—that would contain a few drops of dried blood.

Today's Sunday.

There's a crest, and a weird little doll, placed inside an old frame.

Now I remember—as if liquid spots were falling—this *mute poetry* of the kind Ullán talked about.

A car passes in the distance, and I'm tossing and turning with the unknown coloring—but what could an unknown coloring be?—in which some cloaks of silence are wrapped.

It's very strange, what I'm saying.

An arena. Quiet and ugly arena. Although a little pitcher of water is in the end always thrown into the arena.

So there's no light? Yes, there's a little light, but… But, sometimes, as if the light (was this in 1934?) were turning into the phantom's dust that was in my father's drugstore (and in what corner of the drugstore did I invent that color, light brown, identical to an evening's?).

There was also a doorbell. But the best thing is to say no more.

Aquella pena, lejanísima al acercarse a un vaso de agua. Fue cuando rodeando al año 1937, o fue en el mismo 1937. Mi padre en el restaurante con tantas sombras debajo de las mesas, tantos cuchillos de sombras. ¿Cristales? Mi padre riéndose. Lo que estaba tijereteando. Ahora, si pudiera, yo guardaría toda esa en una mandolina que tocaba un zapatero italiano, llamado Canterofio. La pena, debo añadir, era también como el agua, o el cartón que podría llegar a ser.

¿Un circo de minúsculos objetos? Un cartón, un circo. La posibilidad de ser un autista al utilizar los ojos, entonces, y esto para entender la cartelera de un cine.

Estrellitas azuladas. Estrellitas azuladas, metidas dentro de un pequeño pedazo de acera (¿quién me inventa eso?).

Pero no sé cómo traerle un sueño a lo que, sin dejar de ser el pedazo de acera, también fuera una caja vieja –¿en qué telón de la infancia? –, carmelita y absurda.

Ahora no sé qué puerta abrir, pues una puerta se tendría que abrir.

Por otra parte –¿cómo? –, convertido en color viejo un rincón del recuerdo, rincón que estuvo, en plena zafra, el Central Australia.

Me digo que, también, volvería a sacar unos trapos rojos. Pero ¿esos trapos siempre fueron rojos?

Yo salí de una barbería cuando el envión—piernas de una mujer fatal retrocediendo, lentamente, hacia atrás –, vista en la escena de una película silente donde se derramaron copas de champán, hizo que, por un instante, el Sol resultara ser una pieza zodiacal y bastante pequeña.

Ahora, veo un azul en el avión. En el avión que estaba colgando sobre el pozo que había en el patio de la casa de mi abuela.

Siempre fue así. Siempre estuvo detenido, a las doce del día, el avión sobre el pozo que estaba en el patio.

Repito, ahora veo un azul.

That sorrow, so distant upon approaching a glass of water. It was somewhere around 1937, or it was in that same 1937. My father in the restaurant with so many shadows under the tables, so many knives of shadows. Windowpanes? My father laughing. What he was gossiping about. Now, if I could, I would keep all this in a mandolin played by an Italian shoemaker named Canterofio. Sorrow, I must add, was also like water or cardboard, which it could end up being. A circus of minuscule objects? Cardboard, circus. The possibility of being autistic by using one's eyes, then, and this in order to understand a movie marquee.

Little blue stars. Little blue stars, placed inside a little piece of pavement (who's inventing this for me?).

But I don't know how to bring a dream into what, without ceasing to be the piece of pavement, would also be—in which curtain of childhood?—an old, absurd, light-brown box.

Now I don't know which door to open, since a door has to be opened.

On the other hand—how?—changed into an old color is a corner of memory, a corner in which, at the height of the sugar harvest, was the Australia Sugar Mill.

I tell myself that I would again take out some red rags. But were those rags always red?

I left a barber shop at the moment of the push—legs of a femme fatale slowly receding into the background, seen in a silent film where glasses of champagne were spilled, made, for a moment, the Sun into a zodiacal and rather small piece.

Now, I'm seeing blue in the airplane. In the airplane suspended above the well that was in the courtyard of my grandmother's house.

It was always like that. It was always suspended, at noon, that airplane above the well that was in the courtyard.

I repeat, now I'm seeing blue.

"Ensalada de violetas con nafta," decía el menú de Marinetti. Pero este menú ¿qué tiene que ver con el azul del avión que estaba sobre el pozo de mi abuela?

Pero el supuesto azul del avión también ahora lo restriego sobre esta calle de la Playa Albino donde vivo. ¿Qué puede ser, en este momento, una ensalada de violetas? ¿La ensalada de violetas, entonces, puede ser igual a un piano? El plomo, entonces, ¿qué color pueda tener?

Lo que se detiene parece que también detiene mi pie, y eso sin dejar de tener un color.

Pero, como estoy bajo una capa de aburrimiento, no sería imposible que se encontrara esa camiseta: la camiseta ensangrentada por ese amarillo que, hoy, también se ha mostrado—pero ¿cómo puede ser eso?—a través de la lluvia fina que no ha dejado de caer.

Temperatura del Agua Bendita: fue cuando, simulándome un cuerpo amarillo, me vi en el fondo del pozo, convertido en avión. Una experiencia con miel, sin duda, que Beuys habría tenido que explicarme.

No simulé nada. ¿No hubo simulación? Mi padre me llevó, aquella vez, a la fonda donde había unas sombras.

La cabeza—del ladrón soñado, la cabeza—me hizo sospechar la posible aparición del Brujo. ¿Qué fue aquello?

¿Había, en realidad, una miel tallada con un hueso? Ésa es otra pregunta que a Beuys le podría haber hecho, pues eso, también, pudiera haber estado relacionado con la temperatura del Agua Bendita.

Hay que empezar a entender, me digo hoy, precisamente en el momento en que cae la tarde.

Los senos fueron hechos con hilos. Y esto fue el resultado de haber soñado con una palma de plata, la cual estaba al lado de una oreja de alambre. Fue en el momento en que una figurita inmovilizada pareció, bajo el techo de una cajita, sonreír. Y esto bajo la luz de este día. Una luz muy extraña. ¿También hecha como con hilos? Verdaderamente, muy extraña, la luz de este día.

"Salad of violets with naphta," said Marinetti's menu. But what does this menu have to do with the blue of the airplane above my grandmother's well?

But I'm now also scrubbing the alleged blue of the airplane over this street of the Albino Beach where I live. At this moment, what could a salad of violets be? Can the salad of violets be equal to a piano, then? Lead, then—what color could it have?

Whatever is being held back also seems to be holding back my foot, and that without ceasing to have a color.

But, since I'm under a cloak of boredom, it wouldn't be impossible for that undershirt to be found, the undershirt bloodied by a yellow that, today, has also shown itself—but how can this be?—through the gentle rain that hasn't stopped falling.

Temperature of the Holy Water: it was when, simulating a yellow body, I saw myself at the bottom of the well, changed into an airplane. An experience with honey, no doubt, which Beuys would have had to explain to me.

I simulated nothing. There was no simulation! My father brought me, that time, to the tavern where there were some shadows.

The head—of the dreamed-of thief, the head—made me suspect the possible apparition of the Sorcerer. What was that?

Was there, in reality, honey carved with a bone? This is another question I could have asked Beuys, because this also could have been related to the temperature of the Holy Water.

One must begin to understand, I tell myself today, precisely at the moment when evening falls.

The breasts were made of threads. And that was the result of having dreamed of a silver palm, which was next to a wire ear. It was at the moment in which a small immobilized figure appeared, beneath the lid of a box, smiling. And that beneath the light of this day. A very strange light. Also made as if of threads? Truly, very strange, the light of this day.

¿La literatura es para ver el mundo con alambritos y figuritas? ¿Todo puede reducirse a figuritas y alambritos?

Y ahora, también me parece entender el ruido; el ruido, como si fuera lo mismo que el silencio.

Colores sucios de la arena. Colores sucios del humo. Y un león: "Si un león pudiera hablar, no lo entenderíamos", dijo Ludwig Wittgenstein.

Y es que me pongo a pensar, y aparece un cubo que no se parecía a un cubo—o sea, algo que está tirado en un rincón feo, descolorido, de mi infancia.

Sería como un par de zapatos, descansando frente a un ventilador que no sólo ostenta—pero ¿ostentar es la palabra adecuada?—el color del mercurocromo, sino que, además, será inmóvil.

Yo me pondría, entonces, a colocar esparadrapos, y esto con la esperanza de poder expresar el color de un día que no tiene color.

Artilugio, y como si lo moviera el sonido de un tamborcito. Pero ¿cómo? Esto no tiene explicación. No, no la tiene. Aunque, eso sí, no deja de haber una rara capa de polvo ectoplásmatica. Una capa, con el polvo regado sobre el suelo del cine de Jagüey Grande donde estuve, en mi infancia.

Aunque es verdad que, si intento inventar un recuerdo, lo único que imagino son alambres. ¿Qué pudiera hacer con esos alambres? Y...otra pregunta: esos alambres, ¿qué relación pudiera tener con esto albino, y no-paisaje, que me rodea?

Tric-trac con colores, el explosivo dedo del rostro del Brujo. O quizás pueda tratarse del vestuario extraído de la caja de plomo de Osiris. Pero... ¿quién puede saber eso?

O el tric-trac que ha corrido por la verruga del Brujo. O quizás esa glosolalia, inspirada por el color lila, que ha teñido la cara de la vieja del Home. Pero, repito, ¿quién puede saber eso?
¿Quién, desde el trampolín, se puede tirar en el color?

Is literature for looking at the world with bits of wire and little figures? Can everything be reduced to little figures and bits of wire?

And now, I also seem to be hearing the noise; the noise, as if the same as silence.

Dirty colors of the arena. Dirty colors of smoke. And a lion. "If a lion could speak, we wouldn't understand him," said Ludwig Wittgenstein.

And I'm starting to think, and a bucket appears that doesn't resemble a bucket—that is, something that's been tossed into an ugly, discolored corner of my childhood.

It would be like a pair of shoes, resting in front of a fan that not only flaunts –is "flaunts" the appropriate word?—the color of mercurochrome, but which is immobile besides.

I would then start sticking on Band-Aids, in the hope of being able to express the color of a day that has none.

A gadget, and as if the sound of a little drum were moving it. But how? This has no explanation. No, it doesn't. Although, certainly, it doesn't stop wearing a strange cloak of ectoplasmic dust. A cloak, with dust scattered over the floor of the movie theater of Jagüey Grande where I went, in my childhood.

Although it's true that, if I attempt to invent a memory, the only one I imagine is wires. What could I do with these wires? And… another question: these wires, what relationship could they have with this albino non-landscape that surrounds me?

Firecracker with colors, the explosive finger of the Sorcerer's face. Or perhaps it could be about the costumes taken out of Osiris's lead box. But…who could know that?

Or the firecracker that ran down the Sorcerer's wart. Or perhaps this glossolalia, inspired by the color lilac, which had dyed the face of the old Lady of the Home. But I repeat, who could know that? Who, from the trampoline, could plunge into the color?

La libertad—una libertad minúscula—era un pasaje de cartón, de color carmelita, que llevé en un bombacho, en 1936. No sé si llovía, no podría decir si llovía, pero las líneas movidas que todavía recojo, todavía me hablan de algo muy raro que sólo en aquel tiempo conocí.

¿Cómo era la cosa? Ahora, ya sólo puedo decir de una cuchara, continuada por el hilito negro que envolvía lo azul de un insecto petrificado.

Nada de esto, por supuesto, era para hacer reír.

También—sigo recordando, aunque sin saber de dónde procede mi recuerdo –, una diminuta escoba negra, apoyándose en un serrucho diminuto.

Y, no sé por qué, sueño con triángulos colocados sobre triángulos, pero esto, si no es que está metido dentro de una bolsa autista, bien puede ser considerado como lo perteneciente al discurso del "no decir".

Y es que también, en los momentos en que me siento asiático, quisiera, junto al color, colocar en estos aforismos dos tercios de vacío. Traduzco lo que François Cheng dice sobre el lenguaje de la pintura china: "En un cuadro, un tercio de lleno, dos tercios de vacío".

Pues, me explico: ¿los dos tercios de vacío no pueden ser expresados, traducidos, como el exabrupto autista registrado por un delirante que, al oír un ruido, le pareciera estar frente a un silencio?

La pequeña sombra, junta a la puerta del baño de una estación de autobuses. Recordé, sin saber por qué, que esta pequeña sombra se mezclaba con el sabor del agua caliente que había bebido, con repugnancia, en un vaso plástico de color verde limón.

Querido Baruj Salinas, pintor, la pregunta es la siguiente: ¿intentas, cuando te encuentras con dos nubes, hacer una mezcla? Hay un poeta argentino, Arturo Carrera, que habla de esa mezcla, por lo que quisiera entender (ya que me he pasado años en la Playa Albina, donde vivo, mirando una colchoneta vieja tirada en un solar yermo) cómo es que eso se logra.

Saludos a Marilín. Lorenzo.

Freedom—a minuscule freedom—was a cardboard landscape, brownish-colored, which I carried in a pocket of my plus-fours, in 1936. I don't know if it was raining, I couldn't say if it was raining, but the blurred lines I still recollect, still speak to me of something very strange that I only knew at that time.

What was this like? Now, I can only speak of a spoon, continued by the little black thread that enveloped the blue of a petrified insect.

None of this, of course, was a laughing matter.

Also—I keep remembering, although without knowing where my memory's coming from—a tiny black broom, supporting itself on a tiny handsaw.

And I don't know why, I dream about triangles atop triangles, but this, unless it's been put inside an autistic bag, could well be considered as belonging to the discourse of "unsaying."

And it's also that, in the moments in which I feel Asiatic, I would like, next to the color, to place two-thirds emptiness onto these aphorisms. I translate what François Cheng says about the language of Chinese painting: "On a painting, one-third full, two-thirds empty."

So let me explain: cannot the two-thirds emptiness be expressed, translated, like the autistic sally recorded by a lunatic who, upon hearing a noise, would think he was facing silence?

The little shadow, next to the bathroom door of a bus station. I remembered, without knowing why, that this little shadow blended with the taste of the hot water I had drunk, with disgust, from a plastic lime-green colored cup.

Dear Baruj Salinas the painter, my question is as follows: do you try, when you encounter two clouds, to make a blend? There's an Argentine poet, Arturo Carrera, who speaks of this blend, which is why I would like to understand (since I've spent years in Albino Beach, where I live, looking at an old mattress tossed onto a vacant lot) how this can be achieved.

Say hello to Marilín. Lorenzo.

from

El oficio de perder (Memorias) / The Vocation of Losing (Memoirs) (2005)

Part One

6

I'm on Section 6, and that's why I think we're now entering those galleries of the Labyrinth that are related to the head of gold.

You already know, I've said so before, that my childhood is the head of gold; afterwards, 1936 and adolescence are in the silver age; then, my youth (so to speak) is the age of copper; followed by the goddamned iron of my maturity without maturity, in the age of iron; until finally, in Albino Beach, enjoying the age of mud, I undertake these *memoirs* and hope to bring them to an end.

Memoirs then, but however I am able, or in my own style, beginning with the gallery through which I can enter, and continuing through the gallery through which I can continue.

I'm not going to follow any order because, quite simply, I don't really know how I can put up with an order. And besides, I have another reason for proceeding in this manner: I want to display myself, in these pages of a Labyrinth, as having a paradoxical discipline: the discipline of the *immature*. What do I mean by this?

One of my hobby-horses for part of my life (the part of my life that began when, already near the silver of my left foot, I became acquainted with Witold Gombrowicz's *Ferdydurke*) has consisted of wishing to assume my *Immaturity*. But what do I mean by that?

Let us recall what Witold said in *Seduction*:

"And the individual is a constant producer of form: he secretes form indefatigably, like the bee secretes honey.

"But on the other hand he struggles against form itself. *Ferdydurke* is a description of man's struggles with his own expression, of the torture of humanity on the Procrustean bed of form."

That is, it seems to be (and I say *seems to be* because, as I warned earlier, I only play the piano by ear, so what I think I'm hearing is perhaps just a figment of my *immaturity*) that however much I strive to present in these pages the image of a statue with a head of gold, shoulders of silver, etc., I'll never be able to free myself of the innate (perhaps ontological) clumsiness of my lamentable immaturity.

So, therefore, since I'm immature, the best I can do is proceed as such and abandon any kind of struggle with form.

Let the Reader, then, adapt to my inborn clumsiness. I can do nothing other than segregate form, but a form that's as if smeared by the greasiness (what a bother it is to accept this!) of my immaturity. That is, a form that can be left to itself, that can be accepted, as it was left to itself, as it was accepted, in childhood, that unbearable dangling part of... that leftover part of the sleeve of a woolen shirt that was too big for us.

Really, the whole thing was unbearable. The sleeve of the woolen shirt, once donned for the first time, almost covered half our hand. What desperation! There was nothing to be done! We had to resign ourselves, and accept that the horrid wool, proto-matter of immaturity, would scrape our hands, for a time that seemed interminable, and that, to compound the curse, would make us feel horribly guilty.

Well then, has the Reader understood this? Rubbing my hands, I feel that horrid wool of my immaturity which, before, was a shirtsleeve.

But now I'm going to enter a gallery of my Labyrinth where heroism will be found, and where there'll even be a meeting with the *modernista* poet Agustín Acosta.

Let's see.

Heroism. Before all else, then, the following must be said: to speak of a vocation, to speak of any vocation, and especially to speak of the vocation of losing, is to speak of heroism.

The hero before all else. One learns a vocation in order to be the hero.

Just as, when one wants to build a Labyrinth, it's because one wants to know what 's inside heroism.

I've wanted to learn the vocation of losing since boyhood, but ever since then I've wanted to be a hero.

I was, like all boys, a narcissist, and like all narcissistic boys, I had a heroic calling.

Of course, at the outset my ambition was about wanting to be a warrior. I wanted to grow up to be Simón Bolívar. I said to myself that I would liberate the Isle of Pines, the island enslaved by Cuba.

But afterwards, following a long and thorny process, the heroic calling and the vocation of losing were united. And once the union had been cemented, the whole thing became my destiny.

Because I was on a rooftop, saluting the multitudes with the straw hat that belonged to my father. It was 1934, a year before Carlos Gardel died.

At noon, with the sun cracking the stones. I ascended (the staircase like a spiral) until I reached the roof of my childhood home, in Jagüey Grande. Once on the roof I looked downwards, towards the deserted street. Below, in front, was the Precinct. There were no prisoners in the Precinct, but there was a bored dog, sprawled on the ground in the doorway.

I remember that midday street as if it were today. There were some elm trees, which they cut down a short time afterwards (the Cuban, among other things, hates trees). The midday street, had it not been for the cart passing by at that moment, would have been completely deserted.

The cart (closely resembling, by the way, a cart driven by Death which, a few years later, I saw in a French film), was coming from the Slaughterhouse to supply the town's butcher shops.

Later, I converted that cart into the symbol of that lamentable filthy well where the excremental collective unconscious of Cuba's decrepit towns resided.

But back then, on that midday in 1934, that cart was just another detail, amidst the multitude greeting me below.

Cries of the multitude. I brandished a straw hat to answer the cries of the multitude. A straw hat that not only had belonged to my father, but also to Colonel Mendieta, the hero of… (Cunagua or Cumagua? Many years have passed, and now I don't remember.)

Mendieta had just installed himself as President of the Republic, after a phony revolution, the revolution of 1933. My father was the de facto Mayor of Jagüey Grande.

In that Cuba of the 1930s, the straw hat was part of the heroic getup. The student martyrs of the struggle against the Tyrant wore it. Maurice Chevalier, the popular singer, wore it.

From the terrace of the Presidential Palace, with my straw hat, the President saluted the multitude. I was a boy, I was the President, surrounded by a retinue of marble derby hats. God only knows what kind of a lunatic a boy, touched by the heroic calling, could become in a town called Jagüey Grande!

The scene that promoted heroism was a phony revolution, with a soap-opera struggle against a Tyrant. Of course, there were unforgettable young leaders, who fell with their straw hats, bloodstained, beneath the murderous bullets of tropical henchmen, but all this, in Cuban style, had for its fife-and-drum-type background things like the films of Carole Lombard and the unforgettable Art Deco monuments.

But regardless of straw hats, or even Carole Lombard, the important thing about that scene was that it promoted, at midday on a deserted street of a rural town, the fact of one's entry into a slightly odd heroism: the heroism that, by way of a corridor of the Labyrinth, would lead me to the vocation of losing.

So that... Perhaps I could go back to talking about immaturity, and how immaturity got entangled with heroism for me, but I'm going to say something else. Something else about having ascended to the roof, and also my having donned Colonel Mendieta's hat. A strange necessity compels me to talk about this.

I'm saying... Let's see if I can make myself understood. In 1934, in a deserted street, a boy was saluting the multitude.

It was indeed a deserted street, because, looking closely, there was only the garbage cart, and the dog stretched out in the doorway of the Precinct.

But there was something else besides. There was...besides...the Tower of Panoramas.

Meaning what?

I was saluting the crowd on the roof of a 1934 midday. That's how it was. I was saluting with a straw hat, a year before Carlos Gardel died. Yes, that's exactly how it was. But there was more.

There were other rooftops in the town.

There were other rooftops, near the one on which I, the President, was standing.

And it was then—or did I dream it—that one, among the nearby rooftops, struck me. I was struck by the rooftop that belonged to the only house in town with an upper floor, the house of the *modernista* poet Agustín Acosta.

A rooftop from whose center rose a pergola.

A pergola on a Jagüey Grande roof? Might I not have dreamed it?

But the most amazing thing is not having dreamt a pergola in Jagüey Grande, but having dreamt the fiction that that pergola was the Tower of Panoramas.

How could this be?

I repeat: this fiction consisted of seeing the Tower of Panoramas.

Because in Jagüey Grande, of course, neither I nor any other boy ever saw this Tower.

So?

The Tower of Panoramas, invented at the beginning of the century by the Uruguayan Julio Herrera y Reissig, was a social gathering for lunatics. "There's no madhouse for that much lunacy," someone in that gathering said.

So?

The only house in town with an upper floor, on which the roof with a pergola could be the Tower of Panoramas, was the house where the *modernista* poet Agustín Acosta lived.

Agustín Acosta was not only the town Notary, but the *modernista* poet who in 1926, the year of my birth, published "La Zafra (The Sugar Harvest)," a poem in which the Australia Sugar Mill arose, that is, the place where not only did I come to experience a strange *desiccation* (sic), but where I also saw a snowfall for the first time (but I'll talk about that later).

The thing is, I remember it as if it were today (or I'm making it up as if it were today), I made my debut in heroic life with the poor, kitschy, risible qualities of the atmosphere in which I was born. I made my debut with a kitsch hero's straw hat, surrounded by marble derby hats. But since I was also a boy destined for the vocation of losing, I couldn't avoid seeing, on that midday of my childhood, the Slaughterhouse cart and Herrera y Reissig's Tower of Panoramas, located on the poet Agustín Acosta's roof.

How to explain all this? Must I resort to Theosophy? Must I seek out a theosophist, an expert in reincarnation, so that he could not only tell us if I, an old Uruguayan from 1900, saw the Tower of Panoramas before dying, but also tell us if I, a boy reincarnated in Jagüey Grande, was able to see, in the pergola of the Cuban *modernista* Agustín Acosta, the tower I had already known in that other incarnation.

This remains to be seen.

A Uruguayan boy who, reincarnated in Jagüey Grande, looks at Herrera y Reissig's Tower?

But...maybe I'm biting off more than I can chew.

And this always happens, I bite off more than I can chew; I start off in more or less good shape, but immediately I descend into talking nonsense.

Now then, let's see, am I sure I saw the Tower of Panoramas in Agustín Acosta's pergola? Well...truth to tell, I don't know.

So?

So, the one thing for sure is that I saluted the multitude on that midday of my childhood, but because things are the way they are, it turns out that what Theosophy says is true. And if what Theosophy says is true, then it could be that, although it seems nonsensical, in reality I did see the Tower. One never knows.

So why am I confused? Why am I getting all mixed up, going round and round in circles?

Well, no doubt about it, life has a lot of peculiarities. Yes, life, if you take a good look at it, is filled with peculiarities. So if life has peculiarities, why couldn't the Tower of Panoramas exist in Jagüey Grande?

Years, many years later, I met Agustín Acosta. And by then there was no longer any rooftop from which to greet the multitude.

Nor did the Tower of Panoramas appear to be there.

We'd left Jagüey Grande. We were living in Havana.

In my childhood, Agustín Acosta was the first appearance of the hero as poet.

In Jagüey Grande, Agustín Acosta had been the poor notary, just like the theosophist and spiritualist who read his cards, Caridad *Macho* (*Macho*, of course, was a nickname), the town medium who, among many other things, presided over the destruction of the rose garden in the patio of my aunt María's house, because, with a single clairvoyant's glance, she perceived it as a dangerous "haunt of evil spirits."

And so in Jagüey, that very poor Jagüey of my childhood (a time in which a daily liter of milk was all the fee a lawyer would receive), Agustín, with his poem "The Sugar Harvest," became not only the soap-opera hero who confronted that dark force, the Tyrant Machado, but also the most famous Cuban poet of those 1920s in which I was born.

A soap-opera conquistador, Agustín had opened, for a boy from Jagüey Grande, nothing less than the possibility of a heroic stage set.

But in 1934, after a phony revolution during which the Tyrant fell, Agustín Acosta ceased to be the theosophist notary of Jagüey and became the Secretary of the Presidency of the Governor of Colonel (all those capital letters!) Mendieta (Mendieta, the hero, was fond of writing unpublished verses, whence his predilection for Agustín Acosta). And that was one year before Carlos Gardel's death, which made it possible for me, a boy with a straw hat, to greet the multitude on that midday in Jagüey.

Life, like the mambo, has its peculiarities. You couldn't make up a better soap-opera than this one.

As I said, years later I met Agustín Acosta. After eight years as Senator of the Republic, he had retired from politics for lack of a public.

Weeks before, I'd sent him my first book, *Suite para la espera* (*Suite for Waiting*).

Agustín, an old theosophist, said that a book justified itself with a single line. "A single line that would be predestined to be read by a single reader. The line which that reader's astral body needed," he concluded.

But Agustín felt (and he almost couldn't conceal) a boundless hatred for Lezama and for everything the *Orígenes* group meant. And he practically couldn't conceal the disdain that my *Suite* merited in his eyes (later I found out that he told somebody, "It's a book of long verses and short verses.").

Fortunately, though, none of this matters any more. What matters for me now about that afternoon I met Agustín Acosta was that he, although he despised my talent, wanted to connect me with Julio Herrera y Reissig.

Could it be that the old theologian suspected my Uruguayan incarnation?

And it happened that Agustín, seated in an old Cuban armchair, but an armchair that inevitably summoned up memories of a *modernista* Assyrian throne, after he ordered coffee, ushered me into the awe-inspiring Tower of Sphinxes.

He recited well, Agustín did. He was a thoroughgoing rhetorician. As a result, his histrionic demeanor, against a backdrop of the splendid light of a tropical afternoon, made visible for me both the green gesture of the sky and the unbalanced laughter of a lubricious satyr sick with green absinthe.

Because of this, the afternoon was unforgettable, no doubt about it. An afternoon for talent.

Agustín, in order to teach me what bombarding with real metaphors was all about, entered the Tower of Sphinxes, but after a short while, since he couldn't stop being the incurable romantic he was, abandoned that path in order to embark upon the soap-opera trail of the White Berceuse.

Unforgettable!

So unforgettable was it that, because of that recitation of the Berceuse, I long ago forgave Agustín Acosta for despising my *Suite for Waiting*.

The scowling Spanish servant appeared with the poet's coffee. But with the terrifying gesture of a *modernista* Dragon, the Poet, transforming her into Medusa, detained the servant so that he could continue having fun with Herrera y Reissig's "Berceuse":

Breathe in her incorporeal lightness of Ulalume
On her temples shine transparencies of treetops:
and the autumnal brown circles beneath her eyes are soaring
like wandering fireflies in a heliotropic evening

All good things must come to an end! That was the sort of thing for which you could rent out balcony seats. I don't remember well enough to provide the exact details. I only know that the servant transformed into Medusa. I only know that in the end the scowling Spanish woman served us coffee. The details all fell into the black hole.

The details are all gone, but the important fact of that afternoon was that, due to one of those strange things that can happen, what with all that fun with the Berceuse I left convinced that I'd previously seen, crowning Agustín Acosta's house in Jagüey Grande, the Tower of Panoramas.

I left convinced, after seeing the poet Acosta reciting Herrera y Reissig, that when I, many years earlier, had harangued the multitude from a rooftop, I'd also seen the Uruguayan's Tower from that rooftop.

I'd never seen the Tower, but I already knew that I'd seen the Tower.

How did this happen? Why, years later, did I see what I'd seen in 1934?

How did this happen? Was it that the theosophist Agustín Acosta, evoking Herrera y Reissig, awakened the vision of a previous, Uruguayan incarnation? Who knows?

What can't be doubted is that things happened that afternoon: Herrera y Reissig, and pagodas, and gold of Byzantium, and Gothic cupolas, and even the blessed demon.

I mentioned that I had just published *Suite for Waiting*, that book in which I had written: *Into the water with Apollinaire*.

Agustín, the disdainful notary from Jagüey, couldn't understand why Apollinaire fell into the water.

But it was sad that he understood nothing, because, given the kitsch that Agustín and I enjoyed thanks to the Berceuse, I think we could have joined forces. Because, when all was said and done, Agustín and I were bound by kitsch: the kind of kitsch that led him to be a winner, even to the point of becoming a Senator of the Republic, though it led me to the vocation of losing.

Kitsch and the vocation of losing. A strange combination. I repeat: life, like the mambo, has its peculiarities. So that now it's helpful to remember that saying of Gómez de la Serna's that *corniness is any sentiment that isn't shared*. Because nothing can be less shared than the vocation of losing?

But now, now that I've talked about all this, now that I've talked about my entrance, with Agustín, into the Tower of Panoramas, I cannot end this Chapter without saying that Lezama too, drowned these verses of Herrera in the steam of his explosive laughter, endlessly repeated, in the cafes of Old Havana:

and gloomily I pursue in my shadow
my own entity in flight.

Though Lezama, also involved with the kitsch of the Tower, as a conclusion, crowned whatever topic we were discussing by quoting these other verses of Herrera y Reissig thousands of times:

Everything sustains the weariness
of some psychophysical land

in the metaphysical pole
of silence and weariness

It's all very peculiar. I'll say it again, life has many peculiarities.

16

I'm at a bad moment of this narrative. A moment where I've come to a halt and don't know what to do.

A few nights ago Carlos Victoria came over, I read him what I'd written, and after the reading, I felt depressed.

I didn't like what I'd read to Carlos Victoria. It seemed confused, thorny, and worse, it seemed to be a narrative that was slipping from my grasp.

What depresses and upsets me most is that I can't figure things out. If I'm writing a narrative, what narrative am I writing? Am I trying to write a Labyrinth where I'm going round and round the same thing? Am I trying to build a Labyrinth where I move forward through circularity?

But if that's what it is, if I'm trying to write a Labyrinth in the form of a Labyrinth, why don't I stick to it? why haven't I prepared a *draft labyrinth* to write in the form of a Labyrinth?

Why am I trying to write memoirs if what I want to build is my Labyrinth?

Because what's starting to obsess me now, driving me to depression, is that perhaps I've been writing something that's attempting to be *the vocation of losing*, that is, that's attempting to be something like an autobiography of my vocation of non-writer writer, and at the same time I'm trying to write a *Don't Die Without a Labyrinth*, that is, the narrative of my kaleidoscope, of my circularities, of my corridors that end in the same corridor, etc.

Am I getting pointlessly entangled?

I have to clear this up. It's taken me two years (maybe more, maybe less, because these last few albino years I've been living through are becoming forgotten and confused; for example, I don't even know how long I've been in this vocation [that one, too] of *bag boy*) with this *vocation of losing*, and although every month at night I've had the privilege of reading what I've written to a novelist I respect, Carlos

Victoria (incidentally, during these readings, a truly novel-worthy situation's been happening, for while Carlos Victoria, who's young enough to be my son, is also reading to me his splendid texts in which he can be seen obsessively searching for his lost father, I'm reading him some texts of mine with the emotional temperament—you already know and will yet know how neurotic I am—of someone searching for his Father. That is, a highly unusual thing is happening—unusual, if I weren't neurotic –in which I'm looking for the Father in someone who's young enough to be my son. A son who also, to complicate matters further, is searching for his own Father at the same time) and I don't know if I've made it clear what I'm driving at.

Okay, to begin with, I have to convince myself that this narrative of a *vocation of losing* has to be the same as my proposal to build a Labyrinth.

I have to know that I want to write my autobiography (an autobiography in the Orteguian manner, without nature but with history), but that this story is at the same time about a Labyrinth that attempts to construct itself before the Reader's very eyes.

Can I do that?

Can I go back to the beginning, without eliminating everything I've written? That's the question, and that's the question that's depressing me.

But despite that, in accordance with the title I stole from Dardo Cúneo, what I have to do is write a consistent narrative of a writerly vocation, I think I should continue to take the risk of writing a narrative where my vocation of losing is indissolubly linked to the construction of a labyrinth.

Despite everything, despite my depression and doubts, yes, I believe I should risk the disaster of writing a confused, even autistic narrative where, to the hundred pages I've written, I can add even a *draft* of what I'm going to write afterwards, because although I don't know how to explain it well, I have something like an unconscious conviction that my vocation and my Labyrinth are the same thing.

But I repeat, I can't explain it. Sometimes reasoning deserts me. Or sometimes my explanation can appear so involved that the best thing to do would be to cut it short. That's the way things are.

I can't explain it, and that's absurd, and I was writing about a childish novel in Neptune's house; now, claiming that I'm depressed, I jump up and start ranting about maybe attempting a *draft* for this text of which I have more than a hundred pages, but what can one do? There's a whole shitload of justifications for doing what I'm doing.

But I don't have to enumerate them all; the main one will do, the fact that at seventy years of age I'm only a bag boy who, although he has an out-of-print book, *The Orígenes Years*, will, apparently until his death, always remain a non-writer writer—a *promising young talent.*

So? So to whom must I justify myself? A bag boy, like a Protestant, has only his conscience to justify himself in the face of nothingness, with no need for a sacrament. Farewell.

17

Beuys spent four days living with a wild coyote. A fine thing, but I, living like a bag boy in an Albino Beach, how could I live with a coyote? In the circumstances I'm living in, what could be like that coyote? A while ago I saw an exhibition of Joseph Beuys. It interested me greatly, the way Duchamp and Joseph Cornell interest me. I felt, when I left, that what I'd seen could help me support myself on what the vocation of losing left me. How so? Well then, the answer it gave me was *askesis*, that is, settling for a reduction: the components of my images converted into pieces. Why this? To achieve a human (in psychoanalytical terms?) transcendence. That is to say, what I'd like to say, is that perhaps, entering this askesis that would consist in reducing images to their component parts, this exercise could contribute to the success of an ultimate nakedness, an ultimate humanity (could this be what Otto Rank said about the Artist become Psychoanalyst?). But I see that what we have here could be a myth, a type of religiosity.

Myth? What myth? "What we have to save is the human soul," said Beuys. To save the soul, to build ourselves a soul, build ourselves a Labyrinth. *Don't die without a labyrinth.*

But then, to save the images, the unexpressed, what is practically unknown about how a soul is composed.

But then, to save the larvae, the kaleidoscope's tiny crystals. Larvae of images, incomplete dreams, in order to construct boxes with them. To build boxes, in order to establish relationships with them ("The artist must not invent anything, but rather discover relationships"). And finally, to establish relationships in order to reach the place they're located: the Labyrinth.

Myth? what myth? Breaking the barriers between art and life? Once this has been achieved, one can write without any concern for whether the writing is published, nor with any concern for whether what's published fills our rooms with crates. Should one not seek to make the act of writing consist solely of something that can bestow life? Were such the case, one would then write or make art with the same disposition as the people I saw in a Paris park doing Chinese exercises: a pure discharge of energy.

Part Two

I

I'm clicking, I love making that click, click, click sound. I love it. I love all that mechanical shit. Click, click…etc. I'm opening this Part Two of the Vocation of Losing. Welcome!

One must proceed with the greatest possible care. Let's see now! There's something like an absurd illumination (characteristic of neon light? I'd love to write a Chapter on neon light), which, doubtless, must contain a question that's also absurd: why are my teeth—I say my teeth, though in reality I've lost, with old age, a good many of them—metaphors? But I've found a quote from Goethe (it's always good to be supported by a quote from Goethe) which goes like this: "All I possess floats off in the distance / all I've lost becomes reality."

I'm listening to Nancarrow while reading an interview with Olga Orozco: "I confess," says Orozco, "that I've never put together a book. I've never organized it as a book, with a specific theme. What's happened is that there've been themes that have seized hold of me at a moment in my life and then that wave which brought the theme has returned and repeated itself; that's why a few books have formed themselves in a consistent direction." Since I enjoy entanglements and Labyrinths, I'm mixing up Nancarrow with Olga Orozco, so that I can then begin to say that it wasn't only at the end of my golden head that I fell into that hole that was 1936, and also to say that I've never prepared a book either. *Spirals of the Withe*? And *The Orígenes Years*? Especially *The Orígenes Years*—I wrote that without preparation. The book was written in between bottles of Scotch, speeches by Octavio Armand, a phantom New York (did I really live in New York?), and the usual fucking-up, though back then it was off the charts.

So, because I also like Olga Orozco's entanglements, I'm going to propose (something I already pointed out/I always repeat myself), in this Part Two, to build the Labyrinth even as I write it.

Is that clear? The thing is, if I'm really a nutcase, it's worth it for me to show myself exactly as I am (a little further down, you'll see how, by plagiarizing Pessoa's business of the heteronyms, I've positioned myself as a Protestant preacher in bed with a surrealist).

But will I be able to build the Labyrinth? Why should I keep asking myself about the same thing?

DREAM—*I'm buying some pastries. Do I put them in a shopping cart? Where am I? Does my mother appear?*

To combine a Diary, a kaleidoscope, a corridor of the Labyrinth, my own story. A Myth. In spite of everything, could this substance of today—today in which nothing's happening—contain some part of the Myth? What do I mean by this question? am I asking something that makes sense?

What sort of a thing is Myth? Perhaps Myth was when, in Jagüey Grande, I went up on a rooftop to salute the multitude. Perhaps Myth was when I wanted to bring to Havana a little piece of pink glass through which to look at the city.

Sometimes, I get the feeling that, through the golden head of my childhood, I found the Myth I later collected in *Spirals of the Withe.*

I found a Myth, and have been struggling with it since childhood, since precisely 1936, when I entered the city I couldn't understand.

But did I lose this Myth? Did I lose it in 1936? I remember the swimming pool once more. The swimming pool in the Jesuits' place. The shouts of the others were there. Splashing in the water. Light entering on all sides. But I couldn't go in. I had to keep apart from the others' joy. That's when my autism, my illness, began. I had lived a Myth in childhood, but from that point on, always, what I was to live would be outside me.

But what is this thing: a Myth? Was it really what I lived during the age of my golden head? was it what I lost in cabalistic 1936?

Because it was the Myth I lived and lost, it's also the Myth I'm unable to grasp.

The Myth…sometimes I can't know if I truly lived it.

Did I really live the Myth? When I was in Jagüey Grande and I left the Harrison Circus weeping, did I really live the Myth? Yes, I lived it. That night was the night of the dilapidated car from the 1930s, when the little blades of grass were moving. Once and for all, something happened. Once and for all. Was that the Myth? Once and for all?

I lived the Myth, but often one forgets having lived the Myth. The various "I's" we were go away as if they erased themselves. And in old age they go away as if they were blending together, those different "I's."

Sometimes, one comes to believe one had different "I's."

Sometimes, one believes one's only dreamt of different "I's."

Sometimes, in old age, there are moments when one doubts whether, in reality, one manages to touch some Myth.

One doubts.

Because it concerns what's dramatically entangled. Although one's old and has lived a good long while, one doesn't understand it. Or maybe it's about old people understanding less than anyone.

Entangled, dramatically entangled. So much so that on a hybrid day when nothing happens, like today, I reach the height of absurdity when I ask myself, as I'm asking myself now, if the substance of a useless day like today could not, in some way, be related to the supposed Myth. But what does it mean to ask such an absurd question?

How can I ask myself such an absurd question?

Above all, how, asking myself questions as absurd as the one I've just asked myself, will I be able to continue telling about this *vocation of losing*?

Isn't it too utterly fucked-up, what's happening to me?

How can a day—this day—the day when nothing's happening, be related to the Myth that an old man doesn't know whether, in reality, it existed or not? How fucked-up! What a question! It would even be better—sometimes I think so –not to keep writing.

(Who was the Box Builder? How did he get mixed up in my story, in my "vocation of losing"?)

Has it been three years, or more than three years, since I began this *vocation of losing*? At the outset, I was writing it like a Diary, writing it as a prolongation of my *Faces of the Reverse*. With it, I proposed to narrate the present, but in a way that, from that perspective, all the parts of my statue would appear: golden head, silver shoulders, etc.

That is, I dreamed of changing this present in Albino Beach into something resembling a space where this Labyrinth that's been my life could be built.

Building the corridors of my Labyrinth even as the different parts of my present were being recorded. Isn't this delirium?

When one decides to write, delirium lurks.

The present, space of my past: continuation of my *Faces of the Reverse*.

Or, what amounts to the same thing, walk through (while building) the Labyrinth, even as I also, with my shopping cart, walk through the substance of today's Albino day, the substance of this day when nothing happens.

That's what I proposed.

Putting myself with Marta, then, in an *Old People's Home*, where even before entering, in the corridor of the Shopping Center, I found the tune of the little plastic horse that the kids climb on.

A palimpsest, then, at the beginning of this *vocation of losing*.

A palimpsest where, on the first page, there's the little plastic horse with its little tune, since I thought that afterwards, once this first page had been built, I'd easily find the writing of the Labyrinth of my past.

But...

But, sadly, afterwards, this attempt at a palimpsest got messed up.

Doubts came.

Would the Diary be the appropriate path to lead towards a Labyrinth of the path that would simultaneously be a statue with a golden head, silver shoulders, etc.?

I then doubted whether this *vocation of losing* would be restricted to what a continuation of *Faces of the Reverse* would imply.

Perhaps, I said to myself, it could be that the Diary, the *Faces*, would swallow up everything, and once that happened, I'd find myself alone, almost reciting a monologue about this present (present?) of this Albino Beach.

But now, with the passage of time and still more time (and also, with the passage of a Martían eagle over the sea), and, now that I feel calmer about the spill I took when in these pages I ran into 1936, I can go back to my first attempt: the Labyrinth built starting from a present.

I repeat: the Labyrinth of what was is what has to be within my present, in this Albino Beach.

Listening to John Cage's piano. A piano, in this narrative.

This piano can't stop being here.

Belén, the Jesuits' place, or whatever part of my past I could recount. This, today, I hear in the piano.

Today my past is tinged with piano music. I can't establish a distance.

Or, putting it otherwise, today I open my kaleidoscope, and the bits of glass, today, contain John Cage's music.

The piano, and again I confirm that these memoirs of the vocation of losing, in my attempt to combine them with this Labyrinth which I must build before dying, mix everything up for me.

They get everything tangled up.

And besides, John Cage's piano, with this entanglement of the vocation of losing in the Labyrinth, shows that, behind whatever pattern my kaleidoscope's little pieces of glass might make, there is always that 1936 present in my *Variations on Something Like a Verdict for a Sun of Other Doubts.*

During this time when I interrupted this *vocation of losing*, I entered several territories.

I dreamed of a review that a literary critic would write of a book of Poetry inspired by boleros.

I wanted to write a story that would refer only to four identical rows, each made up of identical sandbags.

I continued with *Bileville*, city of dreams—I continued to record my dreams in the little notebook on my bedside table.

I continued turning and turning with Duchamp (my *Homage* hadn't come out yet) and Beuys. I turn and turn with Duchamp and Beuys's final drying-up; I speculate about the autistic limit that can be reached with them.

Finally, I entertained myself with *Chemical Garden of Delights*, a bouquet of autistic aphorisms I'd been composing at that time.

Thus, I interrupted *The Vocation of Losing* in order to do something like going elsewhere, but in the last dimension, I feel I'm in the same place.

It's that I feel that four rows of sandbags, or recording dreams in a little notebook, or turning with Beuys's drying-up, or attempting autistic aphorisms, never cease being (albeit in a way that I can't fully understand) something like a space, or something like a substance, which, in the unconscious, never ceases to identify itself with the construction of a Labyrinth, or with my attempt at writing the vocation of losing.

Part Three

9

And after my *cardiac strolls*, and my visits to the couch, there was my entry into the Publix, as a *bag boy*. A fine ending!

"We're the faithful dead," says an old *bag boy* while we're waiting to punch in. The *boy* is a veteran of the Korean War, and he's just had his prostate operated on.

Time is becoming mechanical. The time of the clock when one punches in.

Deflates, it's a time that deflates.

And when I began the vocation of *bag boy*, I was writing my *Palindrome: Homage to Duchamp*. I'd been writing, for part of my life, my *Faces of the Reverse*, but okay, now I was looking for something like a semantics of *the reverse*, or I wanted to find a description of the space and the matter of a landscape that would follow this directive of Duchamp: "*Graphically, this road will tend towards the pure geometrical line without thickness (the meeting of two planes seems to me the only pictorial means to achieve purity.*

But in the beginning (in the chief of the five nudes) it will be very finite in width, thickness, etc., in order little by little, to become without topographical form in coming close to this ideal straight line which finds its opening towards the infinite in the headlight child."

In the beginning I kept the apron I wore in the Publix in a little plastic bag; now I keep it in a stall. The apron was green; now it's black.

"Form = space," according to Duchamp. I took that into account.

When I was starting out at the Publix, it was like a static whirlpool. Back then I almost always left at 6 in the evening, and because of the humidity, there was something that sounded like a cloud of smoke. Generally, evenings were sad and dark. The bus passed by the place where the discarded mattress was. The bus, of course, stopped for traffic lights, and there could even have been a few swallows atop the traffic lights. What more can be said?

But I also remember, in my early days at the Publix, an old customer who came every morning to buy bread. It was a strange moment in the supermarket's morning, because a strange silence would fall. During that silence, I looked at the old man's ears. Trashy ears that looked like a bad copy of Van Gogh.

Or from those early days I remember, I don't know why, the hands of a cashier on the counter where the orders were placed. Were these hands pudgy, or was it that, for a moment, they seemed pudgy to me? But why does this memory persist?

Or, following Duchamp, in the *Palindrome* I was writing, at times I proposed myself the following things: to tell a story about a Box; or to tell something whose elements would decompose, according to this process: a) beginning with the exposition of the argument; and b) crumbling the pieces of the characters, at the same time as, with regard to the landscape, I tried to refer to the *longitude* of its space and the *quality* of its material.

"In general," said Duchamp, "the picture is an apparition of an appearance (see explanation). Put the whole bride under a glass case, or into a transparent cage."

Or, above all, I dreamed of translating, in my own way, Duchamp's warning: "Of hygiene in the Bride, or of the Diet in the Bride."

Three drowned fetuses! Things like that, along with the old man's trashy ears, were what I saw in the Publix, when I started working there.

The fetuses, or what looked to me like fetuses, were three green aprons resting on a table.

The strong light of a bulb fell on the table with the aprons, but at that moment, an employee from the Warehouse arrived and flicked the light switch, as a result of which, in the semi-darkness of the room, what looked to me like fetuses disappeared, and the aprons remained.

The shopping cart...and I worked five days a week; consequently, it seemed that everything was happening too fast.

I was tired, sleepy, and everything was happening too fast. Time was turning into something like scarce money. Money that was spent immediately.

My entire life was going to the Publix.

I was afraid, too.

And my hands kept peeling, as if I had chilblains.

Then I bought some gloves, and since then I've used gloves at work.

There was also a Colombian cashier who, though dressed in uniform, always brought Goya's *Naked Maja* to mind. The cashier smiled somewhat enigmatically, because she looked as if she were sucked into herself. I never decided to speak to her about the Duchess Cayetana; since the cashier probably didn't know who Goya was, nor the *maja* for that matter, and since one never knows how people are going to react, the best thing, I think, was to say nothing.

In the *Palindrome*, I was interested in expressing the different possibilities for a story in a given situation. "Always or nearly always give reasons for the choice between 2 or more solutions (by ironical causality)," said Duchamp.

And when I found this quote, "the phenomenon of stretching in the unity of length," I remembered the Count Largo I had spoken of in my *Cetrería del Títere* (*Puppet's Falconry*).

Or, fully immersed in my work, I tried to dream that the metal was memory and sensation, so that in this way, by emancipating it, it would change into an abstract quality or something to play with. This, from trying to interpret Duchamp's advice: "Emancipated metal of the rods of the sleigh.

Friction reintegrated (emancipated metal)."

Some awful young people are riding their cars through the supermarket parking lot, like an exhalation. Certain evenings are the worst, when the parking lot gets dark and the goddamned rain starts. Then, pushing the shopping cart around is a fucking drag.

The machinery of the image, but making noise as it functions. That's what I heard, when I was writing my text on Duchamp. It delighted me to be able to savor an always admissible surrealism: the surrealism of the mechanics of the image: "The pulse needle should have its source in the life center of the bride. (The bride has a life center—the bachelors have not. / B and C (as they sway,) just strike the circle A, B below, C above."

Like punching the Publix time clock. After walking with my *cardiac strolls* towards the place with the mattress, with the same emptiness I placed my life at the service of punching in at the Publix.

Grounds for confirming the uselessness of time, and now, punching the clock, I confirm something like a whitish stain. "Is there a point of arrival," wondered Krishnamurti, "is there an end for which time is necessary?" But what would Krishna have asked had he punched in at the Publix?

Punching in is like being burned into the void. It makes us more phantasmal than we've ever been.

Punching in is a whitish stain that dissolves, in pennies, the passage of time. The shredder of time.

Punching in, or the *click* of the shopping carts when they're pushed into other shopping carts. You haul two or three carts from the parking lot. Then you put those two or three carts into a row of other carts. *Click*.

But I've always taken some pleasure in my vocation of losing, a gambler's pleasure, because while writing my *Palindrome*, I knew that the mechanical functioning of the image liberates the metal, according to Duchamp's observation: "The friction of the runner on the rail (instead of changing into heat) is transformed into a returning force equal to the going force. (This phen. In relation to the emancipation of the metal which forms the body of the rods of the sleigh)".

Like watching the old women in front of the Publix's counters. Always the same wrinkles, the same griefs, when you get to know the clientele.

The thing is, you could go on counting the sighs of the old women who go to the Publix. At eleven a.m., for example, you can say: "Now we've reached the nth sigh." And that too is like a kind of phantasmal experience.

Just like "she found herself barely held back from a fainting fit by a slender thread," as Juan Emar once wrote. And I, in the Publix, have seen, in front of the counter, a pale blonde woman, with hiccups. With her hiccups, could she find herself held back from a fainting fit, as if by a thread? Not at all! but it's different from what Juan Emar said. The blonde at the Publix counter isn't held back from a fainting fit, but from something else, so that thing could never be a thread, but something coarser. But how, in the supermarket, can I set about unraveling such things?

And an especially interesting situation is when the cash registers stop working. The cashiers stand there as if paralyzed. The public also look paralyzed. We *bag boys* look at each other, but what I did there, and I don't think the others did, was to think about a trapeze artist, designed by Kafka.

But above all, what I wanted to do with my *Palindrome* is to build something like a bridge for a diary of the unconscious. A diary in which I could register, like Duchamp:

"We'll miss, at the same time less" / "3 or 4 drops of height have nothing to do with savagery."

Or, above all: "A transformer designed to use the slight, wasted energies such as:

the excess of pressure on an electric switch.

the exhalation of tobacco smoke

the growth of a head of hair, of other body hair and of the nails."

No doubt about it, with this transformer I could record the time and space of my stereotypes: the rigid position of my hands and feet on some occasions; an inner story (with or without alphabets) of the taste of my breakfasts; my position while stretching out on the sheets at bedtime; and the synesthesia, accompanied by images, that the cold can bring.

With cans of Coca-Cola, cans of Pepsi-Cola. Cans of diet drinks, from the Publix. Pop tinwork. From here it's an easy leap to dreaming of violent films. Fantômas. Electronic kings traversing the cities' underground passages.

Hills of cans. Huge triangles of cans. In the Publix. It's nice to see this.

Then the background music begins and attaches itself to the mountains of cans. A fine symbiosis, like Baudelaire's correspondences, inside a supermarket.

It's a tunnel, a tunnel corridor, which makes the background music communicate with the symmetrical mountains of cans.

I like walking down this tunnel corridor.

I think it's like being in a cardboard paradise.

I think the combination of background music, pyramids of cans, and tunnel corridors, can bring out those electronic dolls that we all carry inside us.

How odd! And all this with the noise of the shopping carts, when they arrange them in a row, in the vestibule. In the vestibule, there's an old man with an idiotic face. The old man looks like he's masturbating, and he's looking around as if obsessed.

So there are races from one place to another. Leaving the parking lot, entering the parking lot, going back into the parking lot. Always with a shopping cart.

But when there aren't many customers, somebody says: "Too many chiefs and not enough Indians." This one's an octogenarian, who was one of Batista's soldiers, and is now a fellow *bag boy.*

The Albino Beach sky, during the last months of the year, starts imitating autumn.

But above all, I've been interested in the possibility that Duchamp offers of relating objects: "Determine the difference between the volumes of air displaced by a clean shirt (ironed and folded) and the same shirt when dirty."

Adjustment of coincidences of objects or parts of objects; the hierarchy of this type of adjustment stands in a direct ratio to the "blunder."

Finally, I get home, where Marta's sister Yolanda has just stopped by as well.

Marta's on the patio, and she's wearing a big palm hat.

The sisters want to take me to an uncle's house, but the part of my Labyrinth that corresponds to uncles now belongs, unfortunately, to another incarnation.

Then, Marta talks about the implosion that has perhaps led me to a black hole. I think I remember that La Maga, in *Hopscotch*, refers to the black hole that Oliviera might be. So I'm afraid that Marta might be going literary on me. You never know.

Notes

The Orígenes Years

"The Gucci Doorman":

Juan Goytisolo (1931-2017), Spanish novelist, essayist, and public intellectual; early supporter and subsequent critic of the Cuban Revolution; see *Count Julian,* trans. Helen Lane (Dalkey Archive, 2007) and *Juan the Landless*, trans. Peter Bush (Dalkey Archive, 2009).

Lezama. José Lezama Lima (1910-1976), Cuban poet, theorist, and guiding spirit of the *Orígenes* group of poets, artists, and intellectuals, whose journal he edited between 1944 and 1956; see his novel *Paradiso*, trans. Gregory Rabassa (Dalkey Archive, 2005), *José Lezama Lima: Selections* (U. of California P., 2005), the poems included in Mark Weiss (ed.), *The Whole Island: Six Decades of Cuban Poetry* (U. of California P., 2009), and *A Poetic Order of Excess: Essays on Poets and Poetry* (Green Integer, 2019). García Vega's complex relationship with his "Maestro" Lezama and the psychological conflicts this brought about were recurring preoccupations in his work.

Fina. Fina García Marruz (1923-2022), Cuban poet, member of the *Orígenes* group; see the poems included in Weiss, *op. cit.* and the memoir *La familia de Orígenes* (Ediciones Unión, 1997).

Cintio. Cintio Vitier (1921-2009), Cuban poet and theorist, member of the *Orígenes* group. As the Origenista who was most concerned with fitting the group's project into the ideology of the Cuban Revolution, Vitier is a particular target of García Vega's criticism. See the poems included in Weiss, *op. cit.*

Father Gaztelu. Ángel Gaztelu (1933-2002), Cuban poet and priest, co-editor of *Nadie parecía*, a precursor to *Orígenes.*

John Cage (1912-1992), U.S. composer, poet, theorist, and visual artist, practitioner of chance operations in musical composition and performance, a major inspiration for García Vega's poetics; see *Silence: Lectures and Writings* (Wesleyan UP, 2013).

Tillich. Paul Tillich (1886-1965), German philosopher and theologian; see *The Shaking of the Foundations* (Wipf & Stock, 2012).

"The Coffer":

Casa de las Américas. A cultural institution founded shortly after the Cuban Revolution to promote the cultures of Latin America and the Caribbean; awards prizes and publishes books and several journals in various fields.

Eliseo. Eliseo Diego (1920-1994), Cuban poet and short-story writer, member of the *Orígenes* group; García Vega alludes elsewhere to a line from his poem "El sitio en que tan bien se está" [The Place That Feels So Right]: "I don't know how to say to him / the Republic." See the poems included in Weiss, *op. cit.*

Boom. A term used to designate a cluster of novels by Latin American authors (notably Gabriel García Márquez, Julio Cortázar, Carlos Fuentes, José Donoso, and Mario Vargas Llosa) published in the 1950s and 1960s and benefiting from broad international acclaim and exposure. Lezama Lima's *Paradiso* is considered to be part of this literary moment.

Fausto Masó. Cuban-born Venezuelan novelist, editor, and journalist.

Víctor Batista (1933-2020), Cuban writer and co-editor of *Exilio: Revista de Humanidades*, which published work by García Vega; later the head of the independent publishing house Colibrí (Madrid), whose list includes many prominent Cuban exile writers and thinkers.

Mario Parajón (1929-2006), Cuban theater director, journalist, and theologian associated with the *Orígenes* group; prefaced the first edition of García Vega's *Ritmos acribillados.*

Alemany. Mariano Alemany, psychologist; friend and classmate of García Vega in the Jesuit Colegio Belén.

Orteguian. A reference to the Spanish philosopher José Ortega y Gasset (1883-1955), whose method may be summed up in his famous declaration "I am I and my circumstance." See *Meditations on Quixote*, trans. Evelyn Rugg and Diego Marín (Norton, 1963).

Carlos M. Carlos M. Luis (1932-2013), Cuban poet, artist, and art critic initially associated with the *Orígenes* group, later working more in a surrealist and visual-poetic mode.

Julián Orbón (1925-1991). Cuban composer and member of the *Orígenes* group.

Octavio Armand (1946). Cuban/Venezuelan poet and essayist, during the 1980s, co-editor with García Vega of the New York-based literary journal *Escandalar.* See *Refractions*, trans. Carol Maier (Lumen: 1993).

Rialta. The name of the mother of José Cemí, the central character of Lezama Lima's novel *Paradiso.*

"The kitsch mystic." A reference to Nicaraguan poet Ernesto Cardenal, specifically his pro-Castro travel memoir *In Cuba* (trans. Donald D. Walsh; New Directions, 1971).

Langston Hughes (1902-1967). African American poet, translator, memoirist, and fiction writer. The quotation here is from his poem "I Too Sing America" (misquoted in the Spanish version of the text by either García Vega or Lezama Lima and corrected here). See *Collected Poems,* ed. Arnold Rampersad (Vintage, 1995).

Aristides Fernández (1904-1934). Cuban painter and short-story writer; pioneer of what came to be called "magical realism."

Gastón Baquero (1914-1997). Cuban poet, essayist, and journalist, on the fringes of the *Orígenes* group; co-editor of the literary journals *Verbum*, *Nadie parecía*, and *Clavileño;* thereafter an editor at the conservative newspaper *Diario de la Marina*, where he published Lezama Lima's chronicles of Havana; after the Cuban Revolution, went into exile in Spain. See the translations of his poems in Weiss, *op. cit.* and *The Angel of Rain*, trans. Greg Simon and Steven White (Eastern Washington UP, 2006).

Torrejas. A sugary toast similar to French toast, generally eaten cold.

Mariano. Mariano Rodríguez (1912-1990). Cuban avant-garde painter, known as the "painter of roosters," associated with the *Orígenes* group, to whose journal he contributed illustrations.

Julián del Casal (1863-1893). Cuban modernista poet, whose "decadent" aestheticism is often contrasted to the "patriotic" poetry of his contemporary José Martí. In recent years, his work has enjoyed a resurgence of critical attention in Cuba. García Vega's essay "The Cuban Operetta in Julián del Casal," first published in 1963 and included in *The Orígenes Years*, is, however, an often-harsh critique that presages his later attacks on what he sees as the illusions and pretensions of Cuban literary culture.

Loveira, Carrión. References to the socially critical novelists of the Cuban Republican period Carlos Loveira (1882-1928) and Miguel de Carrión (1875-1929), authors respectively of *Generales y doctores* and *Las impuras*. García Vega included excerpts from both authors' writings in his 1960 *Antología de la novela cubana*.

"Lola, jolongo, weeping on the balcony." The opening sentence in José Martí's *Diario de campana*; for the complete text, see *José Martí: Selected Writings*, trans. Esther Allen (Penguin: 2002).

Mallea. Eduardo Mallea (1903-1982), Argentine novelist and critic, author of existentialist-inflected essays and fictions. See *History of an Argentine Passion*, trans. Myron Lichtblau (Latin American Literary Review Press, 1983); and *All Green Shall Perish and Other Novellas and Stories*, trans. John B. Hughes (Knopf, 1983).

Céline. Louis-Ferdinand Céline (1894-1961), French novelist, physician, and anti-Jewish polemicist. See *Journey to the End of the Night*, trans. Ralph Manheim (New Directions, 2006).

"...a poetry anthology of Cintio's..." A reference to Cintio Vitier (ed.), *Cincuenta años de poesía cubana* (Dirección de Cultura del Ministerio de Educación; Ediciones del Cincuentenario, 1952).

Seix Barral. A Spanish publishing house that published many of the so-called Latin American "Boom" writers.

Vicentina Antuña (1909-1993). Cuban academic, educator, and founder of the Consejo Nacional de Cultura following the triumph of the Cuban Revolution.

Góngora. Luis de Góngora y Argote (1561-1627). Spanish poet, the most eminent and influential of the Baroque poets in Spain, and a major influence on both the Spanish "Generation of 1927" poets (among them Dámaso Alonso, Vicente Aleixandre, and Federico García Lorca) and the *Orígenes* group. See *The Solitudes,* trans. and ed. Edith Grossman (Penguin, 2012).

Juan Ramón. Juan Ramón Jiménez (1881-1958). Spanish poet, critic, and editor; leading voice of the so-called "Generation of 1898" which emerged following Spain's defeat and loss of her colonies to the United States; winner of the 1956 Nobel Prize in Literature. One of Lezama Lima's most famous poems is his youthful "Colloquy with Juan Ramón Jiménez," which explores the two writers' divergent poetics. See *Selected Writings of Juan Ramón Jiménez,* trans. and ed. H.R. Hays (Farrar Straus Giroux, 1999).

Max Henríquez Ureña (1887-1968). Dominican writer, critic, and literary historian, author of a two-volume *Panorama histórica de la literature cubana.*

"The unnameable feast." An ironical allusion to a line from Lezama Lima's poem "Noche insular, jardínes invisibles" ("Insular Night, Invisible Gardens): "since being born here is an unnameable feast." "Here," of course, is Cuba.

"The rich guy." A reference to José Rodríguez Feo (1920-1993), writer, translator, and patron of the journal *Orígenes* and subsequently, following a falling-out with Lezama Lima, the journal *Ciclón*, which published many of the writers from the so-called "Generation of the 1950s." His correspondence with Wallace Stevens is an important literary document, and available as *Secretaries of the Moon*, ed. Beverly Coyle and Alan Filreis (Duke UP, 1986).

Bauta. A small town in the Havana area. Ángel Gaztelu was a priest at its parish church where the *Orígenes* gatherings were held.

"...a painter of the *Orígenes* years." A reference to Mariano Rodríguez.

Espuela de Plata. A literary journal published between 1939 and 1941 and edited by Lezama Lima, the art critic Guy Pérez Cisneros, and Mariano Rodríguez, it was the immediate precursor of *Orígenes.*

Wallace Stevens (1879-1955). U.S. American poet, whose correspondence with José Rodríguez Feo led to the creation of the poems "Someone Puts a Pineapple Together" (inspired by a painting by Mariano Rodríguez) and "A Word with José Rodríguez Feo."

Eugenio Florit (1903-1999). Spanish-born Cuban lyric poet, translator, anthologist, critic, and longtime professor at Barnard College and Columbia University.

Jaeger's *Paideia.* A reference to the three-volume study of ancient Greek educational practice (Harvard UP, 1961) by German Hellenist philologist Werner Jaeger (1886-1961).

Unamuno. Miguel de Unamuno (1864-1936), Spanish/Basque philosopher, essayist, and writer of fiction. See *The Tragic Sense of Life in Men and Nations*, trans. Anthony Kerrigan (Princ UP, 1978).

Alain Robbe-Grillet (1922-2008). French novelist and filmmaker, pioneer of the so-called Nouveau Roman in post-World War II French fiction. See *Jealousy* and *In the Labyrinth*, trans. Richard Howard (Grove, 1994).

Jorge Mañach (1898-1961). Cuban philosopher, cultural critic, and politician, central intellectual figure of the 1930s generation. See *Martí: Apostle of Freedom*, trans. Coley Taylor (Devin Adair, 1950).

Luis Felipe Rodríguez (1884-1947). Cuban author of realist, socially oriented fiction and drama.

Phantom Plays the Game

"Homage to Senghor":

Senghor. Léopold Sédar Senghor (1906-2001), Senegalese poet, theoretician, and politician; co-founder of the negritude movement and first president of independent Senegal; see *Collected Poetry*, trans. Malvin Dixon (U. of Virginia P., 1998).

Cortázar. Julio Cortázar (1914-1984), Argentine novelist, short-story writer, and poet; see *Hopscotch*, trans. Gregory Rabassa (Pantheon, 1987).

St. John Perse (1887-1975), Guadeloupean-born French poet and diplomat, winner of the 1960 Nobel Prize in Literature. See *Selected Poems*, ed. Mary Ann Caws (New Directions, 1982).

Aimé Césaire (1912-2008), Martinican poet, theoretician, dramatist, and politician; co-founder of the negritude movement and long-time mayor of Fort-de-France and member of the French National Assembly; see *The Complete Poetry*, trans. Clayton Eshleman and A. James Arnold (Wesleyan UP, 2017).

"Old Maldoror":

Maldoror. Title character and protagonist of a hallucinatory, blasphemous, blackly humorous prose-poetic work by the Comte de Lautréamont (Isidore Ducasse, 1846-1870); see *Maldoror and the Complete Works of the Comte de Lautréamont*, trans. Alexis Lykiard (Exact Change, 2004).

"Martían Text":

José Martí (1853-1895), Cuban poet, journalist, and revolutionary; iconic figure of Cuban culture claimed by all Cuban political tendencies, and hence a suitable target for García Vega's demystifying approach. See *José Martí: Selected Writings*, trans. Esther Allen (Penguin: 2002) and the translations of his poems by Mark Weiss in Jerome Rothenberg and Jeffrey C. Robinson, eds., *Poems for the Millennium, Volume Three: The University of California Book of Romantic & Postromantic Poetry* (University of California Press, 2009).

"A Reading for Doctor Phantom":

Bachelard. Gaston Bachelard (1884-1962), French philosopher of poetry and science; see *The Poetics of Space*, trans. Maria Jolas (Beacon, 1994) and *The Poetics of Reverie: Language, Childhood and the Cosmos*, trans. Daniel Russell (Beacon, 1960).

"I'm Not Being Clear":

Juarroz. Roberto Juarroz (1925-1995), Argentine poet, author of *Poesía vertical*, which brings together most of his work; for a bilingual English-Spanish selection, see *Vertical Poetry*, trans. W.S. Merwin (North Point, 1988).

A Cushy Deal down the Drain

"The Tablets of Armand Schwerner."

Armand Schwerner (1927-1999), U.S. poet. García Vega is here referencing and paying parodic homage to Schwerner's major work *The Tablets* (National Poetry Foundation, 1999).

Bileville

Clarice Lispector (1920-1977), Brazilian novelist, short-story writer, and chronicler; see *Complete Stories*, trans. Katrina Dobson (New Directions, 2015).

Roberto Fernández Retamar (1930-2019), Cuban poet and essayist; editor of the journal of the *Casa de las Américas* since 1965; member of the Cuban Council of State; see *Caliban and Other Essays*, trans. Edward Baker (U. of Minnesota P., 1989) and the poems included in Weiss, *op. cit.*

A Little Walk Until Being Seated

"Song":

Alessandra Molina (1968). Cuban poet. See the poems included in Weiss, *op. cit.*

The quotation from William Blake (1757-1827) in the epigraph is from Chapter 9 of his burlesque work *An Island in the Moon*.

Palindrome in Another Lock: Homage to Duchamp

Marcel Duchamp (1887-1968), French anti-artist, anti-philosopher, and chess player; see *The Writings of Marcel Duchamp*, ed. and trans. Michel Sanouillet and Elmer Peterson (Da Capo, 1989), from which García Vega's quotations from Duchamp have been taken.

"The Story of a Clip-on Tie":

Vallejo-like. A reference to César Vallejo (1892-1938), Peruvian avant-garde poet, playwright, and novelist who was a particular influence on García Vega's early work; see *The Complete Poetry: A Bilingual Edition*, trans. Clayton Eshleman and José R. Barcia (U. of California P., 2009).

"Rubén Darío Park":

Rubén Darío (1867-1916), Nicaraguan poet, pioneer of *modernismo*, the symbolist-inflected movement which revolutionized Spanish-language poetry; see *Selected Writings*, ed. Ilán Stavans and trans. Andrew Hurley, Greg Simon, and Steven F. White (Penguin, 2005).

Luis Buñuel (1900-1983). Spanish-Mexican film director, influenced by surrealism and a master of cinematic black humor. His films include *Viridiana* (1961), *The Exterminating Angel* (1962), and *The Discreet Charm of the Bourgeoisie* (1972).

Jean-Pierre Brisset (1837-1919), French "outsider" linguist and philosopher whose homonymic explorations and speculations (sampled by García Vega) are completely untranslatable into any non-French language.

Textilandia Albina

Rogelio Saunders (1963). Cuban poet, fiction writer, and essayist. See the poems included in Weiss, *op. cit.*

"Is This About a Rose?"

Virgilio Piñera (1912-1979), Cuban poet, playwright, short-story writer, and novelist; member of the *Orígenes* group, with which he later broke; pioneer of what came to be known as the Theater of the Absurd. García Vega shares Piñera's dark, negating humor and iconoclasm, but always insisted on their fundamental difference. See *Cold Tales*, trans. Mark Schafer (Eridanos, 1988) and the poems included in Weiss, *op. cit.*

Two Poems

"Listening to Giacinto Scelsi":

Giacinto Scelsi (1905-1988), Italian composer and poet; noted for his compositions based on a single pitch, some of whose titles García Vega cites in this poem.

"Mantras by Stockhausen":

Karlheinz Stockhausen (1928-2007), German composer, noted for his experimental work in serial composition, electronic music, and opera. "Mantra" is a 1970 composition for two pianos and ring-modulator.

Distributing Scraps when Drops of the Varicolored

"Drops of the Varicolored (Visual Apothegms)":

Octavio Paz (1914-1998). Mexican poet, essayist, editor, and public intellectual; Nobel Prize in Literature, 1990; see *The Poems of Octavio Paz*, trans. Eliot Weinberger (New Directions, 2012) and *Children of the Mire: Modern Poetry from Romanticism to the Avant-Garde*, trans. Rachel Phillips (Harvard UP, 1974).

Lionel Barrymore (1878-1954). U.S. stage and screen actor, noted for performances in Frank Capra's *It's a Wonderful Life* and John Huston's *Key Largo*.

Ullán. Spanish poet and journalist José-Miguel Ullán (1944-2009), known among other achievements for his collaborations with artists and musicians.

Marinetti. Filippo Tommaso Marinetti (1876-1944). Italian poet, novelist, essayist; founder of the Italian Futurist movement, pioneer of visual and sound poetry; see *Critical Writings*, ed. Günter Berghaus, trans. Doug Thompson (Farrar Straus Giroux, 2008).

Beuys. Joseph Beuys (1921-1986), German visual and performance artist and theorist, associated with Fluxus international (anti-)art movement; see *What Is Art? Conversations with Joseph Beuys* (Clairview, 2004).

Ludwig Wittgenstein (1889-1951), Austrian philosopher of language and language-games; see *Philosophical Investigations*, trans. G.M. Anscombe (Wiley-Blackwell, 2009).

François Cheng (1929), Chinese-French philosopher, poet, and calligrapher; see *Chinese Poetic Writing*, trans. Donald Riggs and Jerome Seaton (NY Review Books, 2016).

Baruj Salinas (1935), Cuban painter, sculptor, engraver, and ceramicist.

Arturo Carrera (1948), Argentine neo-baroque poet and translator; see the poems included in *The Oxford Book of Latin American Poetry*, ed. Cecilia Vicuña and Ernesto Livón Grossman (Oxford UP, 2009).

The Vocation of Losing

Witold Gombrowicz (1904-1969), Polish novelist, short-story writer, dramatist, and diarist; lived for many years in Argentina, where he befriended and collaborated with Virgilio Piñera during is twelve years residency, and with whom he shared a taste for the sardonic and grotesque. See *Ferdydurke*, trans. Danuta Borchardt (Yale UP: 2012).

Agustín Acosta (1886-1979). Cuban poet; named "National Poet" during the Batista dictatorship.

Carlos Gardel (1890-1935). French-born Argentine singer and movie star; iconic exponent of the tango.

Maurice Chevalier (1888-1972). French singer and movie star; with his signature boater hat and tuxedo, he embodied the stereotype of the debonair Frenchman.

Carole Lombard (1908-1942). U.S. American movie star, famed for her combination of physical beauty and comedic flair.

Herrera y Reissig. Julio Herrera y Reissig (1876-1910). Uruguayan *modernista* poet and playwright, whose work is situated between art-nouveau decadence and emergent vanguardist tendencies in Latin American literature.

Tyrant Machado. Gerardo Machado (1871-1939). Cuban veteran of the War of Independence and eventual dictatorial President of Cuba, overthrown in the revolution of 1933.

Gómez de la Serna. Ramón Gómez de la Serna (1888-1963). Spanish avant-garde novelist, dramatist, essayist, and aphorist; noted for his startling, often blackly humorous apothegms which he dubbed *greguerías*. See *Aphorisms*, trans. Miguel González-Gerth (Latin American Literary Review Press, 1990).

Carlos Victoria (1950-2007). Cuban novelist and short-story writer, one of the most distinguished figures in the so-called "generation of Mariel," named after the massive 1980 exodus from Cuba; one of the dedicatees of *El oficio de perder*. See *A Bridge in Darkness* (Pureplay, 2005).

Dardo Cúneo (1914-2011). Argentine historian, political analyst, and biographer, and one of the dedicatees of *El oficio de perder*.

Joseph Cornell (1903-1972). U.S. American visual artist whose mysterious, poetic boxes composed of seemingly disparate elements inspired García Vega's poetics.

Otto Rank (1884-1939). Austrian psychoanalyst, pioneer of object-relations theory; anticipated Gestalt therapy. See *Art and Artist: Creative Urge and Personality Development*, trans. Charles Francis Atkinson (Norton, 1999).

Nancarrow. Conlon Nancarrow (1912-1997). U.S. American avant-garde composer, famous for his *Studies for Player Piano*.

Olga Orozco (1920-1999). Argentine surrealist poet and short-story writer. See *Engravings Torn from Insomnia*, trans. Mary Crow (BOA Editions, 2002).

Boleros. A genre of popular song that first emerged in Cuba and spread throughout Latin America. Slow in tempo, a bolero generally sings of love lost or anticipated.

Duchess Cayetana. María Teresa de Cayetana, Duchess of Alba, said to be the model for the painting *The Naked Maja* by the Spanish artist Francisco de Goya y Lucientes (1746-1828).

Krishnamurti. Jiddu Krishnamurti (1895-1986). Indian philosopher and teacher. See *The Book of Life: Daily Meditations with Krishnamurti* (Harper, 1995).

Juan Emar (1893-1964). Pseudonym of Álvaro Yáñez Bianchi. Chilean avant-garde writer, art critic, and painter; his experimental writing found no public acceptance, which led him to withdraw from the world in order to work on his immense (5,000-page) novel in five "pillars" *Umbral* (Threshold). In many ways his uncompromising work anticipates García Vega's.

Fantômas. Mysterious criminal mastermind at the heart of a series of popular novels by Marcel Allain (1885-1969) and Pierre Souvestre (1874-1914).

La Maga, in *Hopscotch*. A reference to a central character in Julio Cortázar's novel, the lover of the protagonist Horacio Oliviera.

Books by Lorenzo Garcia Vega (1926-2012)

Suite para la espera (poems). Havana: Orígenes, 1948.

Espirales del cuje (novel). Havana: *Orígenes,* 1952. Winner of the Premio Nacional de Literatura.

Cetrería del títere (short stories). Havana: Universidad Central de Las Villas, 1960.

Antología de la novela cubana, edited, introduced, and annotated by LGV. Havana: Dirección General de Cultura, Ministerio de Educación, 1960.

Ritmos acribillados (poems). Introduction by Mario Parajón. New York: 1972.

Rostros del reverso (1952-1975). Diary. Caracas: Monte Ávila, 1975.

Los años de Orígenes (memoir/essays). Caracas: Monte Ávila, 1979; reprinted in 2007 by Bajo la Luna, Buenos Aires, and in 2019 by Ediciones Rialta, Mexico City.

Poemas para penúltima vez (1948-1989). A comprehensive collection of previously published and new poems. Miami/Caracas/Santo Domingo: Escandalar/Saeta Ediciones, 1991.

Variaciones a como veredicto para sol de otras dudas: Fragmentos de una construcción 1936 (poem). Miami: La Torre de Papel, 1991.

Espacios para el huyuyo (fictions). Miami: La Torre de Papel, 1993.

Collages de un notario (memoir, testimony, essay, short story). Miami: La Torre de Papel, 1993.

Vilis (prose). France: Ediciones Deleatur, 1998.

Palíndromo en otra cerradura: Homenaje a Duchamp (micro-fictions). Venezuela: Pequeña Venecia, 1999. Reprinted in 2011 (Barcelona: Barataria) with an introduction by Patricio Pron.

Cómo hacer un cuento con Guido, seguido de Un cuento con Guido Llinás (plaquette). Montreuil: Ediciones del Peral, 2003.

El oficio de perder (memoirs). Puebla: Benemérita Universidad Autónoma de Puebla, 2004. Reprinted in 2005 (Seville: Renacimiento/Ediciones Espuela de Plata) with an introduction by Antonio José Ponte.

Papeles sin ángel (micro-fictions). Miami: La Torre de Papel, 2005.

Cuerdas para Aleister (micro-fictions). Introduction by Rafael Cippolini. Buenos Aires: tsé-tsé, 2005.

No mueres sin laberinto: Poemas (1998-2004). Edited and introduced by Liliana García Carril. Buenos Aires: Bajo la Luna, 2005.

Devastación del Hotel San Luis (novel). Buenos Aires: Mansalva, 2007.

Lo que voy siendo: Antología poética. Edited and introduced by Enrique Sainz. Havana: Torre de Letras, 2008; reprinted by Ediciones Matanzas, 2009.

Antología. Casa General de Ahorro de Canarias, 2009.

Son gotas del autismo visual (micro-fictions). Guatemala City: Mata-Mata Ediciones Latinoamericanas, 2010.

Erogando trizas donde gotas de lo vario pinto (micro-fictions). Madrid: Ediciones La Palma, 2011.

Ping-pong zuihitsu: Proyecto de novela epistolar (in collaboration with Margarita Pintado). http://pingpongzuihitsu.blogspot.cz. 2011.

El Cristal que se desdobla (diaries). Edited and introduced by Pablo López Carballo, with tributes by Miguel Casado, José Kozer, and Antonio José Ponte. Madrid: Amargord, 2016.

Rabo de anti-nube: Diarios 2002-2009. Edited and introduced by Carlos A. Aguilera. Leiden: Almenara, 2018.

Ficción en cajitas (posthumous anthology). Edited and introduced by Pablo de Cuba Soria. Ecuador: Fondo de Animal Editores, 2016. 2nd ed.: Blurb, 2019.

Cuaderno del Bag Boy (diaries). Edited by Carlos A. Aguilera and Pablo de Cuba Soria. Richmond, VA: Editorial Casa Vacía, 2016. 2nd ed: Blurb, 2019.

About the Author and Editor/Translator

Lorenzo García Vega (Jagüey Grande, Cuba, 1926—Miami, USA, 2012) was the youngest member of the Orígenes group of poets and artists centered around José Lezama Lima. He left Cuba in 1968 and lived in Madrid, Caracas, New York City, and finally, Playa Albina (his sobriquet for Miami). He was awarded the Cuban National Prize for Literature in 1952. His experimental, frequently obsessive writing spans and transgresses a variety of genres, from poetry and narratives to essays, memoirs, and diaries. In the 1980s, he was rediscovered and championed by a younger generation of Latin American writers.

Christopher Winks (Editor and Translator) is Professor and Chair of Comparative Literature at Queens College/The City University of New York. He is the author of *Symbolic Cities in Caribbean Literature* (Palgrave Macmillan, 2009), and he has published essays, reviews, and translations from French and Spanish in many journals and edited collections. He is the editor and co-translator with Adriana González Mateos of *Los danzantes del tiempo: Antología poética,* a bilingual English-Spanish anthology of Kamau Brathwaite's poems that received the 2011 Casa de las Américas prize. Recent translations include Lila Zemborain's poetic sequence *Soft Matter* (Quantum Prose, 2023).